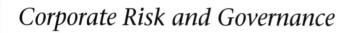

*Corporate Risk and Governance*

# Corporate Risk and Governance

An End to Mismanagement,
Tunnel Vision and Quackery

ALAN WARING

GOWER

Published by
Gower Publishing Limited
Wey Court East
Union Road
Farnham
Surrey
GU9 7PT
England

Gower Publishing Company
110 Cherry Street
Suite 3-1
Burlington
VT 05401-3818
USA

www.gowerpublishing.com

Alan Waring has asserted his moral right under the Copyright, Designs and Patents Act, 1988, to be identified as the author of this work.

**British Library Cataloguing in Publication Data**
Waring, Alan.
  Corporate risk and governance : an end to mismanagement,
  tunnel vision and quackery.
  1. Risk management. 2. Corporate governance.
  I. Title
  658.4'013-dc23

**The Library of Congress has cataloged the printed edition as follows:**
Waring, Alan.
  Corporate risk and governance : an end to mismanagement, tunnel vision and quackery /
by Alan Waring.
      pages cm
  Includes bibliographical references and index.
  ISBN 978-1-4094-4836-5 (hardback) -- ISBN 978-1-4094-4837-2 (ebook)
-- ISBN 978-1-4724-0244-8 (epub)  1. Risk management. 2. Corporations--Corrupt practices.
3. Corporate governance.  I. Title.

  HD61.W37 2013
  658.15'5--dc23

2013007497

ISBN 9781409448365 (hbk)
ISBN 9781409448372 (ebk – PDF)
ISBN 9781472402448 (ebk – ePUB)

Printed and bound in Great Britain
by MPG PRINTGROUP

# Contents

# List of Figures and Tables

## Figures

## Tables

# List of Cases

# About the Author

Dr Alan Waring has 35 years' experience in risk management. His books include *Managing Risk* (1998), co-authored with Prof Ian Glendon and *Practical Systems Thinking* (1996). He has presented over 20 conference and seminar papers on risk issues at major events in the UK, China, Iran, Hong Kong, Singapore, Australia, Cyprus and the US. He has written numerous articles published in, for example, *Strategic Risk, Catastrophe Risk Management, Corporate Governance Asia, InfoRM* and *Risk Management – An International Journal*.

As a full-time risk management consultant since 1986, he has undertaken client assignments for over 80 organizations in 15 countries across many industry sectors. Typically working with boards, board risk committees, individual directors and senior executives, his assignments have included governance-related corporate risk reviews for large organizations as well as a wide range of strategic and operational risk issues.

He has conducted assignments and written reports submitted to the King's Cross Fire Inquiry (1988) and the Sea Empress Inquiry (1997) as well as implementation assignments for numerous clients following the King's Cross Fire Inquiry and the Piper Alpha Inquiry. He has also participated in independent studies of the Barings Bank collapse, the NHS reforms and Iran in transition to an economy-without-oil.

From 2007–2009, he was Adjunct Professor, Centre for Corporate Governance and Financial Policy, School of Business, Hong Kong Baptist University. He has also been a visiting lecturer or visiting professor at other institutions in the UK and China. In 1998, he helped found *Risk Management – An International Journal*.

He may be contacted at PO Box 41029, 6309 Larnaca, Cyprus, waringa@cytanet.com.cy.

# Foreword

Having worked closely with Alan Waring on a number of projects stemming from our time together in the UK during the 1980s and 1990s and subsequently, and also as his PhD supervisor, I can attest to his being as much at home in the applied practitioner field as in the scholarly conceptual domain. It is evident that his attention to the details of an issue, in tandem with his ability to appreciate its social and political context, is present in this, his latest book, *Corporate Risk and Governance: An End to Mismanagement, Tunnel Vision and Quackery*.

Targeting board-level thinking and action in particular, this book reflects the essential global dimension of risk management. In this field the author is very much at home, having practised and consulted on strategic risk management across several continents. Among many other issues, the importance of broad-based multi-disciplinary education and continuing professional development for senior managers, and all those charged with risk management responsibilities, becomes salient. The author's impressive range and depth of practical experience, spanning 35 years as a risk professional, is brought alive through the numerous international case examples, many of which are based on his own work.

The impressive number of case studies range from family-owned companies to international relations, revealing both the ubiquitous nature of risk management issues and their diverse impacts on corporate risk and governance. A high proportion of the cases described are contemporary, meaning that this is a very up-to-date text, while there is useful cross-referencing between case examples. The delicate balance that contemporary technology engenders, which is increasingly implicated in several celebrated cases of financial institutions' collapse, is also well illustrated throughout this insightful book.

Readers may well identify similarities between some of the case descriptions and contemporaneous events within their own organization, which could presage reflective thought, followed by appropriate action. Even one such revelation could make this book worth your while reading. While eschewing prescription, guideposts include the need to be proactive when managing risk, in particular not relying on reactive approaches that include exclusively insurance-based strategies. 'Quantification only' approaches are also to be avoided. Other dictums include avoiding bias to financial/accounting risk as the only or primary risk, the book stressing the need also to take account of risks arising, *inter alia*, from within the political domain, as well as through corruption and fraud, intellectual property, brand or product risks, human/employment relations, and environmental/major hazards.

Several cases remind readers that crises may build up over many years, even decades, before spilling over into organizational failure. However, what becomes clear as one reads through the case examples and their interpretations, is that what we might label in hindsight as 'disasters' are merely part of the continuously changing fabric of our contemporary world. How we create disasters helps to define our place in the world.

We might plan against them and perhaps mitigate their worst effects, but ultimately we can never completely control them. What can take years to create, develop and nurture, can be destroyed in a moment. Like the proverbial trust, the potential for disaster often arrives on foot, but leaves on horseback.

Throughout this very accessible book the author's flowing yet parsimonious style makes for easy reading. Most chapters open with jargon-free definitions of key concepts. Each chapter is kept relatively short so as to encapsulate the essential points on the topic at hand. This feature allows the reader to dip into the text to find an item of particular interest or to locate a chapter with particular relevance to a current problem or issue. Aside from its analytical approach, the book is also a valuable compilation of many risk management failures, which serve to remind managers of the great variety of risks that must be managed.

Described as a 'thinking aid' rather than a prescriptive account, the author is at pains to explain that neither simple nor simplistic 'solutions' are available to address risk management failures, such as those that he describes. The benefit of hindsight may reveal only broad generic lessons from the seemingly disparate and increasing frequency of 'disasters' now being documented. Retaining situational awareness of what can go wrong is an important element. More critically, ethical issues pervade many risk management failures, to the extent that trust, integrity and honesty shine through as the real beacons against such occurrences. Acknowledging these basic human values as the ultimate shield, the author is scathing in his condemnation of those who, through ignorance or neglect, should shoulder responsibility for often devastating outcomes of risk management failures on individuals and communities.

The author identifies numerous points at which risk management issues are likely to become salient, which are many and varied, including the importance of organizational and national cultures. For example, the author refers to 'corruption of the spirit' as being systemic within the culture of many countries. Aside from its generic insights, this book also provides a useful summary compendium of many risk management failures, not just those relating to corporate governance. This is a book for anyone with responsibility for, or interest in, managing risk within organizations or across broader social groupings, such as government agencies. Important as these elements are, it becomes clear that we can never rely on the twin pillars of legislation and enforcement in managing risk effectively. As much as anything, risk management is a state of mind, in particular a state of perpetual preparedness and readiness for action.

A. Ian Glendon
Associate Professor, School of Applied Psychology
Griffith University
Queensland, Australia
July 2012

# Acknowledgements

The author would like to thank the following for their assistance with the substance and preparation of this book:

Associate Professor Ian Glendon, School of Applied Psychology, Griffith University, Gold Coast, Queensland, Australia for contributing the Foreword and for many years' collaboration on risk management issues, including co-authoring their previous book *Managing Risk* (Waring and Glendon 1998).

Masis der Partogh, Publisher and Editor of *Financial Mirror* (www.financialmirror.com), for encouraging the author's Risk Watch Column since 2004 and for his kind permission to draw on some of these articles where appropriate.

For stimulating debates over the years on the subject matter of this book and/or for reviewing all or parts of the manuscript:

Chris Brett, formerly Group Risk Manager for a number of publicly listed companies, including membership of board risk committees, and a proponent of better corporate governance through better risk management.

Andreas Chrysafis, writer and commentator on governance, justice and social issues.

Tasos Coucounis, barrister-at-law and Senior Partner, Andreas Coucounis & Co.

Socrates Coudounaris, Senior Manager, PricewaterhouseCoopers LLP, London, a prominent Fellow of the Institute of Risk Management and a proponent of better corporate governance through better risk management.

Petros Florides, Regional Governance Adviser, World Vision Middle East/Eastern European Region.

Dr Peter French, chartered psychologist and formerly a professor at the Chinese University of Hong Kong.

Dr Sadegh Gharavi, Managing Director of Rah Shekan international civil engineering company, international business developer, adviser to governments on bi-lateral trade agreements, and recognized authority on earthquake protection of buildings.

David Glinski, Group Environment, Health and Safety Manager, Prudential plc.

Michael Howard, founding Chairman and Chief Executive, Frontier Software Plc.

Nigel Howarth, former international management consultant, now sponsor of Cyprus Property Buyers online information and advice centre.

Gavin Jones, former business owner and entrepreneur, now a writer and commentator on governance, justice and social issues.

Robert Lowe, formerly a senior executive with the 3i investment group and a former financial controller in large corporations.

Neil Maloney, former Group Head and Acting Director at the Independent Commission Against Corruption (ICAC), Hong Kong, former Head of Integrity Services, Hong Kong Jockey Club and now independent consultant.

Andrew McClay, litigant for property buyers' rights.

Ken McWhinnie, Director of Risk Management within a large conglomerate based in the Far East and a proponent of better corporate governance and better risk management.

Michael Mooney, Director, Operant Risk Management Ltd.

Cornelius O'Dwyer, campaigner and litigant for property buyers' rights.

Denis O'Hare, former senior banking executive and founder of the Cyprus Property Action Group.

Eleni Papacharalambous, barrister-at-law, Senior Partner and Head of IP Law Department, and Coralia Papacharalambous, advocate, Papacharalambous & Angelides LLC.

Paul Roth, senior regional representative in the aero engines business.

Hermes Solomon, writer and commentator on governance, justice and social issues.

Graham Walker, former senior police officer and owner of multiple businesses in Africa.

Robert West, offshore driller for oil and gas exploration companies in Asia, Africa, Middle East and South America.

Robert Youill, Managing Director, Shanghai office of FTI Consulting, and formerly Regional Anti-Piracy Director for Asia Pacific for the international music industry.

Evdokimos Xenophontos, President of the Cyprus Institute of Directors, a board member of the Bank of Cyprus and proponent of better corporate governance and better risk management.

Barbara Maurizi, for steering the author through file handling, formatting and other software issues in preparing the manuscript.

Jonathan Norman, the Gower Publishing Director, and his team for their professionalism throughout and their many suggestions for ensuring a successful outcome.

The author's wife Mehri, for her patience and support during the drafting of the manuscript.

# List of Abbreviations and Acronyms

| | |
|---|---|
| AGM | Annual General Meeting |
| AKEL | Progressive Party for the Working People, effectively the Communist Party in Cyprus |
| ALARP | As Low As Reasonably Practicable |
| AP | Associated Press |
| APB | Asia Pacific Breweries |
| AR&M | Availability, Reliability & Maintainability |
| AS | Australian Standard |
| ASNZ | Australian–New Zealand Standard |
| | |
| BA | British Airways |
| BCCI | Bank of Credit and Commerce International |
| BCP | Business Continuity Plan or Business Continuity Planning |
| BLEVE | Boiling Liquid Expanding Vapour Explosion |
| BMC | Business Media China |
| BMIIB | Buncefield Major Incident Investigation Board |
| BP | British Petroleum |
| BoBS | Board of Banking Supervision (UK) |
| BPAL | British Pipeline Agency Ltd |
| BRICS | Brazil, Russia, India, China, South Africa |
| BS | British Standard |
| BSS | Barings Securities Singapore |
| BSkyB | British Sky Broadcasting |
| BSL | Barings Securities London |
| | |
| CBA | Cyprus Bar Association |
| CBI | Central Bureau of Investigation (India) |
| CBE | Commander of the Most Excellent Order of the British Empire (a UK honour) |
| CCTV | Closed Circuit Television |
| CD | Compact Disc |
| CEO | Chief Executive Officer |
| CFO | Chief Finance Officer |
| CIMAH | Control of Industrial Major Accident Hazards |
| C-level | Chief |
| CIPD | Chartered Institute of Personnel and Development |
| CMP | Crisis Management Planning |
| CNOOC | China National Offshore Oil Corporation |
| COMAH | Control of Major Accident Hazards |
| COO | Chief Operating Officer |

| | |
|---|---|
| COSO | Committee of Sponsoring Organizations of the Treadway Commission (US) |
| CPAG | Cyprus Property Action Group |
| CPI | Corruption Perceptions Index |
| CPSC | Consumer Product Safety Commission (US) |
| CRO | Chief Risk Officer |
| CSE | Cyprus Stock Exchange |
| CY | Cyprus Airways |
| | |
| DBA | Disciplinary Board of Advocates |
| DEFSTAN | Defence Standard |
| DVD | Digital Video Disc |
| | |
| EAC | Electricity Authority of Cyprus |
| EC | European Community |
| ECHR | European Court of Human Rights |
| ED | Enforcement Directorate (India) |
| E&P | Exploration & Production |
| ERM | Enterprise Risk Management |
| EU | European Union |
| | |
| FDA | Food and Drug Administration (US) |
| FRC | Financial Reporting Council (UK) |
| FSA | Financial Services Authority (UK) |
| FSU | Former Soviet Union |
| *FT* | *Financial Times* |
| | |
| GDP | Gross Domestic Product |
| GMP | Good Manufacturing Practice |
| GRECO | Groupe d'Etats Contre la Corruption (Council of Europe) |
| | |
| HAZOPS | Hazard and Operability Studies |
| HBOS | Halifax-Bank of Scotland |
| HKBU | Hong Kong Baptist University |
| HKJC | Hong Kong Jockey Club |
| HOSL | Hertfordshire Oil Storage Limited |
| HR | Human Resources |
| HSE | Health and Safety Executive (UK safety regulators and enforcers) |
| | |
| IACC | International Anti-Counterfeiting Coalition |
| ICAC | Independent Commission Against Corruption |
| ICI | Imperial Chemical Industries |
| IMF | International Monetary Fund |
| INTERPOL | International Criminal Police Organization |
| IoDC | Institute of Directors Cyprus |
| IP | Intellectual Property |
| IPO | Initial Public Offering |
| IPR | Intellectual PropertyRights |

| | |
|---|---|
| IPT | Immovable Property Tax |
| IRM | Institute of Risk Management |
| ISO | International Standards Organization |
| IT | Information Technology |
| | |
| JV | Joint Venture |
| | |
| KPI | Key Performance Indicator |
| KRI | Key Risk Indicator |
| | |
| LNG | Liquefied Natural Gas |
| LOCA | Loss of Coolant Accident |
| | |
| MAPP | Major Accident Prevention Policy |
| M&A | Mergers and Acquisitions |
| MBA | Master of Business Administration |
| MGN | Mirror Group Newspapers |
| MNC | Multi National Company |
| MoD | Ministry of Defence |
| MEP | Member of the European Parliament |
| MP | Member of Parliament |
| MPA | Motion Picture Association |
| | |
| NED | Non-Executive Director |
| NIORDC | National Iranian Oil Refineries and Distribution Company |
| *NOTW* | *News of the World* newspaper |
| NPL | Non-Performing Loan |
| | |
| OIM | Offshore Installation Manager |
| OSHA | Occupational Safety and Health Administration (US) |
| | |
| PLC | Public Limited Company |
| PoA | Power of Attorney |
| PR | Public Relations |
| PRC | People's Republic of China |
| PRMIA | Professional Risk Managers' International Association |
| PTW | Permit-to-Work |
| PV | Present Value |
| PVC | Polyvinyl Chloride |
| | |
| QA | Quality Assurance |
| | |
| R&D | Research & Development |
| RBS | Royal Bank of Scotland |
| | |
| SARS | Severe Acute Respiratory Syndrome |
| SEC | Securities and Exchange Commission (US and some other countries) |

| | |
|---|---|
| SFO | Serious Fraud Office (UK) |
| SHE | Safety, Health and Environment |
| SIA | Singapore International Airline |
| SIBL | Stanford International Bank Ltd |
| SMART | Specific, Measured, Appropriate, Realistic and Timed |
| SME | Small and Medium Size Enterprise |
| SMS | Safety Management System |
| SOASAC | State-Owned Assets Supervision and Administration Commission of the State Council (PRC) |
| SocGen | Société Générale |
| SOE | State Owned Enterprise |
| SOX | Sarbanes Oxley Act 2002 |
| | |
| TCO | Temperature Cut-Out |
| TNT | Tri-nitro Toluene |
| TSB | Trustee Savings Bank (part of Lloyds TSB) |
| | |
| UBS | Union Bank of Switzerland |
| UFAB | Union des Fabricants |
| UN | United Nations |
| UNCAC | UN Convention Against Corruption |
| USFDA | US Food and Drugs Administration |
| USTR | US Trade Representative (Office) |
| UVCE | Unconfined Vapour Cloud Explosion |
| | |
| VAR | Value At Risk |
| | |
| WEF | World Economic Forum |
| WHO | World Health Organization |
| WMD | Weapon of Mass Destruction |

# Introduction

The book describes, analyzes and discusses a range of interrelated corporate risk and governance issues, which the author has found during his professional career to be of special relevance to risk professionals, corporate board members, senior executives, risk committee members, financiers, insurers and a wide range of professional advisers, regulators and legislators. All these categories form the target readership of this book.

Over the past 25 years, there has been a growing realization that failure to implement robust risk management in an organization is likely to lead to damage to corporate finances, overall performance, reputation, share values and access to capital. In extreme cases, corporate survival can be at stake. However, despite greater awareness and risk control efforts, major corporate risk failures continue to arise.

The Barings Bank collapse in 1995 seemed destined to bring about a radical improvement in finance sector risk management (see, for example, Chapter 11 'The Collapse of Barings Bank' in Waring and Glendon, *Managing Risk*, 1998). The revelations of boardroom and senior management attitudes and general behaviour within the Barings organization, and the lack of even the most basic risk management systems that might have stopped the 'rogue trader' Nick Leeson, were astonishing. Yet, in 2007 Société Générale was hit with a €4.9 billion trading loss, following 18 months of rogue trading by Jerome Kerviel in a case that was remarkably similar in many ways to Barings. Then, in September 2011 Union Bank of Switzerland (UBS) in London was hit with a €1.5 billion trading loss following rogue trading by a senior employee. After Barings, tougher regulations and risk management requirements covering the finance sector were implemented in tandem with the wider corporate governance discipline placed on stock exchange listed companies. All of this failed to control numerous risk exposures such as sub-prime mortgages, complex derivatives and other dubious practices that led to the collapse of banks such as Lehmans, Icelandic banks and Northern Rock, scandals at Royal Bank of Scotland and Lloyds TSB (and more recently on other matters at Barclays and HSBC) and the world financial crisis in 2008–2009, all of which continues to aggravate economic performance and the sovereign debt crisis of many countries.

From the 1980s onwards, corporate fraud cases in the UK such as BICC, Polly Peck and Mirror Group Newspapers (MGN) as well as the Barings collapse provided the impetus for corporate governance initiatives, resulting in 1999 in the Combined Code. In the US, the 2001 collapse of Enron and its negligent auditors Arthur Andersen led to the Sarbanes-Oxley Act (SOX) in 2002, all of which was intended to inject greater corporate governance and risk control. Yet, despite such efforts, Ponzi fraud schemes such as Bernard Madoff's (US$57 billion) and Stanford International Bank's (SIBL) nearly US$8 billion fraud flourished for several more years and, as noted above, high-risk instruments and practices were still widespread throughout the finance sector right up to 2008. There is every reason to be concerned that new (or even old) high-risk activities with inadequate controls may arise. As one former Chairman of the Board Risk Committee of a national bank in the

European Union (EU) stated in 2011, too many directors of large organizations still think in terms of 'What can we get away with?' and some also just will not accept that anything bad will happen and that risk management needs tightening up.

However, although the finance sector has provided many of the high-profile examples of risk mismanagement, the oil, gas and petrochemical sectors are also not immune, for example, British Petroleum (BP) (Alaskan Prudhoe Bay environmental damage 2006; Texas City Refinery explosion 2005; Deepwater Horizon 2010 fire, explosion, deaths, injuries and environmental damage) and PetroChina 2005 (Jilin chemical plant fire, explosion, deaths, injuries and environmental damage to the Songhua River across China and into Russia). The railway industry has also provided numerous examples of major accidents, for example, in the UK, Clapham (1988), Paddington (1999), Potters Bar (2000); several major railway accidents in China in 2011.

History often appears to repeat itself. For example, the UBS and Société Générale rogue trader incidents, years after the Barings collapse; the BP Texas City oil refinery fire and explosion had uncanny similarities to those at its Grangemouth Refinery in 1987 and 2000. The author introduces other examples from his own experience where 'failures of hindsight' (Fischhoff 1975, Toft 1990) and defects in organizational learning (Turner 1994) played a role in repeat incidents.

Although financial risks are likely to be significant to most organizations, the book emphasizes that all organizations are subject to multiple risk exposures and many of these will also be significant to particular organizations on a case-by-case basis. For example, many sectors such as pharmaceuticals, fashion, cosmetics, drinks and automobiles are vulnerable to product counterfeiting and intellectual property (IP) theft by international criminal gangs. The immovable property sector in countries having weak statutory and regulatory controls and a *laissez-faire* attitude to fraud and corruption have discovered too late that their entire industry can be brought to its knees when corporate as well as individual foreign buyers and investors are alerted via the Internet and other media exposés. The gaming and casinos industry is vulnerable to infiltration and control by international organized criminal gangs because of the cash-rich environment and the opportunities for money laundering and tax evasion. The pharmaceutical industry in many countries is increasingly subject to government policy changes, imposed price controls and a requirement for hospitals to buy cheaper generic drugs rather than more expensive branded versions. The threat to margins is causing pharmaceutical manufacturers and distributors to re-work their assumptions, business models and financial projections. Questionable boardroom structures, especially joint Chief Executive Officer (CEO)/ Chairman arrangements in family-controlled businesses including listed companies, can also be a significant risk to corporate stability, reputation and survival as well as the interests of minority shareholders. Failure by organizations to recognize corporate social responsibilities and corporate implications of changing demographic and health issues in the population at large may be a longer-term risk exposure.

Based on the author's professional experience working with corporate boards and executives in Europe, Asia and the Middle East, the book provides some key reasons and insights into why increased regulation and ever more elaborate corporate risk 'systems' have failed, and continue to fail in many cases, to result in a proportionate increase in actual risk control. Boards in many large organizations often suffer from limited knowledge and understanding of risk and a tendency to confuse and conflate pure risk and speculative/opportunity risk exposures. An overall bounded rationality limits the scope of what they consider to be significant risks. For example, only a minority of organizations (less than 50 per cent in the UK) has continuity and crisis plans and few recognize such threats as pandemics, oil supply interruptions and a potential major military conflict in the Middle East as being significant to them. An 'out of sight, out of mind' mentality results in defective planning for crises and business continuity. Some individual board members and senior executives also hold negative attitudes and false beliefs about risk (for example, that risk management interferes with 'proper' business management) and an exaggerated sense of their own risk management skills, all of which play a part in creating a dysfunctional climate as far as risk management is concerned. Opportunities for growth and gain and a confused 'risk appetite' may be used to gloss over, play down or even ignore significant threats. The analysis in *Human Safety and Risk Management* by Glendon et al. (2006) of risk cognition and competing models seeking to explain risk decisions and risk behaviours is referred to.

Other relevant themes in the book reflect those discussed at length in *Managing Risk* (Waring and Glendon 1998), such as organizational cultures, power relations, management systems and organizational change, Gower/Ashgate books edited by Burke and Cooper such as *Risky Business* (2010), *Corporate Reputation* (2011) and *Occupational Health and Safety: Psychological and Behavioural Aspects of Risk* (2011) and books on situation awareness such as Banbury and Tremblay (2004).

The substantive content of the book and its selected case material is organized as 15 chapters under the following sections, which the author believes provide a selective but nonetheless rich flavour of contemporary issues in corporate risk management:

- Enterprise Risk Management (ERM) and Corporate Governance
- Corporate Due Diligence
- Fraud, Corruption and Organized Crime
- Intellectual Property and Product Risks
- Man-Made Disasters

Although not intended to be a controversial book, there are some chapters and passages that may raise hackles among those readers having a rigid, narrow or purist view of particular issues, especially those individuals who prefer corporate risk issues to be reduced to 'neatly stackable and fixable' terms rather than accepting that they are frequently complex, messy, interdependent and not as predictable as one would wish. If any reader responds to a particular chapter or passage with 'I cannot see what this has to do with corporate risk and governance', then they are probably failing to grasp the fact that risks rarely appear as a simple set of conveniently labelled 'pigeonholes' and may not always seem immediately obvious, especially to those who are relatively inexperienced in risk management.

The book is predominantly a thinking aid rather than a prescription for guaranteed success in corporate risk management (which claim, in any event, would be suspect). As noted in *Managing Risk* (Waring and Glendon 1998), the author is firmly against 'salvation models' that purport to offer an easy, trouble-free route to a risk nirvana. The book is, therefore, not a risk management 'cookbook' that presents step-by-step risk mitigation 'recipes'. Reference is, however, made to suitable guides such as ISO 31000, PAS 200, ISO 22301 and the revised UK Corporate Governance Code (FRC 2010) and many of the chapters do contain summaries of key points intended to assist the reader's practical application to improvement of corporate risk management.

# PART 1

# *Enterprise Risk Management and Corporate Governance*

# 1 Risk Management and Governance in Context

## Corporate Governance

In a superficial sense, corporate governance is something of a fancy term for good corporate management. However, the term 'good management' perhaps lacks the gravitas and locus of accountability implied by 'corporate governance', which is very much the primary responsibility of the board of directors. Corporate governance refers to the system by which companies and other organizations are directed and controlled (FRC 2010).

A board's governance responsibility encompasses the expression of corporate values; setting the desired tone and attitude; issuing policies, strategies, control standards and criteria for accountability, transparency, probity and risk; monitoring and reviewing performance; and demonstrating leadership with a clear focus on sustainable success.

Ultimately, corporate governance is all about ensuring that the interests of shareholders and other stakeholders (for example, employees, customers, the public) are protected. Without an effective risk management system, it is self-evident that no board could ever claim convincingly that the organization is under good governance. Boards should take a comprehensive approach to what 'all significant risks' means. Governance therefore requires that *all* significant risks to the business should be identified, analyzed and managed appropriately, whether by elimination, avoidance, reduction, control or other means (Waring 2001a). Although differing in emphasis and some aspects of principle and practice, this is the thrust of the original and revised Turnbull code in the UK (London Stock Exchange 1998, Turnbull 1999, FRC 2005), as well as other national codes, for example PRCCCG (2002), HKCCG (2005) and SCCG (2005) and generic international guides such as ISO 31000 (ISO 2009).

## Corporate Risk Exposures

The World Economic Forum's (WEF) annual Global Risks Report for 2011 (WEF 2011) emphasizes that business leaders and decision-makers need to switch to longer-term thinking for mitigating increasingly complex and interlinked global risks. Organizations are exposed to multiple and often complex and interacting areas of risk, including mergers and acquisitions (M&As), treasury risks, credit risk, integrity risks, security, marketing, product liability, contracts, capital projects, health and safety, major hazards, environment and many more. Above all these, two over-riding and critical issues are corporate reputation and brand, both of which take years to build up and perhaps only hours or days to destroy. Share values, market confidence and willingness of other companies to engage with yours all depend on reputation and brand and ultimately the very survival of the organization can be put at risk. Examples include:

**Table 1.1    Some high-profile examples of business risk failures**

| Organization | Year | Losses/Damage | Proximate Cause |
|---|---|---|---|
| BP | 2010 | Loss of Deepwater Horizon offshore oil installation in Gulf of Mexico following fire and explosion; 11 deaths and 17 injured; environmental disaster; BP set aside US$41 billion initial compensation fund; federal prosecutions pending and financial penalties expected; BP's corporate reputation severely damaged | Well blow-out preventer failed; widespread safety management failures implicated |
| Stanford International | 2009 | US$7 billion Ponzi-type fraudulent investment scheme; SIL in receivership; class action lawsuits by aggrieved investors; prosecutions of key SIL figures completed 2012 | Falsification of investment data and misleading of investors, prompting Securities and Exchange (SEC) investigation |
| PetroChina | 2005 | Jilin chemical plant explosion; deaths, injuries, environmental catastrophe across three provinces and into Russia; foreign investors dump PetroChina stock | Poor control of major hazards |
| China Aviation Oil | 2004 | US$550 million losses; suspension of trading | Incompetent trading in derivatives |
| Parmalat | 2003 | US$16 billion; receivership | Share price manipulation and false accounting |
| WorldCom | 2002 | US$4 billion; corporate collapse | Share price manipulation and false accounting |
| Enron | 2001 | US$15 billion; collapse of Enron | Energy price manipulation and false accounting |
| Sumitomo Corp | 1996 | US$2.6 billion | Rogue copper trades |
| Barings | 1995 | US$1.4 billion; collapse of Barings Bank | Rogue trading; weak internal controls |
| Union Carbide | 1984 | 4,000 dead; 30,000–40,000 seriously injured; 200,000 others affected; US$470 million settlement plus incalculable consequential and collateral losses to many parties; UC eventually sold to Dow Chemical | Massive toxic release from Bhopal factory |

*Source:* Developed from tables in Waring (2005, 2006a and b).

China in particular is vulnerable worldwide to the fall-out from highly publicized cases of corporate fraud, environmental disasters and safety disasters in its industries (Waring 2005), such as Jilin/PetroChina and coal mines. Officially, well over 120,000 people are killed and over 600,000 handicapped in workplace accidents in China every year but the real figures are likely to be higher owing to under-reporting. In 2004, the official cost to China of its workplace accidents was 2 per cent of gross domestic product (GDP) (Wang 2005). China has achieved a momentous industrial expansion and has secured inward investment from numerous Western corporations who have set up factories in China while others queue up to buy Chinese-made goods. These same companies are now nervous about ensuring that safety standards in their Chinese factories are as good as those back home. No Western CEO wants a public scandal with criticism in the media (for example, see cases 13.1 to 13.4 in Chapter 13) and major shareholders demanding his or her resignation for damaging the company's reputation and share values.

## The Global Marketplace

Today, we all operate in a global marketplace and have to think and act in a way that reflects the demands of the marketplace. Those demands now include a clear demonstration that the organization in all aspects of the undertaking meets the requirements of good corporate governance, including sustainability, corporate social responsibility and risk management. Many large companies in Asia, the Middle East and South America now want to be seen as global players and establish strong business relationships with the West: how will they be accepted if they ignore or pay only lip service to corporate governance as understood in the global context, including risk management standards? A poor risk management record will damage the mutual trust and confidence upon which inward investment and trade depend.

Equally, many enterprises in Asia, the Middle East and South America are now buying companies abroad and entering into joint ventures (JVs) and capital projects overseas. They will therefore need to undertake risk evaluations of the other parties and the contexts in which they will be operating. Such pre-contract 'due diligence' audits, which are relatively familiar to Western multi-national companies (MNCs) (see Chapter 8), are quite novel in Asia and the Middle East. Such audits need to cover not only the obvious areas such as finances/accounts and legal/contracts but also environment (who wants to discover too late that they have acquired major contamination legacies with horrendous clean-up costs?), human resources (HR) (who wants to discover too late that the corporate cultures do not match and they have entered a 'marriage made in hell'?) and political threats (who wants to waste time and money pursuing a foreign asset whose acquisition is likely to be blocked by their government?). For example, the attempted US$18.4 billion purchase of Unocal by China National Offshore Oil Corporation (CNOOC) in 2005 and the US$6.8 billion takeover of six US Ports by Dubai Ports in 2006 were thwarted by objections in the US Congress.

## The Problems of Growth

The so-called BRICS Group (Brazil, Russia, India, China and South Africa) have shown higher economic growth rates in recent years than most developed countries. China's economy, for example, has grown on average 10–12 per cent per annum for the past decade and only in 2010 began to show signs of a modest fall in growth rate. The benefits of growth are self-evident in China's rapid modernization, its rising standard of living and consumer culture. However, the rapid economic growth which has been on the back of phenomenal industrial expansion has also brought problems (Barton et al. 2004), for example:

- few planning controls, leading to major hazards sites located in urban centres (for example, PetroChina/Jilin);
- poor process and waste controls, leading to major environmental damage (for example, Pearl River Delta);
- poor health and safety management, leading to many accidents, injuries and occupational ill-heath (Wang 2005);
- potential over-heating of the economy;
- raw material and energy deficits;
- the temptations of fraud and corruption;
- magnification of urban–rural gaps in economic and social benefits, leading to social tensions and unrest.

Steps have been or are being taken by the People's Republic of China (PRC) Government to address some of these issues (for example, SOASAC 2006, Yuanyuan 2004) but a lot remains for individual enterprises, whether State Owned Enterprise (SOE) or private, to do their part in prevention, control and general risk management. There remains a huge gap between the fine words of state regulations and codes on risk management topics and what actually gets implemented. There is, as yet, very little evidence that Chinese corporations are engaging seriously with corporate governance and risk management principles as outlined in this book (see Waring 2006b and c). Without such engagement and ongoing commitment and programmes, the disparity in standards between Chinese companies and the expectations of their overseas investors and customers is likely to cause them increasing problems with inward investment, their external operations and overseas markets. A similar picture emerges for companies in other Asian countries, the Middle East and elsewhere. The US$multi-billion so-called 'Rajagate' fraud and corruption case involving several mobile telephone companies in the Indian telecoms industry and a former government minister is just one example (see case 9.3 in Chapter 9). As recent World Economic Forum Global Risks Reports (WEF 2011, 2012) observe, economic disparity and global governance failures are exacerbating and driving a range of other risks, especially illicit trade, crime, corruption and state fragility. Economic imbalances contain the seeds for future financial crises.

## The Purpose of Risk Management

As the Institute of Risk Management Guide to Enterprise Risk Management and ISO 31000 states (IRM 2010), a successful ERM initiative can affect the likelihood and consequences of risk materializing, as well as deliver benefits related to better informed strategic decisions, successful delivery of change and increased operational efficiency. Other benefits include reduced cost of capital, more accurate financial reporting, competitive advantage, improved image and perception of the organization, brand enhancement and, in the case of the public sector, enhanced political and community support.

Risk management provides a means to cope with a multiplicity of different kinds of risk and risk exposure so as to enhance beneficial outcomes and reduce harm and detriment. Risk management seeks where possible to reduce the uncertainty over how big an impact the risk would have if it materialized and how likely it is that the risk would materialize. However, there are two distinct types of risk exposure likely to affect an organization. The first type of risks are the so-called 'upside risks' which the author prefers to call speculative/opportunity risks, for example marketing, cash flow, product innovation, M&As, JVs, business investment. With these, the aim and expectation is to maximize beneficial outcomes and minimize detrimental ones. In reality, both beneficial and detrimental effects often occur in tandem and the art of effective risk management is to ensure that the balance is always heavily in favour of beneficial outcomes. The other type of risks is the set of pure risks, where success is determined by nothing bad occurring, for example health and safety, environment, fire prevention, security and information technology (IT) reliability.

In the author's experience, there is a tendency for many directors and executives to believe that they should concentrate on speculative/opportunity risks, as these represent 'normal management' whereas pure risks such as health and safety, fire, security and other technical risks are 'nuisance' issues to do with tedious compliance requirements imposed from outside. This somewhat bizarre attitude is usually based on their often limited personal experience rather than any tutored knowledge of risk and its management. Associated with this line of thinking is the equally bizarre belief that pure risks are typically 'operational' and therefore less important and not a matter for the board. This demonstrates a confused understanding of what 'strategic' means, that is, to such individuals, strategic matters are of high importance and for the board's purview whereas operational matters are far less important and should be kept away from the board. Of course, on the contrary (Waring and Tunstall 2005), the world is awash with examples of apparently workaday operational risks that, owing to poor risk management, suddenly became huge strategic risks for the organization (for example, the BP Deepwater Horizon case). A board should always know which operational risk exposures it needs to keep a close eye on and which it can safely delegate to executive management. See Chapters 3 and 4 for further discussion.

## Corporate Culture, Risk Appetite and Risk Aversion

According to Turnbull (1999) and FRC (2005), the sound system of internal controls required for good governance *'should be embedded in the operations of the company and form part of its culture'*. Organizational culture is a complex subject that can only be touched upon within the scope of this book. Briefly, organizational culture may be regarded as: a set of unwritten, and usually unobtrusive, attitudes, beliefs, values, rules of behaviour, ideologies, habitual responses, language expression, rituals, quirks and other features which characterize a particular organization. For deeper insight into organizational culture in relation to risk see Douglas (1992), Turner (1992, 1994), Glendon et al. (2006), Waring and Glendon (1998) and Waring (2001b).

A survey of 1,419 business executives conducted jointly by Zurich Insurance and Harvard Business Review Analytic Services in 2011 found that, although the importance of risk management had risen in organizations since 2008, companies still have a long way to go in building an effective, risk-aware culture. Although two-thirds of respondents agreed that the importance of risk management had increased in their organizations, only 10 per cent reported that their executive management was 'highly effective' in creating a strong risk management culture. The implication is that senior managements are having difficulty with risk management implementation. This finding echoes the author's experience over the past decade. The increasing attention by regulators, investors, the public and the media on risk issues, coupled with external reporting and scrutiny, inevitably has pushed risk management up the managerial agenda. However, despite what may seem a non-controversial subject having obvious benefits, as noted above many directors and executives still regard risk management as something rather alien and unwelcome, an imposed nuisance that 'gets in the way of' what they see as normal management. Such an attitude makes many reluctant to do much more than soft-peddle on risk management. See Chapters 3 and 4 for further discussion.

One test of the strength of an organization's culture is to compare, on the one hand, risk management objectives that either the organization and/or professional advisers consider to be desirable with, on the other hand, the actual level of achievement against these objectives. Table 1.2 summarizes what in the author's experience is found typically in many large organizations anywhere in the world but those organizations operating under corporate governance requirements and adopting ERM principles tend to reach the desirable objectives more quickly and with more lasting results.

**Table 1.2    Disparities between some desirable risk management objectives and typical level of achievement**

| Desirable Risk Management Objectives | | Typical Level of Achievement |
|---|---|---|
| Integrated risk management | v. | Fragmented reality of risk management |
| Strong, cohesive culture of responsible risk-taking | v. | Organizational 'silo' structures and sub-cultures, often not in harmony |
| Safety should have a very high priority | v. | 'Safety first' rhetoric and 'safety last' reality |
| Robust risk management systems | v. | Simple checklist prescriptions |
| Risk management system validation audits as well as compliance audits | v. | Checklist compliance inspections |
| Need for disaster/crisis management and business continuity planning | v. | 'It will never happen to us' |
| Need for closer attention to organizational, cultural and business risk issues | v. | Over-reliance on narrow technical prescriptions |

*Source:* Adapted from Waring (2005).

The board's appetite (or propensity) for speculative or opportunity risks needs to be properly recognized and understood. It represents the motivational engine for growth and success. However, as the Institute of Risk Management Guidance Paper on Risk Appetite and Tolerance notes (IRM 2010), different functions and locations lower down in the organization are also likely to have different risk appetites and it will be important for the board to get these aligned and in harmony with those of the board so as to avoid potential distortions to the company's risk profile and the creation of unwelcome exposures.

Responsible risk-taking requires that speculative or opportunity risks should be taken in an informed way and with adequate risk controls, so as to counter a reckless gambling or cavalier approach. Equally, there should be a healthy aversion to any pure risks that lack adequate risk controls.

The next 10–15 years will test the ability of many organizations to change from a culture of complacency and minimal compliance with a narrow set of risk-related regulations to one of a culture of responsible risk-taking that seeks to protect all the stakeholders' interests and addresses the full array of risk exposures enterprise-wide. The development of such a mind-set requires strong leadership and a demonstration by the board and senior management that enterprise risk exposures have to be managed competently and effectively.

## Risk Management Frameworks and Standards

Over recent years, a range of risk management frameworks and standards has been published and applied widely in businesses and other organizations. For several years, the Australian and New Zealand standard ASNZ 4360 proved very popular around the world as a useful guide to ERM. Other frameworks and standards have found favour in particular countries or with particular sectors or disciplines, for example Sarbanes-Oxley (SOX 2002) and COSO (2004) (the US and accountants), Basel II (2004) (banking and finance sector), DEFSTAN 56 (the UK defence sector and project managers). All of these have strengths and weaknesses but all share in their various ways a common thrust of requiring the assessment of significant risks and the implementation of suitable risk responses. This requirement is now expressed in the international standard ISO 31000: 2009 which applies to all kinds of organization regardless of sector. The overall risk management process expounded by ISO 31000 has the following essential components:

- Establishing the Risk Context (both internal and external).
- Risk Assessment (identification, analysis, evaluation and prioritization of risks, reference to board's risk appetite, tolerance and acceptability positions; reference to legislation and standards both internal and external).
- Assessment-Based Risk Treatment (appropriate combination of control/mitigation options including cessation, avoidance, deferment, reduction, sharing, transfer and risk financing).
- Monitoring of Effectiveness (including routine surveillance, internal reporting, periodic internal and independent external audits and reviews).
- Communication (including internal and external reporting, information dissemination and consultation).

To support the risk management process, there should be an enduring framework comprising the following elements:

- Risk Architecture: specification of the formal risk roles and responsibilities of the board, its committees, executive and line management, professional advisers and employees; the 'noticing system' for identifying new or changing risks, whether internal or external and whether short, medium or long term; specification of the risk communication system, risk management training arrangements and the risk reporting structure.
- Risk Policy and Strategy: statement of the board's policy on and strategy for risk and its management; expression of the board's risk appetite and the board's expectations of how all employees will think and act on risk matters.
- Risk Protocols: formal procedures, rules, guidelines, methodologies, tools, techniques, standards, acceptability/tolerance criteria for risk assessment, risk treatment and risk monitoring.

Although ISO 31000 is now regarded as the universal standard on risk management for all sectors and disciplines, and the author recommends it as the best currently available, he cautions against slavishly following this, or indeed any standard, to the dogmatic exclusion of other relevant material. No standard and no adoption of it can ever be perfect. Experience shows that regarding a standard as a salvation model (Waring and Glendon 1998), which can offer complete protection if followed to the letter, often deceives and disappoints. A self-confident and pragmatic approach which uses such a standard as a prominent guide among an array of relevant references is likely to be more rewarding.

## European Union Corporate Governance Framework

In April 2011, the European Commission issued a Green Paper on The EU Corporate Governance Framework (EU 2011). In a forthright section on risk management, the Green Paper reiterated the basic principles of the board's responsibilities for risk management and raised a number of issues for the public at large to consider. More than two-thirds of the respondents (individual, corporate and institutional) agreed that the board should approve and take responsibility for risk matters, including the identification of key risks. There was almost unanimous support for the principle that the board should ensure that risk management arrangements are effective and commensurate with the company's risk profile. However, some respondents felt that a distinction needed to be drawn between the strategic and corporate responsibilities of the board and the day-to-day responsibilities of executive management.

Overall, respondents did not see any justification for further EU intervention in this matter and this view is in keeping with the EU's position that corporate governance codes are best left to member states to determine.

# 2 *Corporate Risk Management in Practice*

## Self-Regulation versus Compliance Approaches

Since the 1970s, the emphasis of UK Government legislation concerning risk topics has been on self-regulation, which requires the creators of particular risks and those who have to deal with or work with them to demonstrate convincingly that they have the risks under effective control. Each particular piece of legislation provides the broad framework of what needs to be achieved in that particular risk area (the goals), and which class of legal entity or person has the duty to achieve it, while as much technical detail as possible regarding acceptable response options by duty holders is relegated to subordinate regulations, codes of practice, standards and guidance documents. Compliance is judged by the relevant regulator or enforcing authority not just on technical compliance but also on whether the higher order goals have been attained. It should be noted that under this kind of regime visits to companies by external enforcement officials are rare and, generally, organizations are left to get on with regulating themselves. However, if and when a serious incident occurs or the authorities have other good reason to investigate and the company is found not to have managed the particular risk adequately, penalties can be severe and especially if there is evidence of poor management systems and a 'What can we get away with?' attitude. The scale of penalties for non-compliance also reflects this model, with some laws specifying the possibility of unlimited fines and several years in jail for those found guilty of higher order offences.

The Health and Safety at Work etc Act 1974 in the UK was one the first major pieces of legislation to adopt the above approach. Despite perennial complaints from diehard reactionary elements, who object to any form of such regulation on the dubious assertion that it reduces industrial efficiency, burdens businesses unduly and interferes with managerial freedom, in general the Act and its implementation have been accepted as having transformed for the better the previous 140-year history of workplace safety legislation in the UK. Environmental legislation in the UK from the 1970s onwards has also followed a similar path to that of the Health and Safety at Work Act, as have the requirements of many of the EU Directives to member states concerning safety and environment. A similar self-regulatory goal-directed ethos runs through the UK corporate governance codes and guidance from the late 1990s onwards (Turnbull 1999, FRC 2005, FRC 2010).

A number of other countries have adopted a broadly similar line to the UK's, for example Australia, New Zealand and Singapore but thus far most countries do not favour a self-regulatory emphasis over compliance-only. The compliance bias is probably an artefact of national history, judicial traditions and cultural expectations rather than any intellectual evaluation of its relative effectiveness. Countries whose populations traditionally pay more lip service than observance of legal regulations and formal requirements generally are more likely to favour the rigid rule-following requirements of a compliance-only regime. The requirements are relatively easy to identify – and ignore – until and unless the duty holders may be forced grudgingly to comply *de minimis* simply to avoid penalties. It is a chance that many feel they can take because in such countries the enforcement regime is probably weak, the imposition of penalties is very unlikely and the potential to bribe enforcement officials is culturally acceptable. Those countries with authoritarian cultures and traditionally governed by authoritarian regimes, such as China and Russia, are also likely to favour the rigid compliance-only model, as it fits quite naturally with the beliefs and norms of the population.

The US also favours compliance-only over self-regulation. Specific dos and don'ts, including sometimes quite technical prescriptions, are typically written into American legislation. However, practically it is virtually impossible to cover every eventuality and so omissions and loopholes are legion in such legislation. The author recalls that on a number of visits to the Occupational Safety and Health Administration (OSHA) and its National Institute for Occupational Safety and Health in the US in the 1970s and 1980s, officials he met were bemoaning the fact that their safety legislation (principally the Occupational Safety and Health Act 1970) had become a straightjacket because of its rigidity, incompleteness and absolute wording, which perversely allowed companies to circumvent the intent of the legislation. Any hazards or risk responses not specified in the legislation bore no compliance obligations and so were often ignored. Responsibility for avoidance of accidents was seen by many companies as residing with the law enforcement authorities and not the individual company. Success was seen as absence of an OSHA citation (an enforcement instrument) rather than minimal accidents, injuries and ill-health. The officials confided that they would much prefer a broader self-regulatory approach but it was now too late as Congress had been persuaded otherwise by powerful business interests. A similar picture of compliance-only emerged in the US with the Sarbanes-Oxley Act (SOX 2002).

A self-regulatory regime necessarily requires companies and duty holders to think actively and broadly about risks, their management and the goals to be achieved, whereas a strictly compliance-only approach encourages a narrow and rather sterile 'tick box' attitude. In the author's experience, those business executives who favour compliance-only tend to have a lazy attitude towards risk management, which they regard as an unnecessary imposition. One cannot say absolutely that a compliance-only approach can never work but it allows too much scope and opportunity to evade the specific wording of the legislation and makes it much more difficult to achieve effective corporate governance via this route. See Chapter 3 for further discussion.

## Robust Risk Management Systems

As this is not a 'how to' book, Chapter 2 only summarizes the main elements of corporate risk management in practice. The principles of ERM and the basic framework and process advocated by ISO 31000 are set out in Chapter 1. Together, the latter enable an organization to create a robust Risk Management System.

The concept of a system is one in which a number of components are interconnected and interact in a structured, organized way. Processes act on inputs to produce outputs which are largely controllable and predictable. Control, monitoring and communication are important characteristics of any system and there may even by identifiable sub-systems for these. For a comprehensive introduction to systems thinking and practice, see Waring (1996a).

Management 'systems' are more accurately described as process control models, as they are used to secure prediction and control of particular management processes. An effective risk management system would need to include the following essential structural and process components:

- risk policy, strategy, objectives (or Risk Strategy in IRM (2010));
- risk organization, responsibilities, planning, resources, communication (or Risk Architecture in IRM (2010));
- risk procedures, methodologies, standards, guidelines, techniques (or Risk Protocols in IRM (2010));
- risk identification, analysis and evaluation regime, including risk criteria, risk tolerance and risk appetite, all resulting in risk profiles (or Risk Assessment in IRM (2010));
- risk mediation/risk treatment;
- special sub-systems for capital projects, safety, health and environment (SHE)/major hazards, emergencies/crises/business continuity;
- monitoring and measurement of risk treatment performance;
- risk management audit and review regime.

The following diagram (Figure 2.1) shows how the key components of an effective risk management system interact.

While somewhat different to those depicted in IRM (2010), this diagram, which is based on that in Waring and Glendon (1998) and subsequent adaptations, for example Waring (2006b), does not suggest anything fundamentally different in concept and requirements to those in IRM (2010) and ISO 31000 (ISO 2009). What is important practically is that all the essential elements are addressed and implemented. The diagrammatic representation, if any, to follow is really only a matter of personal preference and not of substance. The following sub-sections outline the key requirements.

## RISK POLICY, STRATEGY, OBJECTIVES

The organization needs a clear written policy on risk management, which sets out the fundamental requirements from the board. The policy statement should include an indication of the overall risk management strategy for the foreseeable future as well as the enduring objectives.

Organizations often under-achieve in business because they set their sights too low. This is no less so in risk management. For example, if the policy and strategy refer only to the objectives of complying with legislation then there is little chance that staff will be innovative or strive for excellence. An effective risk management system therefore needs robust and challenging objectives to be stated and an indication of the high standards to be achieved Equally, an organization may under-achieve if its members are encouraged by ill-conceived statements in policy and strategy documents to treat risk management systems as an externally imposed and unproductive burden that stifles initiative and deters responsible risk-taking.

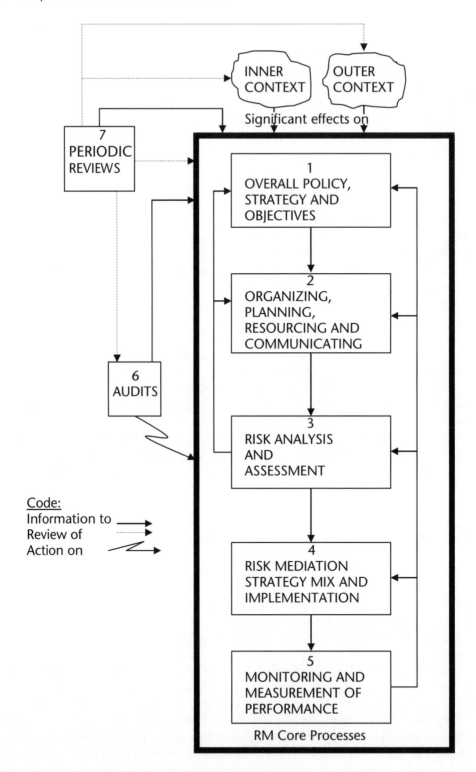

**Figure 2.1   Overall model of the risk management process**

*Source:* Adapted from Waring and Glendon (1998).

## RISK ARCHITECTURE (ORGANIZATION, RESPONSIBILITIES, PLANNING, RESOURCES, COMMUNICATION)

Although clear policy, strategy and objectives are necessary, without a practical implementation framework they will not progress beyond being noble intentions and wishes. Key responsibilities and accountabilities need to be allocated and a formal risk management organization identified. Board risk committees, non-executive directors (NEDs) and professional risk managers and advisers are discussed separately later in this chapter.

Risk management planning should include, at the very least, an annual action plan which is implemented under project management discipline to ensure that plan objectives are met and timetables adhered to.

## RISK ASSESSMENT REGIME

Before sensible actions can be taken to manage risks, it is necessary to understand the nature of the particular risk exposure, who or what is affected by it, the current state of mitigation, the scale of consequences, the frequency of occurrence and so on. On the basis of the identification, analysis and evaluation, judgements can then be made as to whether the risk (as currently mitigated) is acceptable or not and whether further actions are needed to reduce, control or otherwise manage the risk. An important requirement for making judgements about risk acceptability will be the need to establish acceptance and tolerability criteria.

The purpose of risk assessment is to inform decision-making about whether current risk levels are acceptable and whether further action is required to effectively manage those risks. A risk assessment addresses such questions as:

- What is the nature of the opportunities, hazards or threats?
- What is the degree of risk? – How big are the benefits or adverse consequences, how likely is it that they will occur?
- Is the risk acceptable?
- Are our present risk controls effective?
- What *could* be done about it? What are the options for mediation or mitigation, that is, treatment?
- What, if anything, *should* be done about?

To answer these questions, the risk assessment procedure comprises:

- define the boundaries of what is to be assessed;
- identify and describe the opportunities, hazards or threats;
- analyze the effects and consequences of the identified hazards, threats and opportunities and estimate the likelihoods of their occurrence;
- estimate risk values;
- evaluate the risk values, for example, high, medium or low;
- decide whether the risk is acceptable or unacceptable by comparing with acceptance criteria;
- decide if control action is required and, if so, what and how.

A systematic approach to risk assessment is needed and this requires firstly identifying both the opportunity exposures (upside risks) and the hazards or threats to which the organization or a defined part of it is exposed (downside or pure risks). There are a wide variety of techniques and approaches to identification, including brainstorming, checklists, group discussion, balanced score card, hazard surveys, Hazard and Operability Studies (HAZOPS).

Identified and evaluated risks need to be formally recorded or logged and typically this will be in a risk register. The corporate risk register acts as a common reference and may also cross-refer to more detailed risk registers and assessments of special topics such as environment, safety, security, supply chains and so on.

Two broad approaches to risk assessment have arisen – the heuristic and scientific approaches. Although a heuristic or 'rule-of-thumb' approach may include some form of quantification, generally it is qualitative and 'subjective', relying on the judgement of an individual or a team or group of individuals. A scientific approach, however, employs quantitative modelling and generally requires formal training in the mathematics used.

It is important to bear in mind that various scientific approaches to risk assessment, which use advanced mathematics and which typically are confined to Quantified Risk Assessment techniques relating to high finance or to major hazards, are not inherently superior to heuristic approaches. Since risk is essentially a product of cognitive processes in the brains of humans, all risk assessment is subjective. It is never free from the biases of human thought, whether those humans are experts or non-experts and whether the technique is heuristic or scientific. Indeed, it is often the case that mis-application of scientific approaches which produce quantified risk assessments may create a spurious confidence in the accuracy and meaning of the risk numbers. Risk assessment techniques therefore need to be selected and applied appropriately and with the necessary skill. For many if not most purposes, heuristic qualitative judgements will suffice.

Heuristic risk ratings are a common analytical technique. For example, for each identified hazard or threat (pure risk), the impact/severity and the probability will be rated as follows:

| **Impact/Severity** | **Probability** |
| --- | --- |
| 1 = negligible | 1 = very unlikely |
| 2 = minor | 2 = unlikely/low |
| 3 = moderate | 3 = conceivable |
| 4 = major | 4 = likely/high |
| 5 = catastrophic | 5 = inevitable |

The two sets of factors combined produce a 5 × 5 matrix of 25 risk levels. For example, an Impact/Severity rating of 4 or 5 combined with a Probability rating of 4 or 5 produce a risk level evaluated as Extreme, whereas an Impact/Severity rating of 1 or 2 combined with a Probability rating of 1, 2 or 3 produce a risk level evaluated as Insignificant. The risk levels are Extreme, High, Moderate, Low and Insignificant and each suggests appropriate action priorities. At the lowest risk level, Insignificant, no action is required.

A similar risk rating approach can be used for opportunity risks but with these the rating process is more complex as an opportunity risk can involve either gain or detriment or both. The Gain/Detriment rating ranges from +5 exceptional gain to -5 catastrophic detriment and two sets of 5 × 5 matrices result, one for gain and one for detriment, plus an additional neutral risk level where there is neither gain nor detriment.

| **Gain/Detriment Rating** | **Probability Rating** |
|---|---|
| +5 = exceptional gain | 1 = very unlikely |
| +4 = major gain | 2 = unlikely/low |
| +3 = moderate gain | 3 = conceivable |
| +2 = minor gain | 4 = likely/high |
| +1 = negligible gain | 5 = inevitable |
| 0 = neither gain nor detriment | |
| -1 = negligible detriment | |
| -2 = minor detriment | |
| -3 = moderate detriment | |
| -4 = major detriment | |
| -5 = catastrophic detriment | |

## RISK ACCEPTANCE CRITERIA

An important requirement for making judgements about risk acceptability will be the need to establish acceptance and tolerability criteria. To a large extent, such criteria are usually determined by the organization's management and its professional advisers and may be written into company risk standards. For some risk criteria, for example those relating to safety and major hazard risks, external regulators may have set legal compliance criteria. For example, for major hazards the As Low as Reasonably Practicable (ALARP) criteria are often imposed to help organizations determine what is a tolerable level of risk taking account of all mitigations (see for example Waring and Glendon 1998), as opposed to the ideal case of negligible risk.

For opportunity risks, risk appetite will be a strong factor in determining risk criteria. As outlined in Chapter 1, risk appetite refers to the prevailing attitude of the organization's management towards risk orientation or risk aversion relating to a particular risk. For example, an organization with a strong risk appetite at a particular time may enter into a rapid growth programme via M&As, the risk criteria including, for example, assets, liabilities, borrowings, market share, legal liabilities, cultural fit and brand image.

Regarding significant actions or new initiatives or ventures, it will be important to make decisions about risk acceptability beforehand. A range of views about and attitudes towards particular risks is likely in any organization and risk appetites may vary from one function to another. Internal workshops may be required to reconcile differences and arrive at agreed criteria for risk acceptability and compatibility with board expectations.

## ASSESSMENT-BASED RISK TREATMENT/MITIGATION

A range of intervention strategies is available to address the assessed risk. Usually a combination of approaches is required for best outcome and these usually involve both active and passive risk management.

Active risk management seeks to ensure that risk exposures are identified and assessed and unacceptable risks are reduced, controlled or otherwise mitigated. Active risk management seeks to change and improve the exposure characteristics. For example:

- investigating incidents;
- prior to JV decisions, assessing the compatibility of other parties for management systems, cultural fit, finances, liabilities, ethics and so on;
- plans and procedures for operating in overseas markets;
- listening to customers and acting on their suggestions/concerns/complaints;
- checking the integrity of job applicants and key staff;
- installing IT security systems;
- removing safety hazards;
- multiple sourcing of key supplies.

The options for active risk treatment are:

- avoidance/cessation;
- limitation;
- reduction (prevention/control);
- enhancement (opportunity risks only);
- sharing;
- deferment.

Any or all of these may be appropriate depending on the particular organization, its context and the particular risk exposure being addressed.

Passive risk treatment is, as the term suggests, a form of risk management that does not primarily involve changing or modifying the risk exposure. Specifically, passive risk management entails the application of finance to reduce or limit the financial impact if a specified risk should be realized. Usually, such risk financing relies on insurance of some kind.

Insurance is an essential component in risk management and it would be irresponsible for any organization not to obtain appropriate insurance cover for particular risks. Nevertheless, insurance cover on its own is not all-powerful and can never adequately address all of an organization's risk exposures or mitigation requirements. Insurance is passive, that is it does not affect in any way the actual risk exposure in terms of hazards, severity of effects (other than some financial impacts) or probability of effects. The best that can ever be hoped for from insurance policies is that they soften the financial blow in the event of specified perils occurring. Moreover, many risks are uninsurable, for example, damage to reputation.

To be sure, some kinds of insurance policy do require the insured party to exercise appropriate preventative or mitigating actions but that in itself is no guarantee that they will be carried out. Experience shows that many insured parties ignore such contractual terms and conditions. They may regret such inaction if and when they make a claim under the policy and the insurer repudiates the claim on the grounds of the insured's failure to mitigate the risk.

Risk financing includes such passive options as:

- transfer (financing including insurance);
- retention (self-insurance including captive insurance companies);
- alternative risk transfer.

In principle, any decision on what level or kind of risk financing to apply in any particular instance ought to be made only after competent risk assessment and application of appropriate active risk treatment measures. Risk financing is neither an alternative nor a superior option to active risk treatment. It is a necessary part of the overall risk management strategy but can only soften the financial blow if some, primarily insurable, risk exposures cause asset loss, liability, business interruption or other specified loss.

The modern approach to risk management is therefore to have, firstly, robust active risk management systems to ensure that risks are identified and assessed and unacceptable risks are reduced, controlled or otherwise mitigated, and then, secondly, adequate and appropriate passive risk management support, that is risk financing and other risk transfer arrangements, including insurance. Active mitigation also needs to include crisis management and business continuity planning.

## MONITORING AND MEASUREMENT OF RISK PERFORMANCE

Monitoring and measuring progress of the risk treatment programme and outcomes enables the organization to keep a check on the effectiveness of risk controls and to decide what, if any, further corrective actions are needed.

Measures of risk performance fall into two categories: active and reactive. Active measures of performance refer to those indicators which relate to current actions, activities or conditions aimed at creating a desirable or favourable effect or outcome. Because they relate to positive effects and current actions, they tend to provide more useful information about the state of risk management. For example:

- meeting business objectives;
- meeting objectives of annual risk management plan;
- reduction of risks assessed as 'high level' on a corporate risk matrix;
- levels of attainment on a risk management training course;
- scores attained in a risk management audit;
- reduction in the cost of risk.

Reactive measures of performance refer to those indicators which relate to past actions or events or historical data. For example:

- percentage of poor performing loans;
- accident rates;
- mortality rates;
- product recall rates.

It is rarely justifiable to rely on reactive measures alone since they usually relate to negative or unwanted outcomes and, by the time they are examined, they will already be out-of-date and can only point towards further investigation to gain more useful information.

Key Risk Indicators (KRIs) are those risk indicators which a particular organization's management judges to be critical to its overall context. For example, out of an array of perhaps 20 areas of risk exposure identified by the organization as significant, the following in Table 2.1 might be judged to be KRIs:

**Table 2.1    Some key risk indicators**

| Significant Risk Exposure | Risk Indicators | KRIs |
|---|---|---|
| Currency | Exchange rate fluctuations | US$/yen |
| M&As | Asset health | Yields; Time/cost to harmonize; |
|  | Systems compatibility | Cultural fit; Bonus levels vs profitability; |
|  | HR | Hazardous substance inventories; |
|  | Residual environmental liabilities | Environmental Impact; Assessment results |
| Product | Design hazards | Product recall policy and history |

Among a potentially large number of different risk management performance indicators, there are likely to be a small number that could be classed as 'key'. Key Performance Indicators (KPIs) are commonly used in many areas of management as the priority indicators for measuring management performance. Examples of risk management KPIs are meeting compliance criteria and meeting objectives of risk management action plans.

In risk management, it is a question of context and judgement as to which measures should be selected as KPIs in any organization. Some KPIs may also be drawn from KRIs where appropriate.

## RISK AUDIT AND REVIEW REGIME

In addition to routine monitoring by management, there is always a need to make a more in-depth and independent examination of how well the risk management system as a whole, as well as particular aspects of it, are functioning and delivering the required results. Independent audits alert management to potential 'blind spots' and provide a test of system effectiveness and efficiency.

An audit is much more than an inspection or a survey, although frequently the latter are wrongly described as 'audits'. An audit is a deep, critical and independent examination of a defined entity (organization, part of an organization, activity, process, equipment) designed to ascertain how far the entity is meeting current, and perhaps changing, requirements. The aim is not to apportion blame for any shortcomings but to help the organization 'see the wood for the trees' and highlight where improvements may be necessary.

The most common type of audit is the verification or compliance audit, which seeks to ascertain how far current standards are being met. Such standards may be in the form of legal requirements, relevant national, international or industry sector published standards, or the organization's own internal procedures or standards. Compliance audits are well known in the accounting and safety worlds.

Compliance audits, typically on an annual frequency, are an appropriate additional check to more frequent routine surveillance. They are appropriate when the relevant organization, strategies, processes, activities and conditions remain relatively stable and are not subject to major change or disaster. These audits do not question the validity of the relevant management systems or address the organizational culture.

Validation audits, however, are likely to be required under the following conditions of major change, instability, disruption or post-disaster:

- merger or acquisition;
- reorganization;
- expansion or retraction;
- new technical processes;
- new premises/relocation;
- new business strategy;
- new product design;
- new business/work in foreign territories;
- if a validation audit has not been done in past three to five years.

Validation audits should question the validity of the relevant management systems and address the organizational culture, in relation both to the current context and any significant changes. During a validation audit, it is quite likely that some compliance checks will also take place to add confidence to the data. However, the focus is more strategic and does not rely on multiple checklists or paper trails.

## Case 2.1    A Common System Defect

In the author's experience, even organizations that do very well in their overall approach to risk management often fail to establish a formal 'noticing and intelligence' system. A risk noticing and intelligence system is an information gathering, analysis and dissemination function designed to identify and monitor significant risk exposure and management issues of such topics as:

*Internal changes and developments*

- M&As;
- company reorganizations;
- consolidation versus growth;
- expansion and diversification;
- new policies and strategies;
- new products.

*External changes and developments*

- regulation and taxation;
- impact of new technologies on, for example, market risks, costs and pricing, competitiveness, resources;
- stability/instability issues in sourcing and operating territories;
- demographic, socio-political and socio-economic factors in operating territories;
- global energy supplies;
- foreign exchange trends.

In one case, a board recognized that such a risk noticing and intelligence system could keep it alert to potentially significant new threats or changes (rapid or subtle) in the company's risk exposures and risk profile. A lack of one would hamper not only strategic oversight but also operational risk management, for example, routine risk surveillance may not be sufficient in scope; feedback to staff on significant issues may not be adequate or may not occur; training needs may not be identified. A system of this kind was also recognized as a help with business continuity and crisis management planning (CMP) (see Chapter 6).

Since auditors need to be independent of the entity being audited, internal risk management audits are only fully defensible if the auditors are assembled from other parts of the organization. However, even in the best-run organizations, internal auditors are not infallible and there is also the potential drawback that however carefully internal auditors are selected some may owe prior allegiances (however subtle) to those being audited or may feel awkward about being too honest in their report. Therefore, independent external audits may also be appropriate from time to time and in some instances are required by statutory legislation. Diverse examples are the UK Companies Act 2006 Part 16 and Regulation 4 of the Singapore Workplace Safety and Health (Shipbuilding and Ship-Repairing) Regulations 2008.

In addition to audits, it is normally part of every manager's job to engage in periodic reviews of the functions, activities, work or systems for which the manager is responsible. Reviews should be as frequent as the context demands. Typically, organizations require a variety of quarterly, six-monthly and annual reviews. Risk management ought to be one of the areas subject to such periodic formal review and, moreover, to comply with corporate governance requirements, 'the board should at least annually conduct a review of the effectiveness of the company's risk management and internal control systems' (Turnbull 1999, FRC 2005 and 2010). Independent external reviews by consultants may be required in any of the same set of circumstances that may require independent external audits. A risk management review is also the recommended starting point for initiating the risk management process (see below).

## Case 2.2    Audit or Review?

For good or ill, the terms 'audit' and 'review' are frequently used as equivalent, although clearly this is not entirely accurate. A risk review does not have to be a 'deep and critical examination', for example, and it does not have to be independent. In many instances, however, a review of a risk management system will be equivalent to a validation audit of it. Much depends on the context and terms of reference of those carrying out the review/audit. Nevertheless, in the author's experience it is not uncommon for boards to make quite an issue of what to call the examination. In one case, the client directors who commissioned the examination insisted that it could not be referred to as an audit either in the proposal, report or other documentation or orally; it had to be termed a 'risks review'. Their reasoning was that in their experience the word 'audit' would be interpreted negatively among directors and executive management. It was felt that 'review' would be interpreted less threateningly and would result in better cooperation and a more useful outcome.

# Board Audit and Risk Committees

The UK Corporate Governance Code (FRC 2005, 2010) states that:

> *the board should establish an audit committee of at least three, or in the case of smaller companies, two, independent non-executive directors (NEDs). In smaller companies, the company Chairman may be a member of, but not chair, the committee in addition to the independent NEDs, provided he or she was considered independent on appointment as Chairman. The board should satisfy itself that at least one member of the audit committee has recent and relevant financial experience.*

The audit committee's main role and responsibilities set out in the code are primarily financial in scope. However, in relation to risk, the code specifies that one of the audit committee's roles and responsibilities is 'to review the company's internal financial controls and, unless expressly addressed by a separate board risk committee composed of independent directors, or by the board itself, to review the company's internal control and risk management systems'.

The distinction expressed in the code between the board audit committee and the board risk committee is both significant and revealing. It betrays the fact that traditionally there has been a financial bias to the perception and understanding of corporate risk and that this bias continues. Financial controls are clearly regarded as the most important risk issue, which the audit committee is required to focus on. The unfortunate implication is that, contrary to the revised Turnbull guide (FRC 2005), the 'internal control and risk management systems' (presumably covering all significant risk exposures and not just financial risks) are seen as secondary issues. The 2010 code clearly implies that the board risk committee is an optional extra and that the audit committee (or even the board) is quite capable on its own of dealing with the full array of risks and risk management issues.

It is also important to appreciate that the existence of a board risk committee does not imply that thereby the board can delegate its supervening responsibility and accountability for risk and its management, even though much of the detailed work may be undertaken by the risk committee.

The typical distinct and separate functions of the two committees are summarized as follows (adapted from IRM 2010):

*Board Audit Committee*

- receive routine reports from Board Risk Committee;
- set annual audit programme and priorities;
- monitor progress with audit recommendations;
- provide risk assurance to the board;
- oversee risk management structures and processes.

*Board Risk Committee*

- formulate corporate risk management strategy, policy, standards and criteria based on risk profiles and risk appetites;

- receive and review periodic risk reports (routine and *ad hoc*) from business units, review risk management programmes and oversee compilation and review of corporate risk register;
- track risk management activity and performance in the business units;
- receive instructions from the board and alerts from the Board Audit Committee on risk issues and respond accordingly;
- oversee the investigation of significant risk incidents (internal and, as appropriate, external), evaluate the findings and consider any implications for risk controls, risk assessment, training and information; report to the board and disseminate any lessons to be learned to the business units;
- commission independent non-financial audits and reviews on significant risk matters;
- make reports and recommendations to the board and to the audit committee as appropriate;
- keep the risk management context under review, for example, operate a risk intelligence and noticing system.

In the author's opinion, there are strong arguments for having a board risk committee because its role and functions are distinct and separate from those of a board audit committee. Whereas the audit committee is expected to concentrate on audits relating to current financial matters and those of the recent past, a board risk committee has a quite different purpose, which is to examine, track, advise and formulate policy on all risk matters (historical, current and future) and reporting both directly to the board and indirectly to the audit committee. The board risk committee should be considering such topics as how the company would cope in the event of major potential crises of various kinds, what should be the company's position on overseas bribery and corruption, what the risk implications are of new technology beginning to enter the industry, what are the company's supply chain risk exposures, and so on. An audit committee might well struggle to deal with such matters effectively in addition to its own demanding financial brief. In the author's experience, it is often the lack of a distinct board risk committee that results in some organizations developing serious blind spots on risk exposures and ending up in an unnecessary mess with adverse corporate consequences.

## Case 2.3    Are Board Risk Committees Necessary?

A very large privately-owned multi-national group was run by a group board. Although in private ownership for over 100 years, the board had decided decades ago to run the business with professional managers and now members of the shareholding family owners were only a minority of directors. The board felt that it was appropriate to follow as far as possible the general principles of corporate governance as if it were a publicly listed company. However, the group board had neither an audit committee nor a risk committee and such structures were left to the subordinate boards to decide. Overall, the group board had a policy of delegated responsibility and accountability, which it was felt encouraged subordinate boards and executive management to develop an entrepreneurial culture. The financial strength and brand reputation of the group and its survival for over 100 years through wars and financial crises, both regional and global, were testimony to the model's validity.

One of the main board directors (who was also an owner) became concerned that, despite the continuing success of the group, there were doubts about whether the subordinate companies (organized into several divisions each with a cascade of operating companies) had an adequate grasp of risk management requirements. His concern had been prompted by a number of risk incidents that involved not insignificant uninsured losses. In conjunction with the Group Chief Executive, he therefore commissioned an independent external review of significant risk exposures in the operating divisions.

Key findings of the review included:

- many common risk exposures across the divisions but no sharing of information, ideas or risk management techniques; 'wheel reinvention' evident;
- silo mentality;
- blind spots regarding particular significant risk exposures;
- limited view of potential crises and of the need for CMP and business continuity;
- no risk intelligence and noticing system in any division;
- divisions having no or weakly qualified professional risk management personnel;
- no risk assessment regime;
- no board risk committees but a few audit committees which included executive directors rather than solely NEDs.

The review report advised that establishing separate board risk committees and providing access to professionally qualified risk managers would be needed to raise the standard of risk management. Moreover, there was reluctance within the divisions to change the *status quo* on risk management, based on a frequently stated but unsubstantiated belief among senior executives that as they were all long-standing experts in their field they automatically knew enough to manage their corporate risks well without recourse to risk committees and experienced risk professionals. This view persisted despite evidence of a number of narrowly averted corporate disasters which should never have occurred if proper risk management systems had been in place. The report discussed at some length the implications of justifying the retention of the *status quo* by reference to 'no actual disaster yet'.

## Case 2.4   A Review for the Board Risk Committee

The newly formed board risk committee of a large multi-national corporation in the newspapers and media sector decided that as a priority they should commission from an external consultant an independent audit and review of health and safety management across the corporate organization. Based in the UK, the latter comprised seven major divisions operating across four continents, including a considerable number of stock exchange listed companies and hundreds of subordinate companies. The audit and review was prompted by a number of recent serious accidents in the organization and a general uneasiness in the board about just how adequate the standard of safety management was.

As is often the case, the external consultant found something of a 'curate's egg' in that some companies had relatively few health and safety issues whereas others needed to make some significant improvements. Again, as is so often the case, the required improvements were mainly in the safety management system (SMS) and management attitudes towards health and safety risks. Such improvements required careful attention and thought rather than financial outlay and certainly did not involve capital expenditure. However, the study also identified that a number of broadly similar businesses had been operating entirely autonomously and did not have a common approach to their common health and safety issues or any other risk management matters. There was already the real possibility of costly 'wheel reinvention' by the separate businesses, with potentially contradictory efforts and possibly unsafe outcomes for some. The report of the audit and review, presented at a meeting of the board risk committee, was fully accepted. One immediate effect of the report, in addition to initiating an action plan to implement its recommendations, was the opening up of a debate in the board about achieving better cost efficiency across the organization and better business-to-business communication while at the same time maintaining sufficient managerial independence for the individual businesses.

## The Role of Non-Executive Directors

The appointment and role of independent NEDs in respect of a unitary board are set out in the UK Corporate Governance Code (FRC 2010). Their primary role is to constructively challenge and help develop proposals on strategy. Among other things, 'Non-executive directors should scrutinize the performance of management in meeting agreed goals and objectives and monitor the reporting of performance. They should satisfy themselves on the integrity of financial information and that financial controls and systems of risk management are robust and defensible.' In other words, they are there to provide independent input to the board and an independent check on board deliberations and decisions regarding corporate risk. They should be selected for their wealth of knowledge, skills and experience which executive directors may lack and this implies that they must almost certainly have a substantial corporate background elsewhere, including time as a main board executive director in other large companies.

The independence of NEDs is all-important, since their input to the board and to any of its committees has to be seen to be devoid of any vested interest that might colour their advice. In large publicly listed companies that are often subject to scrutiny by institutional shareholders as well as by the media and government, the selection of independent NEDs tends to be fairly scrupulous. This may not always be the case with smaller companies, where executive directors' personal friendships may have more influence in the selection of NEDs.

With family-controlled listed companies (see Chapter 5 for further discussion), especially those in countries having slack implementation of corporate governance rules and law enforcement generally and a 'What can we get away with?' business culture, there is always the danger of NEDS being appointed on little more than a *sine cure* basis. Where this happens, their appointment and role are not much more than a gesture and window dressing to give an appearance of probity and good governance. Typically, the NEDs will be invited once or twice a year to a perfunctory board meeting and then whisked off for a jolly nice lunch before being given a cheque (or even a cash 'bung') as their director's fee. In more robust jurisdictions, such as the UK, NEDs are likely to avoid such invitations to join dubious boards because they may well be as fully liable as executive directors for any corporate misdemeanours.

It should be noted that corporate governance codes allow some latitude on how companies should comply and, for example, the membership of some companies' board risk committees comprise a mix of executive directors and independent NEDs instead of exclusively NEDs. If necessary, the 'comply or explain' rule can be used in the annual report to shareholders.

## Case 2.5    An Eclectic Board Risk Committee

A large publicly listed multi-national company based in the UK, whose ownership was still 60 per cent family controlled, had long been run by professional managers. Only the board Chairman, a member of the House of Lords, was a family director and shareholder. A board risk committee had been set up comprising the Group Chief Executive as committee Chairman, the main board Chairman, the Group Finance Director, the Group HR Director, the Group Risk Manager and two NEDs from the main board. The two NEDs had substantial executive director experience in other large PLCs and one had significant experience on a board risk committee.

Over several months, during which time the author was engaged as an external consultant, the wide-ranging topics addressed by the board risk committee included:

- contingency planning for future strikes and other industrial action;
- ensuring skill retention and continuity in an increasingly high churn rate workforce;
- coping with long-serving loyal employees reluctant to learn new technology skills;
- corporate reputation and brand protection;
- safety, health, fire and environmental risk management;
- IT vulnerabilities affecting production, sales and accounting;
- countering aggressive competitors who were using e-commerce and taking customers and market share.

# Professional Risk Managers and Advisers

Increasingly, large organizations are appointing risk managers and risk advisers to their staff in recognition of the expanding scope of risk management demands and the complexities of the subject matter. The need for professional qualifications in risk management is also being recognized more than in the twentieth century. However, many risk managers' jobs are often quite narrow in the scope of risk management issues they are expected to cover and may reflect professional interests and functions that are dominant in the organization rather than the actual array of significant risk exposures. The rise of the so-called Chief Risk Officer (CRO) is an example of a job title found almost exclusively in the finance sector and whose functions are usually heavily orientated towards such topics as credit risk, Basel II and Solvency II compliance rather than ISO 31000. If these CROs possess any professional qualifications in risk management, they are likely to be those of bodies such as the Professional Risk Managers' International Association (PRMIA). The focus of a CRO and the risk concepts and language of the finance sector are quite alien to most other sectors that are more at home with ISO 31000 and employing a Group Risk Manager with a professional qualification from the IRM, for example.

In the last century, many risk management departments were little more than insurance buyers for the organization and concentrated on insurable risks and passive risk management. Important as these aspects of risk management are, on their own they do not enable an organization to be in real active control of all the risk exposures to the enterprise. There is therefore a need to be wary of instances where a job title of Group Risk Manager is a misnomer for Group Insurance Manager.

The primary role of internal risk management departments should be to promote and drive risk management, determine the policy and strategy for risk management, set risk management standards and key criteria, build risk awareness and act as the principal source of professional advice on risk management requirements. Where a board risk committee exists, a Group Risk Manager or someone with a similar title and function should be working closely with the committee to carry out or facilitate many of its activities.

Since the range of potential risk exposures is so large and the methods and techniques needed to address them so varied, it has become increasingly necessary for internal risk management and other functions to call on external consultants for expert advice and assistance when necessary. External risk consultants are appropriate for a range of inputs, such as:

- independent audits and reviews;
- development and improvement of risk management systems;
- risk assessments requiring expert technical knowledge;
- problem-solving requiring expert technical knowledge;
- management training in risk subjects.

Ideally, consultants need to possess:

- advanced formal qualifications in risk by examination, for example a Masters degree obtainable via a number of universities in the UK, Australia and elsewhere;
- enhanced skills beyond mere competence, as evidenced by substantial experience in tackling complex problems or strategic issues;
- many years' practical experience in risk management, probably well in excess of ten years;
- independent opinions and strong sense of ethical standards;
- senior membership of relevant professional risk management bodies.

## A Practical Starting Point for the Risk Management Process

A common problem encountered by organizations that are relatively inexperienced in ERM is where and how to begin. The overall risk management system, including the risk architecture and process, presents a mass of detailed requirements which can seem quite daunting. In the author's opinion, the answer to this 'how to break in?' question has been concisely expressed in ASNZ 4360. Although now defunct and subsumed within ISO 31000, the value of its statement on carrying out an initial Business Risk Appraisal lives on.

The objectives of an initial Business Risk Appraisal (ASNZ 4360) are:

*Before starting to develop a risk management plan, the organization should critically review and assess ... the risk management process ... This review should reflect the risk management needs of the organization and its context. The review should deliver a structured appreciation of:*

- *the maturity, characteristics and effectiveness of existing business and risk management culture and systems;*
- *the degree of integration and consistency of risk management across the organization and across different types of risk;*
- *the processes and systems that should be modified or extended;*
- *constraints that might limit the introduction of systematic risk management;*
- *legislative or compliance requirements;*
- *resource constraints.*

A Business Risk Appraisal is a special review comprising a systematic examination of risk exposures across the enterprise or a defined part of it and the efficacy of the organization's systems for managing them. Such an appraisal might be conducted at any time deemed appropriate by the board, its audit committee or its risk committee and not just as an initiating action for a new risk management regime.

# 3 *Countering Tunnel Vision and Quack Governance*

Chapters 1 and 2 focussed on what organizations ought to do for effective corporate risk management and governance. Despite all the codes, regulations, standards and best practice guidance available on these subjects, the fact remains that there is still a long way to go before it can be stated with confidence that the majority of organizations have fully implemented the requirements in practice and in spirit. Chapter 3 considers why such mismanagement flourishes. In the author's opinion based on 35 years' professional experience, the underlying causes of risk management failure in organizations boil down to a toxic combination of incompetence, tunnel vision, quackery and personal agendas, especially but not exclusively at board level.

## The Seeds of Tunnel Vision

Most people understand what 'tunnel vision' means when used metaphorically but it is perhaps necessary just to define it. The origin of the term lies in medicine and an ophthalmic condition whereby the person affected only has a central cylindrical field of vision (tunnel vision) instead of the normal full field vision. When used metaphorically, it refers to a person, group or organization whose recognition and understanding of a subject is severely limited and excludes much of surrounding relevance and importance while focussing only on a small number of supposedly central issues which they believe fully satisfies requirements. Other correlated visual metaphors include 'myopia', 'blind spots' and 'shooting at the mice while missing the elephants'.

The author identifies, in no particular order, the following seeds of tunnel vision in corporate risk management, which are likely to be an incomplete list:

- failure to recognize risk interdependencies;
- finance bias to risk management;
- bounded rationality, narrow risk-related experience, untutored view/ignorance, unchallenged dogma;
- ignoring people risks and HR risks;
- reaction rather than pre-emption, including failure to exercise due diligence (see Chapters 7 and 8);
- fixation on salvation models;
- insurance and risk transfer bias;
- risk quantification bias and focus on single metrics;
- personal agendas and self-serving calculation.

The following sub-sections examine some of these issues.

## Ignoring Risk Interdependencies

Organizations are subject not only to multiple risk exposures but also to the effects of dynamic interdependencies among these exposures. As Professor Klaus Schwab, the founder and Executive Chairman of the WEF noted in its 2008 Global Risks Report (WEF 2008), 'The interconnectedness of global risks discussed in this report reflects the need for a collaborative framework of response.' Sean Cleary, strategic adviser to WEF noted further that 'The world has become more complex and interconnected with risk becoming systemic. We have to up our game very dramatically.'

Undoubtedly, global risks are important but it is also important for organizations to understand that systemic risk is not something that only relates to external risk exposures and the wider world. Risks within the organization also interact and therefore systemic thinking is required for even day-to-day management of internal risks. Many of the cases cited throughout this book demonstrate all too clearly how one uncontrolled internal risk exposure can exacerbate a number of other risks and sometimes disastrously. For example, both BP's Deepwater Horizon disaster in 2010 and the PetroChina Jilin disaster in 2005 triggered a cascade of consequential exposures (for example, environmental, commercial, criminal and civil liabilities, share values, reputation, brand). In the Mari-Vasillikos disaster in Cyprus in July 2011 (see Chapter 15), failure to store a consignment of mixed munitions safely in a naval base resulted in a huge explosion which, apart from killing and injuring people, knocked out the neighbouring Electricity Authority's power station, which supplied 60 per cent of the country's electricity. For many weeks, the whole country endured power cuts, employers operated part time and the economy went into recession.

In some instances, some of the very internal mechanisms set up to ensure better governance and risk management have themselves now become regarded as sources of risk which interact with other risks. One has only to consider, for example, the growing furore in recent years, and especially since the 2008–2009 global financial crisis, regarding excessive executive remuneration and bonuses in large publicly listed companies. In the finance sector in particular, CEOs and other senior executives continue to draw huge seven-figure salaries plus share options as well as annual bonuses, which often rival the salaries. Some of these same individuals have presided over banks that had to be rescued by the government (that is, the taxpayer). Meanwhile, and in a period of recession, the mass of more lowly employees in those same and similar companies are paid relatively little and are exposed to an increased threat of redundancy.

The recipients of this largesse, widely regarded by the public rightly or wrongly as little more than greedy parasites, typically argue that they warrant such huge bonuses because (a) they have shown exceptional skill and performance, (b) such bonus levels are comparable with others in the sector, and (c) if they did not get them then they would simply move to a competitor company for a higher remuneration package. They may well have shown exceptional performance and warrant a bonus but many observers point out that the bonus levels appear to be stratospherically out of proportion to the claimed merit and related much more to argument (b). If bonus levels are determined by a so-called 'going rate' in the sector, then high and ever increasing rates are almost inevitable as executives compare notes and press for more and more. When (b) is coupled with argument (c), which to many people seems like thinly disguised blackmail by such executives, the mechanism becomes self-perpetuating. This is especially the case where board remuneration committees fail to get a grip on the situation and allow themselves to be, in effect, led by specious arguments and intimidated by unscrupulous executives and the fear of losing self-styled high fliers.

The board and its various governance committees are supposed to act in the overall best interests of the organization and not pander to the self-serving arguments and demands of a minority of selfish executives, no matter how important they are or might think they are. If they fail to discharge this governance responsibility, they run the very real risk of the organization receiving widespread public opprobrium on a scale serious enough to severely damage its corporate reputation and brand. This is, in effect, what happened to the Royal Bank of Scotland (RBS) in 2007–2008.

## Case 3.1    The RBS Scandal

In 2007, the then CEO of RBS, Sir Fred Goodwin, oversaw the €72 billion takeover of the Dutch financial group ABN Amro Holdings NV. However, there were 'underlying deficiencies in RBS management, governance and culture which made it prone to make poor decisions' (FSA 2011). In particular, the CEO and board should have known that RBS did not have the capacity to take over such a large undertaking. Before long, RBS was racking up huge debts and its resources were becoming depleted. By autumn 2008, the bank was in serious trouble and heading for collapse. In October 2008, the Government felt obliged to step in urgently to protect the bank but at a cost to the UK taxpayer of £45 billion in direct financial support, the world's largest ever bank bailout. In addition, the bank received several hundred £billion more in state-guaranteed loans and insurance bonds.

The official inquiry report into the RBS affair (FSA 2011) noted how for several years prior to the near collapse the CEO had had a very bad relationship with the official regulator, the Financial Services Authority (FSA), and had among other things doctored a formal FSA notice to the RBS board so that crucial risk warnings were removed. The official inquiry report noted with some displeasure that despite all that had happened 'no-one has ever been punished'.

Following the bailout, Goodwin was reported to have left RBS with a pension worth £693,000 per annum for life arising from a total pay-off estimated at £17 million. Contractually, he was able to receive the full pension by taking early retirement at age 50 rather than being fired for cause which would have resulted in a substantial loss of pension. Despite widespread public anger and calls for him to return his pension fund to the company, he refused. However, in June 2009, he gave up some £200,000 per annum following negotiations with RBS which, with a £2.7 million tax free lump sum, reduced his annual pension to around £350,000. Seemingly having been rewarded for catastrophic failure and remaining defiant against any kind of censure, he has been vilified constantly in the media. In January 2012, officials acting for the Queen's Honours List stripped him of his knighthood as a further mark of public disapproval, a particular humiliation for such a person now styled just Fred Goodwin and no longer Sir Fred Goodwin.

More than three years after the 2008 RBS debacle and with the bank still backed by a Government shareholding of 66.46 per cent and a total financial interest of 82 per cent, in January 2012 the board nevertheless offered Goodwin's successor Stephen Hester a bonus of 3.6 million shares worth around £1 million. Following much bad publicity, within a couple of weeks he decided not to accept the bonus. The RBS Chairman Philip Hampton also decided to forego his bonus award of shares worth some £1.4 million. In the absence of publicity and mammoth public disapproval and humiliation, these bonus awards would probably have been accepted.

The case demonstrates how badly managed M&A risks can create or aggravate liquidity risks and undercapitalization risks and lead to corporate collapse and irreparable damage to an organization's reputation and brand. Poor judgement and decision-making by the board and its remuneration committee after the bailout then enabled the CEO eventually to leave the company with a £multi-million pension fund and, moreover, the excessive bonus awards for board members continued unabated. Further, the RBS scandal along with several others in large financial organizations resulted in a devastating loss of public trust and confidence in the whole sector.

Removing the culture of boardroom excess and 'reward for failure' in the banking sector has now become a political time-bomb for the UK Government. This culture of excessive boardroom remuneration and reward for failure has become the twenty-first century manifestation of 'the unpleasant and unacceptable face of capitalism', a phrase coined by British Prime Minister Edward Heath in 1973 to describe the highly questionable behaviour of the chief executive and directors of the London and Rhodesian Mining Co (Lonrho) relating to control of the company.

## Finance Bias

There remains a tendency for financial risk to dominate the risk management thinking of many boards. Yet, important as financial risk exposures undoubtedly are, organizations routinely overlook or even dismiss other equally significant risks because their attention is biased towards finance issues. Even in the finance sector, where reasonably one might expect attention to financial risks to predominate, the bias is often excessive. ERM is frequently dealt with as if all that matters are the primary Basel II financial exposures of credit, liquidity and market risks. For example, a survey of financial institutions in Hong Kong in 2008 commissioned by the author and conducted by the Centre for Corporate Governance and Financial Policy found that 70 per cent (more than 60 responding organizations) believed that compliance with Basel II and/or SOX fulfilled most of the requirements of ERM. Only 22 per cent of the responding organizations recognized the existence of ASNZ 4360 (the most widely used general risk management standard available at that time and now replaced by ISO 31000). The report also noted that when such institutions assessed risk exposures of their clients as part of due diligence for M&As, JVs, capital project investments and initial public offerings (IPO) in which the institution had a major stake or interest, they concentrated on accounting/financial risks, legal risks and corporate management risks while ignoring political risks, fraud and corruption, IP and brand risks, product risks, and environmental/major hazard risks.

Many of the major accounting and audit firms have for years been peddling to all sectors what they call ERM consulting services that really only focus on finance and accounting requirements in line with Basel II and SOX and not on the wider spectrum of significant risks to the enterprise. Yet, the underlying risks that, for example, floored Barings Bank, Lehman Brothers and Halifax–Bank of Scotland (HBOS) and greatly embarrassed Société Générale and RBS were actually in the attitudes and cultures of their respective boardrooms and senior executives – the 'people' risks. HR risk management and other operational risk controls that ought to have raised red flags and countered the tunnel vision were either absent or defective. For further discussion, see below and Chapter 4.

## Ignorance and Bounded Rationality

Bounded rationality (Simon 1972) refers to the inherent limitations on what an individual or a group can know and understand about a particular matter. It is impossible for anyone to be all-knowing. However, this is not a ready excuse for ignorance. Board members and other senior executives must be able to show due diligence in acquiring the necessary breadth and depth of knowledge about corporate risk and risk management generally as well as the significant risk exposures of their particular organization. Training comes into it as do good internal communication and intelligence systems. In the twenty-first century, any such corporate custodian who, after a serious incident or calamity, pleads that he or she did not know about the exposure or tries to play dumb about having had a responsibility for avoiding or preventing it, will get little sympathy from corporate stakeholders, state regulators, official inquiries, the courts or the media.

### Case 3.2   What the Board Believed Were the Facts

Following a major fire in which large numbers of passengers, other members of the public and staff were killed or injured, the rapid transit company involved became subject to an official government inquiry. The company's board commissioned a number of independent external reports on, among other things, the company's SMS and the state of safety training and emergency preparedness of operational staff. Prefacing the study, board members advised the consultant team led by the author that, based on their own post-disaster enquiries, they were confident that a robust and efficient safety training regime was in place and they just wanted to see if nonetheless any improvements could be made.

In fact, the consultants discovered that, far from being exemplary, the safety training regime was archaic, inefficient and not fit for purpose. Many operatives, who were supposed to receive regular update training and at least every two years, had never received any, in some cases over an employment period spanning decades. The current employee establishment database was in a shambles and included individuals who had left the company or died years ago. The paper-based safety training records were equally chaotic, with many records missing or jumbled up, for example surnames beginning with M mixed up with those beginning with W and vice-versa. Much of the content of safety training was at odds with the content of the network operational safety manual, which in turn sometimes had a poor fit with actual conditions and requirements at a particular station. Few stations, including deep underground stations, had ever carried out any emergency evacuation exercises. Updates and revisions for the loose-leaf operational safety manual were sent out to each station from corporate headquarters with a standing instruction to replace the old sheets with the new ones. Unfortunately, whereas some stations did precisely as instructed, others failed to replace them while others simply hand annotated the changes onto the old pages. The result was a highly variable and, in some cases, incorrect and unsafe set of instructions all across the network.

When confronted with the evidence, board members had great difficulty in accepting it since it was at such variance with what they had convinced themselves was true. This case not only demonstrates the problem of bounded rationality but also the dangers of boards relying exclusively on subordinates' and business units' own reports on risk management issues, which sometimes may be economical with the truth for a variety of reasons.

Regrettably, despite corporate governance responsibilities being taken more seriously in recent years, in the author's experience, many and perhaps most board members in most large organizations are still woefully lacking in any core knowledge and understanding of risk management. Their knowledge is largely untutored and uninformed; it amounts to little more than accumulated personal experience, with all its limitations, biases and distortions. While experience is valuable, indeed essential, it is no substitute for a modest but accurate grounding in the subject. No one would suggest that board members or other senior executives other than, say, a Director of Risk, Group Risk Manager or a CRO should obtain professional qualifications in risk management. However, board members are notoriously reluctant to spend even half a day on a special briefing or workshop on the subject, which many of them regard as unnecessary as they believe that their prior knowledge and experience are all that is needed. They often put forward the self-deception that their many years' experience helping to run successful businesses is proof enough that they know all about risk management. Organizations where such child-like naïvety and arrogance are prevalent are high contenders for 'accidents waiting to happen'. It is instructive to recall the damning words of Nick Leeson about the ignorance and naïvety of his bosses at Barings prior to the collapse (Waring and Glendon 1998): 'They were always too busy and too self-important, and were always on the telephone. They had the attention span of a gnat. They could not make the time to work through a sheet of numbers and spot that it didn't add up'. No relevant training in risk management was discernible at Barings, at any level, and not even the rudiments of a risk management system existed. So much for preposterous assertions by some company directors that by virtue of their being a director they already know enough about risk management!

In addition, risk management has become an attractive haven for executives and professionals from all walks of life who are looking for a mid-career change. Many such individuals have moved into risk management from jobs in internal audit or in the police and security services. While many of these undoubtedly bring a wealth of knowledge and experience in their albeit limited areas and aspects of risk management, that fact alone does not entitle them to be automatically rebadged as 'risk management experts' in the sense that could be applied realistically to all the varied kinds of corporate risk exposure within the scope and meaning of ERM. Unfortunately, while risk management remains an unregulated profession, it is difficult to stop individuals and companies being 'economical with the truth' in these matters. Organizations hiring risk managers or risk management consultants need to guard against sloppy or *laissez-faire* recruitment and selection criteria so that inadequately qualified persons are prevented from getting in and straying beyond their competence.

## Ignoring People and Human Resource Risks

In the author's experience, most board members are decidedly uncomfortable with dealing with 'people risks'. While perhaps being able to grapple with financial issues such as credit risk, cash flow, treasury risks and currency exposures, there is hesitancy when it comes to threats that are more difficult to pin down because they involve often complex psychological factors of individuals or groups in the organization. In general, anything to do with human behaviour and psychology is seen as mumbo-jumbo, vaguely threatening and best kept locked away firmly in the HR department. There is even more reluctance when the 'people' risks lie in the boardroom itself!

Humans exhibit contrary attitudes when it comes to trusting others. There is an underlying tendency prevalent in humans to trust that others will be as honest and well-intentioned as they are but this sits uncomfortably with the opposite tendency in all of us not to be too trusting of others. One has only to consider the lax and sloppy manner in which so many employees, including senior executives, are hired and promoted with only a superficial check into their character and background (see Chapter 7). The more senior the post, the greater the willingness for prospective employers to rely heavily on the candidate's self-certified CV, plus a couple of interviews and references from a current or previous employer. This approach is very common, almost the norm, in the Far East and Asia. Sometimes, undue influence such as personal friendships, family connections or memberships of particular professional clubs or groups persuades companies and their boards to confer too much trust on individuals, both during and after recruitment. Boards have difficulty in believing that someone who is 'one of us' or who 'was recommended by Fred Bloggs over at XYZ Corp' may possess some serious flaws or that the board's trust will never be abused. This was clear in the televised evidence of board members of the major banks in response to questioning in the House of Commons Treasury Committee inquiry in 2009 into the failure of UK banks. Some were barely able to describe the flimsy recruitment and due diligence process for the hiring of senior executives which they themselves had participated in and gave the vivid impression that it was an extremely casual and unimportant process. The Committee's official report (HOCTC 2009) also commented on how, in the case of the HBOS crisis for its new owner Lloyds TSB the explicit prior warnings from Mr Paul Moore, the HBOS Head of Group Regulatory Risk, to the HBOS Chairman Lord Stevens had not only been dismissed but Mr Moore himself had then been dismissed from his job for being too critical. Paradoxically, the same boards that fail to control 'people risks' may have an excessive reliance on procedural, bureaucratic financial/accounting risk protection such as SOX, Basel II and audit, which often fail to spot the risk 'elephants in the room'. The Barings, Lehman, RBS and HBOS cases are prime examples of such failures.

A number of authors describe in detail the psychological elements of dysfunctional boards or individual leaders that result in increased risk exposures and sometimes crises, for example Bovard (2008a and b), Burke and Cooper (2010), Glendon (2004a and b), Glendon and Waring (2007), Leeb (2006). The characteristics and effects of individual directors summarized variously as 'obstinate', 'authoritarian', 'terrifying', 'capricious', 'a bulldozer' and so on are well recognized but rarely challenged by fellow directors or the board chairman, perhaps because they do not recognize the potential or actual damage that arises, or because they make allowances in view of the positive contribution the director also makes, or because they are intimidated.

## Case 3.3   The Case of the Bulldozer

In 1991, the Brent Walker property, sports and television group collapsed with debts totaling £1.2 billion. The most lasting monument to Brent Walker is the Brent Cross shopping complex in north-west London. The company had been created by former fish market porter and boxer George Walker, a colourful and driving personality. However, in 1994 the Serious Fraud Office (SFO) brought criminal charges of theft, false accounting and conspiracy to defraud against Mr Walker and his former finance director Mr Alfred Aquilina. The charges related to the company's film and television division where it was alleged that prior to the collapse they inflated profits by £19.3 million on the back of bogus film rights in order to lure investors. Mr Walker was also accused of stealing some £17 million.

At the trial, Mr Norman Lonsdale the former director of the film and television division, said in a statement that he had been shocked when the charges had arisen. Regarding Mr Walker, he said: 'While Mr Walker had rough mannerisms, I had never seen anything that gave me feelings that something untoward was going on. I think that he always played it straight.' He went on: 'Mr Walker had a unique management style. He was a bulldozer when making decisions. He asked for opposition but did not like it when he got it. He sometimes intimidated the board but I have never known him use violence or the threat of violence.'

At the end of the trial, George Walker was cleared but his co-accused Alfred Aquilina was convicted, fined and imprisoned.

Dr Michael Walton has studied extensively *in situ* the behaviour of corporate leaders and boards and, in particular, what happens when the bad boardroom behaviour of individual leaders can no longer be explained away or trivialized as exuberance, assertiveness, drive or over-confidence and has become toxic. Toxic leadership is defined (Walton 2007a) as: 'behaviour which is exploitative, abusive, destructive and psychologically – and perhaps legalistically – corrupt and poisonous.' His further writings (Walton 2007b and 2010) provide practical guidance on how to avoid such problems. Burke and Cooper (2010) also examine in depth this problem area.

# Reaction vs Pre-emption

Too many boards and executives adopt a complacent attitude bordering on laziness when it comes to risk management. They are quite content to wait to receive the quarterly or six-monthly risk reports from business units and accept them 'on the nod'. The problem is that a 'cosy pretence' of meaningful risk reporting can take hold. Business units learn how to craft their risk reports so that a 'situation normal, nothing exceptional to report' impression is conveyed, whereas this may be far from accurate. For example, the author is aware of one international company whose refrigerated storage unit at its main warehouse failed and this did not come to light for several days. By then, the entire stock of temperature-sensitive goods had been compromised and had to be destroyed. The total non-recoverable cost ran to several US$million. Failures in both technical and managerial risk controls were evident but, despite the massive disruption to the business and the significant financial loss, the episode only received perfunctory attention from the board. One is left with the stunning conclusion that these directors saw the whole thing as an act of God which no human intervention via risk management could have prevented! Moreover, the senior executive in charge of the warehouse at the time was later promoted, suggesting that the board considered him a 'safe pair of hands'.

In essence, organizations that wait for bad things to happen before taking any action run the additional risk of drifting into a semi-permanent crisis management mode. Reactive risk management is the very antithesis of corporate governance.

## Fixation on Salvation Models

Waring and Glendon (1998) refer to 'salvation models' for risk management systems which enjoy considerable popularity, especially among those who are too lazy to do any serious thinking about their organization's risk exposures and what realistically is required to deal with them. Salvation models are those which are misused so as to create the illusion that simply following the model closely, if not slavishly, will guarantee an excellent outcome (that is, the organization will be saved from unwanted detriment and disasters). In the author's opinion, any formula that purports to offer such a guarantee amounts to quackery. Such misuse is especially, but not exclusively, related to legislation and standards around which cluster compliance audits and third-party certification schemes. Used appropriately, audits are an invaluable tool but Waring and Glendon (1998) note that, when misused, certification schemes for management systems are dangerous because they are so seductive and suggest quick returns and never-ending success which they cannot possibly deliver. In some instances, organizations make vast emotional, intellectual, financial and other resource commitments in their name, with often little in return that is sustainable. There is a danger of management system certification becoming not a measure of high standards but a measure of, at best, mediocrity among weak and average organizations seeking to bolster their image and self-confidence. The inherent commercialization of all the paraphernalia attached to certification (for example, registration, how-to-achieve-compliance consultancy and training, third-party compliance audits and frequent re-audits) adds to the shift of focus and emphasis away from the actual needs of the organization and towards the commercial ends of the external provider industry.

Fortunately, ISO 31000 was issued as a guidance standard, with no possibility of certification attached to it. However, this decision was not reached without a battle between certification proponents, such as the British Standards Institution, and anti-certification proponents, such as the Federation of European Risk Management Associations. The latter argued from experience that apparent compliance with a standard does not guarantee outcome and may raise a false sense of assurance among regulators, customers, financiers, shareholders and others. Also, the certification process may not always be objective and may vary from one country to another. Not all commercial providers in the certification industry are as scrupulous as they should be and there are too many corporate buyers who just want a certificate to 'prove' that the organization is good rather than making any real effort to become genuinely good.

Not all risk-related standards have managed to avoid the curse of certification. Examples of those having a certification option are: ISO 14000 series (Environmental

Management Systems), OSHAS 18000 series (Occupational Safety and Health Management Systems) and ISO 9000 series (Quality Management Systems). In the author's opinion, such standards should only be used as guides.

A huge supply industry also built up around compliance with SOX (SOX 2002). Many of the accounting and audit firms saw SOX compliance as a major revenue generator for them among client organizations. They milked it for all it was worth for several years. However, a growing disenchantment with SOX compliance, its costly and prescriptive burden and its questionable effectiveness in risk control began to emerge within organizations, not just in the US but also in other countries where companies were affected by extra-territorial jurisdiction enforced by the US Government. In 2005, the CEO of the Hong Kong Exchange stated publicly that Hong Kong should avoid introducing SOX-style regulatory controls on listed companies. In 2006, Mr LeLand Graul, the SEC Director of accountants BDO Seidman, told an audience at the American Chamber of Commerce in Hong Kong that SOX had not prevented the collapse of Refco, for example, and that the more flexible and holistic self-regulatory approach of the UK would probably give better protection to investors.

## Case 3.4   The Refco Collapse

The US brokerage firm Refco was one of the largest companies in the derivatives, commodities and US Treasury markets. It had over 200,000 clients in 14 countries. In 2004, it was planning to make an IPO but barely two months before the flotation date it was revealed that the company's CEO had hidden a US$435 million personal loan from the company which was not included in the company's accounts. The IPO prospectus also failed to present the company's true assets and liabilities and the fact that since 1997 bad debts had been hidden from financial reports by an ongoing fraudulent loans scheme benefitting senior executives and some external investors. The US$1.124 billion in fraudulent loans was only uncovered by accident in 2005 by a new employee. Not long after, the company filed for bankruptcy owing clients over US$4 billion but having only US$1.9 billion in assets.

An independent examiner appointed by the Refco bankruptcy trustee implicated both the company's lawyers and its external auditors as being complicit in the fraud. Also discovered were huge pay-outs to executives over the year leading to the collapse. Some appeared legitimate, for example, sale of some of their shareholdings. Other pay-outs included the US$45 million severance payment to the former Chief Finance Officer (CFO), which was not mentioned in the Refco prospectus.

SOX is not a sacred cow or a guaranteed cure-all, far from it. Compliance alone is not a warranty of satisfactory, let alone excellent, ERM. The scope is rooted in finance and accounting protection and not broad-based ERM. Brave attempts have been made to 'bolt on' non-accounting risk exposures and integrate them into SOX, for example COSO (2004) but these have been naïve and unconvincing (Waring 2007b and c). There is also something perverse, if not dangerous, about individuals whose only ERM qualifications and experience are in, for example, banking, accounting, internal audit or Basel II deciding if and when professional advice and judgement on risk exposures such as counter-terrorism, political risks, HR risks, IP, supply chain risks or major hazards are required – or worse still sallying forth themselves to render such advice and judgement. Unfortunately, this is still the kind of unsophisticated state of affairs prevalent in the SOX/COSO environment.

Professor Roberta Romano of Yale Law School (Romano 2004) argues that SOX itself is flawed in its whole approach to accounting and finance protection let alone any consideration of wider enterprise risk exposures. In her words, SOX is 'quack governance'. The time, cost and energy drain of SOX compliance can render an organization exhausted and antagonistic towards genuine ERM. Many executives have been misled into believing that SOX and ERM are identical and, perhaps understandably, some now have a jaundiced view of all risk management.

## Insurance Bias

As noted in Chapter 2, insurance is an essential ingredient within a robust risk management system. However, as a passive tool based on financial compensation, insurance *per se* cannot mitigate actual risk exposures on the ground. At best, it is a long-stop instrument to soften the financial blow in the event of an insured peril actually occurring and does not represent any kind of credible substitute for a proper active risk treatment strategy. Many risks are not insurable, or at least ways have thus far not been found to make them insurable. Brand damage and reputation damage, for example, can be devastatingly real for a company but hard to pin down or to prove as having resulted from a particular event or cause. Regrettably, however, many organizations continue to regard insurance as their main or only risk management strategy. Even then, the payment of the required premiums may be viewed by the board grudgingly as a necessary evil.

Many Group Risk Management functions remain little more than insurance buyers and custodians and administrators of the company's insurance policies. Some complacent boards are more than happy to keep it that way, as they delude themselves that corporate risk management is being delivered and there is nothing more required from the board. Group Risk Managers whose qualifications and background are firmly in insurance broking or underwriting are often equally willing to maintain this *status quo* illusion. However, the author knows of a number of large organizations where newly appointed Group Risk Managers having a broader background and perspective have had a sustained fight against the insurance-only ignorance and resistance of their respective boards towards proper ERM.

## Risk Quantification Bias

Boards often feel most comfortable dealing with numbers and especially financial figures. However, important as quantitative data and financial measures of risk and performance undoubtedly are, on their own and devoid of qualitative information they are likely to convey a very reduced or even misleading picture of enterprise risk exposures (see, for example, Toft 1996). The consequences are even worse where an over-reliance is placed on a single metric such as Value at Risk (VAR). Boards may unwittingly develop a serious blindness to major threats that would not be recognized in such a metric.

In one instance, the chair of a board risk committee asked the author for assistance in drawing up a set of measures of risk and a data acquisition protocol that would provide the committee with a balanced overview of the organization's risk exposures. The request came as a means to counter the opinion of one very dominant member of the committee who had been insisting that the only measure for them to apply was VAR.

A quantification bias can also appear in how the performance of executives is measured and evaluated. The corporate risks that arise when only a narrow range of personal performance measures is applied to senior executives have become all too evident in the array of specific banking failures and the ongoing general controversy over excessive remuneration and bonuses.

## Case 3.5   Performance Appraisal and Reward Structure at Barings

Glendon and Waring (1997) and Waring and Glendon (1998) note that not only had no evidence surfaced of the existence of any substantive HR or personnel function in Barings prior to its collapse but also the company had neither knowledge, nor policy nor intention to implement any systematic form of performance appraisal and management. Individuals' performance was judged largely or exclusively on revenue earnings or how good a subjective impression they made on their superiors. The risks of relying on a combination of a single outcome performance indicator and the likelihood of people untrained in performance appraisal being prey to personal biases, are considerable.

For the individual executives at Barings, their own measure of performance and self-worth appeared to be their annual bonus. The general remuneration and bonuses at Barings were among the highest for comparable organizations in the UK and US and, at the time of collapse in 1995, three directors were scheduled to receive £1 million or more each in bonuses, based on the company's 1994 earnings. After the collapse, a number of directors who approached the Bank of England to discuss a rescue package insisted that they should still be paid their outstanding bonuses! As the official Board of Banking Supervision report notes dryly (Waring and Glendon 1998), there was no evidence that the judgements of Barings managers were inhibited by the possibility that their bonuses might be prejudiced. There is ample evidence that earnings, targets and bonuses had become an all-consuming fixation among Barings executives and had obliterated not only propriety and integrity but also any sense of governance responsibility for managing corporate risk.

When, following the collapse Mr Peter Norris, Chief Executive of Barings Investment Bank Group, presented the Barings case for rescue to a meeting with other banks, the bankers were outraged to learn that proposed bonuses for the previous year would exceed £100 million. After removing profits attributable to Nick Leeson, Barings intended to declare a pre-tax profit of £83 million for 1994 while paying staff bonuses of £84 million. In other words, the Barings directors were paying themselves and their staff more than they declared in profits instead of the more normal 25–30 per cent of profits in the sector. Yet, 13 years later when many UK banks were in deep trouble, the greed and 'reward for failure' culture had become endemic in the sector.

## Personal Biases and Agendas

It would be preferable to imagine that all board members always put their governance duties and the best interests of the organization as a whole way ahead of any personal interests or biases they may have. However, while many directors do strive to meet this noble goal, some fall by the wayside. When individuals or, worse, the majority on a board seek to intellectualize a contrived justification for ignoring sound advice and not adopting sound risk management requirements, their motives and governance credentials automatically become suspect.

In one instance, the author had been carrying out a very high-level corporate risks review for a large long-established organization. His draft reports had been submitted to the lead director who was a major shareholder and had long been a champion of risk management. At a meeting with the author to discuss the drafts, the director expressed his satisfaction with the reports but confided that, although intellectually his fellow directors would understand and accept the reports' findings, arguments and recommendations in principle, he doubted with regret that they would act on them. His given reason was that board members saw themselves as big businessmen engaged with 'the big picture' where they 'automatically' managed the risks. To them, any additional formalized risk management was unnecessary and almost an affront to their dignity and self-image.

Some individual directors have more selfish personal agendas that make them avoid engagement with risk management responsibilities. Individuals who place their own personal career ambitions and remuneration as priorities way ahead of protecting corporate and shareholder interests do not expect to remain in the organization for more than a few years, and maybe only a couple of years, before moving on to a better job elsewhere. They calculate cynically that therefore they should not get too involved in anything potentially controversial or requiring decisions and actions on their part which might attract negative personal consequences if things went wrong. Typically, they will go through the motions and create an appearance that they are engaged with risk management while as far as possible avoiding risk decisions and delaying any serious implementation. Their shortcomings often only get found out after they have left when their carefully constructed window dressing collapses.

As one senior corporate executive who does believe in strong risk management commented, directors can have all the negative views and opinions they like about the value and necessity of robust risk management but they have absolutely no right to allow their prejudices to jeopardize the owners' and shareholders' interests. It is surprising, therefore, just how many such individuals last as long as they do before being called to account.

# 4 *A Culture of Responsible Risk-Taking*

Corporate culture and its implications for risk exposures and risk management were raised in Chapter 1 and were alluded to throughout Chapters 2 and 3. Aspects of organizational culture will be relevant to some degree to many, if not all, the cases cited throughout the book.

Organizational culture may be defined as: a set of unwritten, and relatively unobtrusive, attitudes, beliefs, values, rules of behaviour, ideologies, habitual responses, language expression, rituals, quirks and other features which characterize a particular organization or a defined part of it (Waring 1996a, Waring and Glendon 1998). Organizational culture provides the continuous psycho-social reference backdrop within the organization by which its members interpret their existence within the body and decide what is good and bad, right and wrong, acceptable and unacceptable, imperative and taboo. Organizational culture reinforces an individual member's sense of identity and what it means to be a member. It provides the unique characteristics which distinguish one company from another, despite their apparent close similarity. For example, two large companies in the same sector and having similar operations are usually quite distinct in terms of their respective cultures. The purposive and unobtrusive 'identity protection' function of organizational culture explains why organizational members often resist attempts to change it (see for example Beer et al. 1990, Westley 1990). Its importance in determining what actually happens and how in an organization, as opposed to official policy, is not to be underestimated and this applies as much to risk and risk management as to any other aspect of an organization. See, for example, Douglas (1992), Turner (1988, 1992), Waring and Glendon (1998).

In addition to the seeds of tunnel vision examined in Chapter 3, three particular features of organizational culture that are likely to have a pronounced bearing on risk and its management are:

- risk myths and delusions;
- a 'chancer' culture;
- authority, conformity and groupthink.

## Risk Myths and Delusions

There is a range of staggeringly naïve beliefs about risk that are all too common in boardrooms and among corporate executives and which cloud their judgement (Waring 2010). It should not be overlooked, however, that groups of employees and their trade unions can be as equally naïve and self-destructive in their attitudes as their employers may be about risks to the organization and to themselves. Nevertheless, the responsibility for corporate risk and governance rests with the board and their risk management system should even include elements for industrial relations risks, excessive wage demands and strikes.

Examples of common risk myths and delusions are:

- Business growth is inevitable; we are immune to economic recession (see, for example, the ongoing behaviour within the public sector in France, Greece, Cyprus and some other EU countries despite the 2008–2009 global financial crisis and the Eurozone crisis in 2011–2012).
- The market will bear whatever prices we ask for, regardless of economic or market conditions.
- Life's a gamble so why treat business any differently? We don't need to apply any discipline or methods to risk management, just use our experience and gambling acumen.
- We are making good profits so we must be managing our risks well. As we have never had anything bad happen, is that not good enough evidence we are invincible?
- Lost customers, foreign buyers, tourists and so on will always return soon; we don't have to do anything significant to get them back.
- Bonuses as the main performance criterion and goal of individuals will ensure good risk-free corporate performance.
- Insurance will do the trick and is sufficient to manage all our risk exposures; no active risk management is required.
- ERM is only about finance, accounting standards and internal audit; ERM and Business Risk Management is what accountants say it is; ISO 31000? Never heard of it!
- Superficial risk checks will be enough for corporate due diligence.
- If customers do not demand risk management from us then it does not need attention.

Some of the above may seem embarrassingly familiar to readers of this book as they are depressingly common around the world. They lead to a lack of any disciplined, well-informed framework in companies for managing their risk exposures. To use an analogy, most of these myths and delusions are rather like the attitude of a person who imagines that he or she will never fall ill and so does not need to do anything to prevent ill-health. The 'I-feel-as-fit-as-a-fiddle' deluded soul who every day smokes 40 cigarettes, interspersed with supersize burgers-and-chips all washed down with a six-pack of beer or a bottle of Scotch, does no exercise, is an obese workaholic and thinks he or she will live to 100 without so much as the need of an aspirin. The odds are overwhelmingly stacked against them and their life expectancy will be cut short drastically. Before reaching that final demise, they will probably suffer years of debilitating ill-health. They certainly will not be functioning well and will be pretty miserable.

Frankly, those (whether boards, executives, employee groups or trade unions) who choose to take such a cavalier approach to managing corporate risks deserve to suffer as a result of their own stupidity. However, the fall-out of mismanaged corporate risks unfortunately also damages many other people as well – shareholders, investors, employees, customers, suppliers. The thousands who were damaged by the Bank of Credit and Commerce International (BCCI), MGN, Enron, Lehman Brothers, Stanford, Madoff, RBS, and the mismanagement of the banks and finance sector alone, quite apart from 'basket cases' in other sectors, are testament to such fall-out. As noted in Chapter 3, does any director or executive have the right to gamble so recklessly with other people's money and lives?

## Case 4.1   Security Threats Start Next Year

A huge integrated resort was being built in the Far East at an investment cost of US$ billions, including hotels, cinemas, sports facilities, restaurants, conference centres and gaming halls. Thousands of people would be using the showpiece resort daily, including foreign dignitaries and other VIPs. The design and build phase took several years. Various technical security features had been designed into the site but overall there had never been a proper examination of the security threats and requirements on a life-cycle basis, from design through construction, snagging and testing, handover, operation, maintenance and repair, development and disposal. With another year to go before completion and handover, the position of senior management was that security issues begin with the operational phase from handover onwards. Therefore, they concluded that there was no need to examine the security requirements until then!

Pointing out to them the blindingly obvious fact that the construction phase was the most vulnerable because of the myriad of contractors on site who had access to plans, premises, software and so on failed to persuade them. They just did not want to accept that organized criminals who wanted to plant electronic surveillance and other devices to be activated once the site, and especially the casinos, became operational would have already infiltrated the contractors. Computer files would have been hacked into and copies of plans, wiring diagrams and other intelligence were just a bribe away. Further, there was potential terrorist infiltration in a region with an uncomfortable record of terrorist attacks on the hotels and leisure sector such as the bombings in Jakarta, Bali and Mumbai. Criminals and terrorists do not conveniently switch off their activities and mark time just to suit the timetables and fanciful security delusions of their targets.

## Case 4.2   Risks Don't Exist Unless Customers are Worried

This case is remarkably similar to case 4.1 in that it was a commercial property development and had never had a proper security evaluation on a life-cycle basis. The premises would be a prestige city-centre development, including hotel, conference centre and leased offices. Mid-build, the owners started to sell the commercial leases and were rather surprised to receive some sharp questioning from potential tenants on security, fire and other risk issues and what the provisions were. Some would-be tenants would have a regular flow of foreign ministers and other VIPs – what were the security arrangements provided by the landlord? Some would-be tenants held lots of critically important data and hosted top secret negotiations – what electronic security, counter-eavesdropping and other counter-measures were in place for the building?

The owner–developers had simply swallowed the assurances of the principal architects and contractors that security measures would be built in. In fact, this amounted to little more than closed circuit television (CCTV) cameras and electronic swipe key access and certainly nowhere near adequate as 'the security strategy'.

The owners were clearly worried that they would lose these two prime clients unless they could demonstrate that they were on top of the security issue. However, when the two potential tenants who had raised the issue decided not to proceed, the owners concluded quite wrongly that therefore there was obviously no need to upgrade their security provisions! The risk issue had been resolved, they thought! In addition, the likelihood that other prospective tenants would also raise similar concerns and back away never entered their minds.

## Case 4.3   The Decline of Cyprus Airways

The days when state-owned airlines acting as the national flag carrier could flourish are long gone. The rigours of intense competition, relentless cost-cutting and efficiency demands and being prey to M&As have required management skills and discipline that history shows can only be delivered by the private sector and usually publicly listed companies. Cyprus Airways (CY), however, sought to carry on with its long-standing tradition as a state-owned airline. In the mid-1990s, CY had 40 per cent market share with over one million passengers per year. This had increased by 2004/2005 before dropping back to 1.4 million in 2010/2011. When in 2004 Cyprus joined the EU, however, the company fell foul of EU restrictions on member state governments having both a controlling interest of their national airline and also injecting subsidies and other anti-competitive preferential treatment. As a result of this loss of state subsidies, the company was forced into a genuine competition with other airlines which relatively were much more modern and cost-efficient.

By 2006, CY was heading for bankruptcy and had to go to the EU for a bailout, which it received on condition that it cut its overheads and made itself more cost-efficient. Among actions taken were withdrawal from some routes, sell-off of some aircraft and other assets, the loss of some 400 jobs out of 1,800 and pay cuts of up to 25 per cent. This near bankruptcy, however, revealed just how profligate the company was with over-staffing and salaries and how for such a long time it had capitulated to employee and trade union demands for pay increases. It was general knowledge that even in 2012 this minor airline was still paying its pilots roughly double the salaries paid to pilots of rival airlines such as British Airways (BA) and Aegean. Its cabin crews were reportedly paid almost three times the rates for those of Aegean. As with civil servants and other public sector employees in Cyprus, they enjoyed a jobs-for-life unsackable status with non-contributory final salary pension scheme. Meanwhile, new low-cost competitors such as Easyjet and Ryanair had also entered CY's traditional markets. Since 2006, however, instead of recognizing the dire health of the company and the need for drastic action, employees and their trade unions had remained in denial that their inefficiency, greed and absurd expectations were partly responsible for the company's continuing loss-making situation and near bankruptcy. They only grudgingly cooperated with management on the cost-cutting and efficiency drives and continued to complain publicly that they felt very hard done by. This was at a time when private sector salaries were but a pale shadow of those in CY and private sector unemployment had risen sharply.

The executive chairman Mr George Mavrocostas, who was appointed in 2006 to deliver the company reorganization, cost-cutting and efficiency programme required for the EU bailout and subsequent survival plan, is widely respected for his skills and his determination to succeed in this. The company became more streamlined and efficient but its staff numbers and huge salary bill kept dragging CY into loss year after year. In February 2012, Mr Mavrocostas was on record as stating that further cuts in staff numbers from the then figure of between 1,000 and 1,100 and in salaries and benefits were inevitable if the company were to become competitive and viable. When CY announced its 2011 figures at the end of February 2012, they showed a €19 million net loss. The 2010 figures showed a profit (the first in years) of around €200,000 but only as a result of a one-off compensation payment from the EU of €20 million for excess fuel costs incurred by a Turkish ban on CY flying in Turkish air space. Referring to the 2012 figures, a CY spokesman stated that the company needed to shed a further 150–160 employees as well as gain €45 million of additional capital. The CY problem was also highly politicized in this small country with a coalition government dominated by AKEL, the communist party. Politicians frequently made public statements backing the demands of CY staff and unions, while still demanding that CY could not be allowed to go bankrupt.

The Government, which still held a 69 per cent stake in CY, announced in February 2012 that it would sell most or all its stake as a means to keep CY afloat. However, it was doubtful that a potential buyer (dubbed by the government as a 'strategic investor') would buy such an ailing company without the freedom to make radical changes to its structure, staffing, remuneration and employment practices. Sector insiders and observers agreed that it was more likely that any interested buyer would wait until CY had gone bankrupt and then offer a token price of, say, €1 to buy the assets and cherry-pick its employees under new contracts and new employment practices of the new company.

Nevertheless, three potential investors did express interest but only on condition that the company's radical restructuring plan announced in May 2012 was implemented. This would involve a further €25 million in savings, some €17 million of which would come from staff cuts of 247 from the 1,100 as at mid-May 2012 as well as from cuts to salaries and allowances. Mr Mavrocostas made it clear that without this plan the company could not survive. Following the €31 million in state aid agreed earlier in 2012, the company then requested in December 2012 a further €73 million rescue from the Government as well as announcing further staff reductions of 40 per cent.

The decline of CY is an example of the consequences of a long-standing public sector culture of a divine right of staff to be privileged, greedy, self-serving and unaccountable for their attitudes and actions. Their tunnel vision, myths and delusions blinded them to the existential threats to the company's survival.

Strange and unsupported beliefs about risks often go hand-in-hand with delusions about risk exposures and what constitute adequate risk controls. The combination leads to a naïve reliance on luck or miracles as a strategy for managing risks instead of having proper systems in place. This represents a huge gamble. Managing a business is not the same as gambling in the casino, where the odds are always stacked against the gambler. Active risk management changes the odds in the company's favour. Lack of credible risk management keeps the odds stacked firmly against the company.

## The Chancer Culture

The term 'chancer' is a colloquial expression used in modern Britain to describe someone who, by nature and habit, tends to take high-risk chances that they can do something daring, possibly wrong, possibly disreputable, possibly illegal or just plain stupid and avoid getting caught or harmed. A chancer is usually driven by the prospect of an attractive reward for such risky behaviour and the expectation that they will get away with it. It is gambling in a very basic sense.

The author was once attending a joint meeting of two professional bodies active in corporate risk management and governance for a roundtable discussion on the EU Green Paper on Corporate Governance (Waring 2011a). The other attendees were senior representatives of a range of large organizations in various sectors, notably finance. The discussion revealed that there was little, if anything, in the Green Paper itself that was contentious. However, some very striking comments were made about boardroom attitudes. One prominent attendee, with substantial director experience in large organizations including chairing a board risk committee, complained that, regrettably, some directors often do not really want corporate governance and risk management, as they claim it interferes with them running the company. He added that this seems like an excuse for being allowed to 'see what they can get away with'. For good governance, this 'chancer' culture has to be eliminated. A board should always be insisting that things are done correctly and ethically. Lots of heads nodded in agreement.

When directors ask themselves, whether openly or on a nod-and-a-wink basis, 'What can we get away with?' other people such as shareholders, employees, customers, suppliers and the public are likely to suffer. If 'What can we get away with?' becomes the mantra of the board, the management hierarchy and workforce below are likely to follow suit. Moreover, cavalier actions resulting from undue influence by major shareholding members of the board may damage the interests of minority shareholders and indeed the major shareholders themselves as a result of damage to corporate reputation and marketplace reactions (see Chapter 5 and case 6.5 in Chapter 6).

Clues to the existence of a 'chancer culture' in an organization are likely to be found in the attitudes and actions of any sub-group whose *raison d'être* lies in revenue generation such as sales, marketing, deal making and fee earning where the individuals' personal remunerations and bonus packages are based solely on the money they have brought into the organization. The problem is not one of competitive salaries and fair bonuses, which few would object to, but to reckless behaviour fuelled and encouraged by obscenely high total packages in a *laissez-faire* environment nurtured by complicit, and arguably negligent, boards and their remuneration committees who judge executive performance on the single metric of revenue earnings. The corrosive sales-and-bonuses culture so evident in Barings Singapore has also been and remains a prominent feature throughout the finance sector. The causative role of such a culture in corporate collapses is now well established and referred to frequently in official inquiry reports, such as those relating to Barings, Lehmans, HBOS, RBS and so on. As noted above, board members and other senior executives are not allowed to treat the company as if it were a casino and as if the company's and investors' money were their own private gambling stake. Yet, it is evident that many still do and high sales performers are often protected by the board from close oversight and in some cases are even encouraged to behave recklessly.

# Case 4.4   A Rags to Riches Story

Mr Inostranyets (not his real name) arrived in the UK in the 1950s on his own as a penniless teenager with only a basic education and speaking hardly any English. Working exceptionally hard for many years, eventually he built up a sizeable set of businesses and property assets worth millions. However, along the way it had not all been plain sailing. There had been bad times as well as good but his toughness and determination always drove him on. For example, following the collapse of one of his capital projects as a result of poor risk management, he found himself on the receiving end of creditor foreclosures and lawsuits and in one period of a few terrible weeks he expected to be made bankrupt. However, a stroke of luck suddenly happened which cancelled out his debts and liabilities and saw his business empire resurge like a phoenix from the ashes.

He was by nature and background a hard-nosed, tough businessman whose only knowledge and experience of risk management was on-the-job and dealing with perceived threats as and when encountered. As a semi-professional gambler who was well-known in the London casinos, he acknowledged that his approach to business risks was in a similar vein, although this did not mean that he failed to gather as much relevant information as possible before making business decisions. Moreover, his religious upbringing had engendered a strong belief in miracles and the stroke of luck that had rescued his business from collapse reinforced that belief. Feeling able to rely on luck and miracles reduced in his mind the need to mitigate risks by proper risk management. He was far from reckless but was simply unaware of his company's risk profile and what prudent mitigation was indicated.

On Mr Inostranyets's retirement, his son took over the group of businesses and has since grown it into one of the largest privately owned multi-sector business empires based in the UK and with an international footprint. His son, who is the current Chairman and CEO, features in 'rich lists' and is regularly in the media in relation to his astute and pace-setting business ideas and activities, some of which draw widespread admiration. Like his father, he too received only a basic education and left school to work in the family business. He too manages risk intuitively and eschews most of what, in a publicly listed company, he would be forced to do to meet corporate governance requirements.

One cannot just dismiss Mr Inostranyets and his son as mere chancers. They are both motivated to do the best for the business and are certainly not reckless or, so far as is known, engaged in anything disreputable. However, the very strength and entrepreneurial value of such single-minded self-assured business owner/CEOs can be the company's Achilles heel when it comes to dealing with ERM. Bounded rationality and other features of tunnel vision, especially if encouraged by business successes and 'miracles', can solidify into a fallacy of invincibility whereby risk management 'by experience and intuition only' is deemed sufficient.

Moreover, in addition to regarding corporate risk management as being fully met by decisions akin to casino-style gambling, there is the issue of whose money is being gambled. It is tempting for anyone who has built up a sizeable business fortune to regard it as his or her own personal money pot to do with as they wish, whether for reckless projects, embezzlement to fund a lavish lifestyle or whatever. There is often a great reluctance for many self-made big businessmen to accept that much of the corporate wealth they have created is legally owned by the body corporate and not by the person who created it. An instructive example is the conviction in the UK in August 2012 of the former Polly Peck International owner Asil Nadir, on ten counts of theft from his company between 1987 and 1990 when it collapsed with debts of £550 million. Not unlike Mr Inostranyets, he had built up the £multi-million company from scratch. In sentencing Mr Nadir to ten years in jail, Mr Justice Holroyd praised him for his business skills and achievements but added, 'The company's success was in many ways your success. But the company's money was not your money. You knew that. You nonetheless helped yourself to it. You committed theft on a grand scale.' The amount stolen for which he was convicted was some £61 million in today's money, while the prosecution alleged that, in total, the amount stolen was £150 million. The theft contributed to the collapse of Polly Peck and large losses by corporate investors, pension funds and individuals. His prosecution was delayed for 17 years after he fled abroad to evade prosecution by the SFO.

## Authority, Conformity and Groupthink

Leeb (2006) ascribes the classic herd behaviour of investors to a combination of authority, conformity and 'groupthink'. Instead of recognizing risks and responding rationally, they tend to follow what respected or authority figures appear to be saying or doing and what other investors appear to be doing. Sometimes such herd behaviour results in catastrophic misjudgements, if the markets or a particular listed company's share value does not do as expected. Herd behaviour also affects other groups such as boards or particular departments or functions. Perceptions of risks are often coloured by the culture of a particular department or 'silo' that an individual works in. Authority, conformity and groupthink of the particular sub-culture plus the fear of being perceived as different and no longer trusted by one's peers can create psychological blind spots across the sub-culture which affect both perceptions of and responses to risk issues.

### Case 4.5   It Was an Act of God

Following the King's Cross fire on London Underground in 1987, in which large numbers of people were killed and injured, the author contributed to a consultant's report to the Government's public inquiry into the disaster. The report of the official inquiry chaired by Desmond Fennell QC concluded that the underlying causes of the disaster were a combination of multiple management failures and a poor safety culture and recommended many changes to remedy this situation. However, despite the Fennell Inquiry report's findings, it was not uncommon to hear senior executives of the company many months afterwards insist that the disaster was an act of God and not a result of management failures or a poor safety culture. The herd was still in denial. In common with professional colleagues, the author believed at the time that in view of such ingrained denial and false beliefs about cause-and-effect it would take perhaps ten years to implement a robust SMS in the company and embed a radically different safety culture.

# Forging a Culture of Responsible Risk-Taking

Responsible risk-taking implies that people in the organization will both seek to take opportunity risks in an informed way and with adequate risk controls, and be averse to any pure risks which lack adequate risk controls. A speculative or opportunity risk is one which may have both beneficial and/or detrimental outcomes, for example investment, HR, product innovation, M&As. A pure risk is an absolute risk or one which relates only to harm. With a pure risk, the best that can happen is that nothing bad happens.

The development of such a mind-set requires strong leadership and a demonstration by the board and senior management that enterprise risk exposures have to be managed competently on a continuous basis. Any culture change in any context will take time. The overwhelming experience of research and consulting experience by the author and many others is that any substantive culture change in an organization will take several years, typically five or more years, to become truly embedded. The author once asked a senior executive of a client organization how long he thought it would take to effect a culture change that the board was seeking. Quick as a flash, he answered: 'Six months.' When asked why he was so certain of this timeframe, he answered: 'Because that is what has been allowed in the change management programme.' Such an approach to what is always a complex, delicate and lengthy task contradicts all knowledge of organizational culture and experience in changing such cultures. A five to ten year period would be far more realistic. This six-month 'quick fix' expectation is a classic example of the naivety of many change programmes (see for example Beer et al. 1990, Westley 1990) and the fallacy of pre-determination (Mintzberg 1994). As Pettigrew et al. (1992) note, the management of any strategic change is the result of uncertain, emergent and iterative processes and 'there are no grand blueprints for long-term success or quick fixes for immediate salvation'.

In addition to boards vetoing 'What can we get away with?' attitudes and reckless gambling when it comes to risk issues, they must also avoid appearing to be remote and disengaged from risk management. Open-circuit disengagement is exemplified by the issuing of occasional directives and the receipt of regular business unit risk reports, but no recognition that closure of the monitoring and control loop requires the board and/or its audit and risk committees to then act decisively when clearly warranted by feedback on compliance. One board director of quality and safety for a large organization told the author rather huffily that it was his responsibility as a director only to issue directives, not to be engaged in any monitoring and control of compliance. This is nonsense. To warrant any claim to have a culture of responsible risk-taking, boards need to say what they mean, mean what they say, monitor, listen to feedback, audit and re-direct if necessary.

Over several decades, there have been a number of deterministic formulae claimed by their proponents to offer improvement in an organization's culture. It is also tempting to look for ready prescriptions for improving more specifically an organization's risk culture. However, although some of these may indeed provide some value to some organizations in some instances, it is difficult to identify all the key factors that may operate in a particular case and then apply a reliable intervention based on an accurate model of risk culture. The result may cause either disappointment at a poor outcome or, conversely, a false belief that a permanent improvement has been embedded. Unless interventions are based on an independently validated model, the results are likely to be variable from one instance to another. The IRM Guidance Document on Risk Culture (IRM 2012), while not a definitive document on risk culture, provides a discussion on models and strategies for improvement of risk culture.

With the above *caveats* in mind, it may be safely said that to forge a culture of responsible risk-taking, large numbers of people, indeed all the organization's members, will need to be engaged in risk management to an extent appropriate to their level and range of responsibilities, for example in risk assessments, project teams and so on. Better selection criteria and procedures which identify and evaluate individual strengths and weaknesses in knowledge, values, beliefs, attitudes and emotional competence are also a key weapon. Another is risk control systems which provide realistic checks and balances on executives, not to deter responsible risk-taking but on the contrary to curb negative behaviour based on unwarranted exuberance, excessive caution, sterile conformity and misguided groupthink in risk decision-making.

Performance indicators of departments, functions and individuals will need to include specific and appropriate examples relating to risk management, which answer the question 'What is in it for me?' Intrinsic motivators alone are usually not enough. It is, however, still unusual to find risk management KPIs embedded within job specifications and this will need to change.

All of the foregoing are positive motivators. In addition to bad examples set by the board and senior management, such as 'What can we get away with?' and disengagement, negative motivators include a predominant emphasis on blaming individuals for risk management failures rather than seeking to learn how to improve risk management. Another negative motivator is allocating or withholding rewards using measures of performance that either are poor or unreliable indicators of risk performance or over which the people affected have no real control.

In summary, for any organization to be successful in developing such a culture of responsible risk-taking the following will be necessary:

- strong leadership, board commitment and engagement;
- realistic timescales;
- patience and persistence;
- robust risk management systems;
- engagement of everyone in risk management, appropriate to their job, level and extent of responsibilities;
- using/reinforcing positive motivators, curbing negative motivators.

# 5 *Family Businesses, Governance and Risk Management*

The term 'family business' may engender images of a small, possibly parochial, company established and run by members of the same family. There are, of course, many family businesses that are and remain small and therefore are unlikely to warrant the attention of a book such as this, which focusses on risk and governance in larger corporate organizations. However, the following good reasons persuaded the author to include this chapter:

- Many small family businesses grow to become corporate giants and, moreover, once they are large they often retain controlling ownership by family members, even if there are other shareholders.
- For the larger family-controlled business, the risk exposures and governance issues are similar to companies that are fully publicly floated but they often have the added risk exposures of lack of capital and skilled resources as well as special boardroom control and governance issues.

This chapter examines the special case of corporate risk and governance in large family-controlled businesses and includes named reference to a number of well-known organizations as well as to others where anonymity has been preserved. Relevant cases in other chapters include 2.4, 2.5, 4.4, 6.5 and 10.3.

## When Family Businesses Become Large

It is widely recognized that SMEs represent the seeds from which much larger companies grow. As the company grows, the founders of many SMEs often appoint family members as co-directors and to other senior posts as well as offering shares. Control of such privately-owned companies can be maintained by ensuring that family shareholdings are always a majority over non-family shareholdings. Some family-owned businesses grow to become US$multi-million and even US$multi-billion turnover enterprises while still remaining under private ownership. Table 5.1 shows that nine out of the world's top 205 companies in terms of revenue are private companies, although not necessarily under family control.

**Table 5.1   Private companies in the world's top revenue earners**

| Ranking Out of 205 | Private Company | Sector | Annual Revenue 2011 US$ billion |
|---|---|---|---|
| 13 | Vitol | Raw Materials | 195 |
| 37 | Cargill | Agriculture | 119 |
| 93 | Trafigura | Raw Materials | 79 |
| 108 | REWE Group | Retailing | 70 |
| 124 | Gunvor | Raw Materials | 65 |
| 130 | Bosch Group | Automotive | 63 |
| 151 | Edeka | Retailing | 58 |
| 154 | Auchan | Retailing | 56 |
| 195 | Chrysler | Automotive | 42 |

*Source:* Abstracted from table in Wikipedia.

When a private company reaches a size such that it meets criteria for potential public flotation, there will be several options open to the owners:

- remain fully privately owned (even if incorporating more private and/or public shareholders) and ignore public listing;
- public flotation of substantial shares but retention of majority control by private (for example, family) owners;
- public flotation of total or majority of shares with control ceded by private owners.

Which option is pursued will depend on the culture of the present owners, their appetite for change, how possessive they feel about the company, the financial robustness of the company, the need for capital injection, their perception of the benefits and drawbacks of each option, and so on. Whichever option they choose will also affect how much of the relevant Codes on corporate governance and risk management they will be obliged to adopt. Any publicly listed company will always be expected to comply but there will also be business pressures on fully private companies to comply at least with the spirit of the Codes. Evasion of compliance standards can adversely affect corporate reputation, market confidence, access to capital and share values. However, some compliance issues often go against the grain of family-controlled big businesses and especially the CEO being expected to relinquish absolute control of the board.

## The Joint Chief Executive Officer/Chairman Issue

Many national corporate governance codes have sections that are voluntary and therefore rely on the integrity and willingness of the particular board to ensure compliance. Codes that recommend a voluntary separation of CEO and Chairman role-holders may result in family-owned or controlled businesses ignoring the recommendation so as to retain a dominant position by the joint CEO/Chairman (Anderson and Reeb 2003). Others may choose to retain a single person for a joint role because they genuinely believe that person to be the best available choice (see Coombes and Chiu-Yin Wong 2004). Ho (2007) has argued in relation to the issue of single joint CEO/chairmen that there is no *a priori* cause–effect relationship between separate post holders and company performance. For further discussion on family-owned businesses and governance issues, see Barton et al. (2004), Gibson (2002), Shea (2006) and Waring (2007a).

It would be both facile and demonstrably misleading to suggest that all family-owned businesses controlled by a powerful individual family member are high-risk candidates for poor business performance and even business failure. Not all such companies are run by 'chancers' (see Chapter 4). One has only to consider, for example, the highly successful career of Sir Alan Sugar who over a 40-year period grew his Amstrad consumer electronics empire from a small family-owned and run company to a giant PLC, of which he was Chairman until the company was acquired by British Sky Broadcasting (BSkyB). He was and remains notorious for not 'suffering fools gladly' and being very exacting and demanding of himself and his staff but he has always commanded great loyalty and respect for his skills, leadership and integrity. There are many other examples in this mould. Treating people fairly if firmly and getting the best out of them are hallmarks of such business leaders and are an important part of managing the 'people risks' of any organization.

However, debilitating conflicts and power struggles involving questionable decisions, and possibly resulting in reputation damage and adverse financial impact, are far more likely where one individual holds too much power which is then abused. A joint CEO/ Chairman enjoying absolute power may regard the company as his personal money pot and fiefdom in which he can treat the rest of the board as compliant window dressing for rubber-stamping his decisions. In extreme cases, such toxic owners may also treat their staff and suppliers very badly (see Walton 2007a and b, 2010).

## Case 5.1   An Abuse of Power

Mr Len Spivak (not his real name) was the joint Chairman and Managing Director of a privately-owned company Len Spivak Enterprises Ltd that he had set up and financed largely by unsecured loans from family members. He was the majority shareholder, with his wife and an executive director as minority shareholders.

His goal was to create a big business with less than 25 people. In the early years, the company grew rapidly into a multi-million pound turnover operation. However, there was a dark side to Mr Spivak's undoubted entrepreneurial skills. He became more and more dictatorial and over-bearing towards the staff and his 'hire and fire' attitude resulted in the average period of employment being only three to four months. Even suppliers were in fear of his notoriously capricious outbursts and spitefulness. One supplier whom he was threatening told him to his face that he was 'like the Mafia'. His co-director was the only person seemingly able to persuade him to take a more moderate course on any contentious issue but, even then, he usually got his own way and behaved as badly and unwisely as he liked.

Eventually, the company had become a group of companies and then Mr Spivak channelled these into a new structure under Spivak Holdings and Securities, with a property and investment division. He brought his young son into the business and then his own brother. However, regardless of growth and diversification, he eschewed the hiring of professional managers and remained Chairman of a board whose function was to agree with his decisions. Visitors to the company's offices remarked how deferential staff were towards Mr Spivak and how his desk in his office was on a raised dias in J Edgar Hoover style, presumably so that anyone who entered was, he imagined, forced to look up and respect him and put at a psychological disadvantage.

After 20 years, his executive co-director had had enough of Mr Spivak's toxic behaviour and, following a final blazing row they parted company, with him retaining one part of the business while his co-director took the rest. Within a couple of years, Mr Spivak had sold his retained businesses for some £8 million. Rather than invest the money and retire, he could not resist starting new ventures, most of which failed or were only moderately successful. He then made a final *folie de grandeur* by buying a minor league football club. Owning such a club was at that time a common status symbol for self-made business tycoons. It allowed Mr Spivak to reign more like the club's emperor than its owner–Chairman. Nevertheless, such clubs are notorious loss-makers and no less so in this case. Within four years, he had lost nearly all his and his family's money on the club.

## Case 5.2    Frou-Frou Biscuits (Waring 2007a)

Alkis Hajikyriakou (Frou-Frou) Biscuits Public Co Ltd (also known as FBI) is a major food manufacturer in the Republic of Cyprus. The company is listed on the Cyprus Stock Exchange (CSE) Alternative Market and is therefore subject to the Cyprus Corporate Governance Code, which is voluntary for this market. Section A.2.4 of the latter requires a clear division of responsibility between the roles of CEO and Chairman. Further, if the two posts are not separated, the Code requires under the 'comply or explain' rule that a justification should be given in part 2 of the board's annual report to shareholders.

The company's major shareholder was the joint CEO and Executive Chairman, Mr Alkis Hajikyriakou, who was reported in 2007 to hold 52 per cent of the share capital. The second main shareholder was the Executive Vice-Chairman his sister Elena (Nora) Dikaiou with a reported 17 per cent holding.

In 2007, the Vice-Chairman had been seeking to get the board to adopt the CSE Code and demonstrate transparency and accountability to shareholders but apparently she met resistance from the joint CEO and Executive Chairman. In response to her attempt to get the topic on the Annual General Meeting (AGM) agenda, she alleges that her brother then sacked her.

Citing the Frou Frou case, the Institute of Directors Cyprus (IoDC) weighed into the Frou-Frou battle by publicly demanding in June 2007 (open letter from the IoDC Chairman published in *Financial Mirror* 6 June 2007) that the CSE and the SEC should make the Corporate Governance Code mandatory for companies listed on the Alternative Market, to bring it in line with the requirements for the Main Market. The IoDC Chairman reminded the CSE and SEC that the aim of the Code was to strengthen the monitoring role of the board, to protect minority shareholders, to adopt greater transparency and to provide timely information, as well as to safeguard the independence of the board of directors in its decision-making.

The company's annual report for 2006 cites ten reasons to justify not adopting the Code. In a scathing critique of the Frou-Frou CEO/Chairman's actions, Michael Olympios, a leading business consultant, stated that 'these explanations not only lack substance but in reality are almost an exact copy of other family firms in the CSE, revealing that this is a symptom of a wider problem of family firms' (Olympios 2007). He noted that, despite corporate reforms, many family firms that are now publicly listed are unable to accept that public companies are accountable to the public. Comments on this case were made to the effect that having executives report to themselves at the board and without robust independent NEDs was like having students grading their own exam papers.

Georgiou (2010) found that family-controlled companies listed on the CSE Alternative Market scored significantly worse on corporate governance variables than counterparts in the Main Market. Further, there were indications that companies fully compliant with the CSE governance code performed significantly better overall on investment returns than did those which were non-compliant, thus implying that family-owned listed companies should comply out of enlightened self-interest.

## Non-Executive Directors

The importance of fully independent NEDs was raised in Chapter 2. Their role is not only to bring invaluable experience and expertise to the board's deliberations but also specifically to challenge lines of thinking, arguments and proposed decisions and actions which they consider inappropriate, unwise or unduly risk-laden. Their independent and non-executive status should render their advice impartial and untainted by any personal or factional interests which might sway the board. At flotation, a company would be required to appoint NEDs in order to comply with Stock Exchange Listing Rules and Corporate Governance Code.

On the board of a family-controlled business, their input is vital to ensure that board decisions are in the best interests of the company, its shareholders and other stakeholders and especially where an over-dominant CEO exists. The NEDs should seek to convince the board that the company's best interests will be served by splitting a joint Chairman/CEO role and appointing a NED as independent Chairman. Alternatively, a family member could become Chairman if the CEO were a professional manager from outside.

Regrettably, some owner–CEOs of family-controlled businesses may appoint NEDs just for window dressing and therefore select the individuals to ensure that they have compliant, *laissez-faire* attitudes. Some NEDs go along with this and turn up for board meetings just to be eligible to take their attendance fees and directors' expenses. However, countries having high expectations of compliance with their governance code may also apply penalties to negligent NEDs. In the UK, for example, a NED is as legally liable as an executive director is for any serious shortcomings of the company. To obtain full value from NEDs, they need to be selected for their knowledge, expertise and experience as well as their integrity, boldness and independence. Above all, NEDs need to be listened to by the rest of the board and their advice to be treated with respect.

## Institutional Shareholders

In addition to independent NEDs, institutional shareholders are another important potential brake on cavalier or unwise decisions and activities, whether in family-controlled businesses or generally. Institutional investors such as pension funds and life insurance companies wield enormous influence as a result of the vast investment funds at their disposal. In recent years, a growing number of boards of large companies have faced stiff criticism from institutional shareholders on corporate governance issues and, in some cases, criticism has escalated into open revolt against such things as alleged unacceptable practices, conflicts of interest and toxic senior executives. The new willingness of such investors to refuse to back executive resolutions, whether on excessive remuneration, loaded board structures, reappointment of weak or toxic CEOs or chairmen, majority shareholder conflicts of interest and so on, and to demand significant change, follows the global financial crisis of 2008–2009. In effect, the scale of revolt has put all boards on notice that they should no longer expect to get away with bad corporate governance.

Table 5.2 summarizes some of the recent challenges by institutional investors on governance issues.

**Table 5.2    Examples of recent governance challenges by institutional investors**

| Company | Nature of Complaint by Institutional Investors | Year |
|---|---|---|
| Mitchells & Butlers | Degree of independence of two sole NEDs; undue influence of largest shareholder. | 2012 |
| BSkyB | Suitability of James Murdoch for re-election as Chairman; independence of Chairman from largest shareholder; conflict of interest; connection of Chairman with *News of the World* scandal. Over 44% of votes refused to back his re-election. | 2011 |
| News Corp | Suitability of Rupert Murdoch, James Murdoch and other directors for re-election; corporate governance and Murdoch family's management; illegal activities and telephone hacking scandal at News International (UK division of News Corp). | 2011 |
| BP | Collapse of Rosneft alliance; Deepwater Horizon disaster; senior executive bonuses; US$1.6 million pay-off to former chief executive; depressed share price. | 2011 |
| Unitech Corporate Parks | Failure to disclose details of unsecured loan to a JV partner; alleged conflict of interest of a director. | 2011 |
| Easy Jet | Executive remuneration proposal, specifically £1.2 million to chief executive to dissuade him from quitting; special payment not linked to performance; over 27% of votes failed to back the proposal; the airline's founder declined to attend and did not vote his 26% of the total shareholdings. | 2010 |
| Cable & Wireless | Dissatisfaction over executive remuneration. | 2009 |
| ExxonMobil | Refusal to commit large-scale capital investment in alternative energy research relating to climate change. | 2008 |

*Source:* Market and press reports passim.

## Protection of Minority Shareholders' Interests

As the Frou Frou case (case 5.2) above shows, an inappropriate board structure such as joint CEO/Chairman may lead to minority shareholders' interests being marginalized or even damaged. If a board having a majority family shareholding or a single dominant shareholder makes decisions that are objectively unsound or risky, minority shareholders are likely to suffer. In addition, if NEDs are non-existent, or compliant with the CEO's wishes or are not truly independent or are subject to conflicts of interest, then any of these factors can also be harmful to minority shareholders.

While not fully guaranteed to be effective, some protection for minority shareholders should arise from having a separate CEO and Chairman, sufficient numbers of fully independent and pro-active NEDs and, where relevant, assertive institutional shareholders.

## Injection of Professional Management

In the early years of a family business, the founders are usually acting as their own experts and few professional staff are likely to be employed. However, as the business grows, reliance by the owner–directors largely on their own expertise becomes less and less realistic. No one can be an expert in everything. Nevertheless, many owner boards find it difficult to face up to the need for injection of expertise from outside. The following cases (cases 5.3 and 5.4) demonstrate the benefits of bringing in professional management to family-owned/controlled businesses whereas cases 5.5 and 5.6 demonstrate the damaging effects of failing to do so.

### Case 5.3    The Morgan Motor Company

Founded in 1910, the Morgan Motor Company has always been in private family ownership and still employs less than 200 people. Its estimated turnover in 2009 was less than £30 million, yet globally the Morgan brand is as instantly recognizable and as iconic as other sporty cars such as MG. In 2009, a Morgan won the FIA GT3 European Championships against other world-class brand marques such as Ferrari. A Morgan car is synonymous with cachet and style and for many people the ownership of a Morgan is a lifetime's ambition. Currently, the range of Morgan cars varies in price from around £29,000 to £44,000 plus extras, although special limited edition models can fetch as much as £100,000. The waiting list for a Morgan is currently between 12 months and two years, depending on model, although years ago the delivery time was considerably longer.

In the mid-1980s, Mr Charles Morgan, the son of the then managing director Mr Peter Morgan, joined the company after ten years in a different career. Charles Morgan began to realize that, despite the company's iconic status and longstanding success, its continued success would require increased growth and profitability and this would depend on producing more cars faster. In 1991, Charles Morgan took a fateful decision to call in Sir John Harvey Jones, the former Chairman of ICI, for advice. Sir John had just begun a BBC television series called Troubleshooter in which he would visit organizations, including family-owned SMEs, that were in the doldrums or in trouble, render a quick evaluation of their problem and make concrete, practical suggestions for how they should proceed to solve it. Sir John had an empathetic and rather avuncular style, and a knack of getting right to the heart of the company's problem quickly. He became a popular hero of sorts and Troubleshooter was an instant TV success which spawned a number of subsequent imitators.

The author was an avid watcher of Troubleshooter and remembers vividly the episode dedicated to the Morgan Motor Company. The next morning, and for days after, this episode was the dominant topic of conversation in the author's office and, apparently, across the country too. With more than a tinge of cynicism, everyone was drawing parallels and analogies between the ills uncovered by Sir John at Morgan and their own place of employment. Of course, this was very entertaining but nonetheless it had opened up the public's mind to how a captain of industry went about evaluating corporate problems and putting forward practical solutions.

What Sir John had found was that Morgan was only producing some 400 cars per year and that this resulted from a combination of an antiquated production line and an absolute insistence that every car had to be literally hand assembled in every respect. A high proportion of wood was used in the bodywork instead of aluminium and hand tools were employed rather than semi-automatic tooling. Sir John's solution was to introduce modern production equipment to boost output and raise prices to boost profits. Together, these would also cut customer waiting lists. The company agreed to consider his recommendations and come up with an action plan.

Some months later, Sir John returned with Troubleshooter to Morgan to see how they were progressing. To his dismay, the directors had rejected his recommendations other than to try to make the current production process more efficient, which would increase production from about nine cars per week to ten per week. A visibly exasperated Sir John then spoke to camera with what became among the viewing public a widely quoted aphorism for any corporate failure 'waiting to happen': 'I don't know when exactly but there will come a day when there is no longer a Morgan Car Company'. Five years was his best guess.

Sir John proved to be wrong in his prediction. However, despite rejecting Sir John's advice in the short term, the company's exposure to his ideas and thought processes later proved its worth. Charles Morgan was spurred on by the experience to gain an MBA. As a result, he realized that Sir John's advice that the company needed to employ a team of professionally qualified engineers to revitalize both the design process and production was sound. He admits that his decision to act on this specifically was crucial to the company's subsequent success. Investment in R&D was increased and other manufacturers' engines were used under licence in some models, thereby releasing finance previously tied up in making their own engines. From 1997 onwards, the modest modernization of the business began to deliver benefits, including production time being reduced dramatically. Improved design pushed Morgan into world-class racing competitiveness. By 2009, profit margins had increased from between 2 per cent and 3 per cent to nearly 12 per cent and production was reported to be around 700 units per year.

## Case 5.4   Triple A Asia (Waring 2007a)

The Triple A Asia Group (not its real name) is a privately-owned conglomerate employing over 10,000 people across Asia in wide-ranging activities including finance, insurance, manufacturing and distribution. It has a solid reputation and, in some areas, it is the market leader. It has been operating as a family-controlled group for over 100 years.

Although family-owned, Triple A Asia took the decision in the 1980s to recruit professional managers, specialists and technocrats to ensure that all the existing businesses had the necessary skill resources to adapt and grow in the global marketplace. A considerable amount of time, effort and money is invested in selecting the best human resources.

The various Group company boards are required to show transparency and accountability and appoint Independent NEDs. This policy is regarded as a necessary part of protecting the interests of all shareholders and stakeholders. Protection of corporate reputation is regarded as an imperative. This policy position presaged a study of the Hong Kong family firm Hutchison Whampoa Limited (Shea 2006), which concurred with previous studies that good practice in corporate governance and social responsibility is not an optional extra for any family firm wishing to put themselves at a competitive advantage both inside and outside Asia.

## Case 5.5   The Demonic Group

The Demonic Group (not its real name) is a family-owned and managed conglomerate whose businesses include civil engineering, cinemas, restaurants, travel and other leisure-related companies operating in a number of countries. The board comprises the company's founder as joint Chairman and Managing Director, his elder son as CEO and Finance Director and his younger son as Marketing Director. None has any professional qualifications and, apart from the father, they have little business experience other than with the company. There are no other directors and no NEDs.

The Chairman and Managing Director is a petulant character who barks instructions at staff, who are always being blamed for some failing or other, real or imagined. Any mistake that he makes will also be blamed on some unfortunate employee. His elder son behaves in a very similar fashion. The younger son spends much of his time travelling abroad on business and is rarely seen at the company's offices.

The directors' main priority is to maximize profits and a large element of achieving this is to minimize staff remuneration and benefits. If and when new professional engineers and architects are required, the company advertises in local newspapers indicating the qualifications and experience required. However, in practice the individuals recruited have much lesser qualifications and experience than those advertised or objectively required. This has resulted in high school graduates with a technical drawing certificate being hired, instead of a fully qualified civil engineer or architect, and then let loose to design bridges and other structures where design safety is of paramount importance. However, the poorly qualified candidates cost only a fraction of the remuneration and overheads of the properly qualified candidates and this is the over-riding priority of the directors. The directors have no concept of what constitutes professional management or the risks to the company in not having it.

### Case 5.6    Heavenly Homes (Waring 2007a)

Heavenly Homes (not its real name) began in the 1990s as a small family-owned house-builder in a Mediterranean country, typically with small projects of up to six houses at a time. The company was run by three brothers and the board was similar in structure to that in case 5.5. Over some years, the company developed a good reputation for quality and price.

Around 2000, the local market started to enjoy a new residential property boom, centred primarily on the growing holiday homes and ex-pat relocation market, some 75 per cent of which involve buyers from UK. The directors saw the opportunity to grow Heavenly Homes exponentially by building series of apartment blocks, typically three to six blocks with 15 to 30 units per block, in up-and-coming villages in tourist areas. Alongside the apartments, they planned for detached houses, typically 50 per site. Large areas of land were bought, licenses obtained and plans drawn up. As marketing accelerated, many people bought off-plan at a discount. Delivery times were typically quoted as 18 months. The expansion plan got underway.

By 2005, Heavenly Homes had at least six major sites at various stages of build and with further land development projects planned. The company was even featured on the leading UK television programme for buyers of foreign holiday homes. However, there were soon growing customer complaints about major defects, poor quality, (very) late delivery and reluctance to close-out snagging lists and deal with complaints. Heavenly Homes soon acquired the tag 'Hellish Homes' among dissatisfied buyers. The joint CEO and Chairman candidly admitted in 2005 that the company had suffered huge damage to its reputation that would take a long time to recover. He asked the author for his advice, who commented that as Heavenly Homes were now running much bigger capital projects, there was an urgent need for proper project management. The CEO was mystified as he had never heard of the term 'project management' before. The author quickly explained and then added that they would also need a much larger number of properly qualified and experienced engineers to run these projects plus competent building workers, electricians, plumbers and so on instead of 'cowboys'. The CEO baulked at the author's suggestion that to find good quality engineers and workers would probably require the services of head hunters for the senior posts and recruitment agents for the rest. He was used to hiring through word of mouth and 'off the street'.

The root cause of the company's problem lay in a combination of greed fuelled by the property boom, the inexperience of the owners in running major capital projects, their lack of knowledge of basic management methods, their tendency to cut corners and their unwillingness to buy-in the necessary expertise. The board of directors lacked both numbers and expertise, including strong independent NEDs. The lack of professionalism coupled with a fear of accepting new expertise and a reluctance to let go typifies many family-run businesses of all sizes in many countries.

## Succession Issues

As the controlling Chairman and/or CEO of a family-owned business gets older, the question of succession will inevitably arise. In the West, where large corporations tend to be publicly rather than privately owned and run, the board usually has some mechanism in place for succession planning. In other regions, such as Asia and the Middle East, large corporations have only really arisen in large numbers in the past 50 years or so and their ageing founders are only just facing up to the fact of their own mortality and the need for an orderly relinquishment of power as they become older and frailer. In countries such as Hong Kong, with a strong tradition of family corporate dynasties being built up since the 1950s, the succession question as a whole has become ever more public in recent years as the corporate patriarchs (and rare matriarch) are now typically in their 80s and 90s and, occasionally, over 100. Succession issues tend to create tensions among the family owners anywhere but, in Hong Kong, they quite frequently degenerate into public and sometimes ugly internecine battles for control of the family empire and fortunes. Recent examples include:

- The ongoing battle between Stanley Ho (in his 90s) and his various wives and children for control of his US$multi-billion SJM Holdings casino empire. Mr Ho senior and his family have long been at the centre of public controversies, including allegations of links to organized crime in Macau. Although never convicted of any crime, some of his business activities and associates reportedly have been the subject over the years of various investigations by police and anti-corruption authorities such as the Independent Commission Against Corruption (ICAC).
- Following the death of Kwok Tak-seng in 1990, his family inherited 42 per cent of Sun Hung Kai Properties Ltd, the largest property developer in Hong Kong by market capitalization. In 2008, his widow aged 79 replaced the eldest son as Chairman and NED. In 2011, the eldest son was removed as a beneficiary of the company's controlling family trusts. In March 2012, the ICAC arrested a former senior government official and two senior executives of Sun Hung Kai (reportedly the two brothers Raymond and Thomas Kwok) on suspicion of corruption under the Prevention of Bribery Ordinance. The two Kwok brothers were subsequently charged by ICAC in July 2012 with bribery of the Chief Secretary for Administration. Other individuals were also charged in relation to the offences. The cases had not concluded at the time of writing.
- Following the death of KamShui-fai, founder of Yung Kee Holdings Ltd, 45 per cent of the shareholdings went to each of his two sons and the remaining 10 per cent to his daughter. In 2009, the family assets were reported to be worth more than HK$2 billion and the company's flagship restaurant was earning HK$51 million (US$6.56 million) in net profits. When the daughter sold her 10 per cent shareholding to one of her brothers, thus giving him a majority shareholding of 55 per cent, the other brother submitted a court petition in 2010 to wind up the company unless his brother bought out his 45 per cent holding. His petition succeeded.

There are arguments for maintaining family control of the boardroom, such as their close understanding of the company's history, standing in the community, traditions, culture and how to get things done, the family's network of contacts and relationships and the fact that they are not beholden to remote, overseas owners. Such factors are very important in a place such as Hong Kong and an outsider, especially one not from Hong Kong, would struggle for years to successfully replace the controlling patriarch or matriarch of a family-owned corporation. Even a close family member would probably find it difficult for a time and there is evidence from drops in share price that markets do not like such transitions. Nevertheless, more and more corporate patriarchs are welcoming back their sons (and daughters), loaded with MBAs and some corporate experience in the West, to take on senior executive positions and be groomed as successors-in-waiting. This was abundantly evident from the contribution of several corporate leaders and their sons to the discussion and debate on Family Businesses at the 2nd Asian Corporate Governance Conference in 2007 held at the Hong Kong Baptist University (HKBU) Centre for Corporate Governance and Financial Policy.

Ultimately, however, it is unlikely that those large corporations which are traditionally family owned and run will be able to survive in the long term unless they accept a realistic degree of professional management (including risk management) and this implies bringing in outsiders as it is unlikely that the number of qualified family members will ever be sufficient. As noted earlier in case 4.4, dominant joint CEO/chairmen in family-controlled large corporations often regard the company as their private plaything and the company's money as their own. Moreover, as a result of their growth and transition to large corporate status, they will be exposed to a number of risk-laden issues which, if they fail to manage competently, can adversely affect corporate reputation, market confidence, access to capital, share values and, ultimately, survival.

# 6 *Business Continuity and Crisis Management*

The word 'crisis' is one of those popular evocative terms that are used to cover an awfully wide range of bad and unwelcome things, many of which are almost certainly not really crises. Nevertheless, bad situations may well degenerate into a crisis and incidents may well trigger a crisis. So, what is a crisis? Here, we hit a slight problem in that there are many definitions.

Some definitions are clearly too restrictive for normal corporate application and, at best, could only apply to very particular circumstances, for example those which refer specifically to information loss or to international conflict and military intervention. Some definitions (for example, in Wikipedia) refer specifically only to 'complex systems (family, economy, society)' and state that 'simple systems do not enter crises', which is self-evident nonsense even ignoring the loose assumptions implied by the term 'simple systems'. The Wikipedia definition implies that individuals and partnerships cannot experience a crisis! Further, it states that one characteristic of a crisis is its unexpected nature and the element of surprise. While some crises certainly are like that, others are characterized by a long build-up that many people are well aware of and sometimes the crisis drags on for years and even decades. PAS 200, the British Standard for crisis management good practice, refers to both 'sudden' and 'smouldering' crises. For example, the News International crises (case 6.5) simmered for years before boiling over. Also, overall the Middle East Crisis has been around for decades, albeit that there have been numerous particular component crises within it along the way (see case 6.6).

The author's working definition of a corporate crisis is: A period of intense and often dramatic conflict and uncertainty about a topic which is central to the organization's current existence and involving loss of control and, if unresolved, possible collapse and chaos. The incubation period leading up to a final period of drama may range from hours to years, depending on how and when a critical mass of negative factors is triggered to create a potentially uncontrollable cascade or chain reaction. Frequently, a crisis involves acutely unstable conditions and leads to enforced major change in the organization that some parties may not want.

## Systems for Managing Crises and Business Continuity

The emergence of a crisis is likely to be evidence that current ERM has not been totally effective in some way. After all, a key purpose of having a robust ERM system is to avoid, deter and deflect crises – to spot the pre-cursors early enough, take preventive action and strengthen the organization's protection and preparedness 'just in case'. That said, not every crisis is readily foreseeable and some arise so quickly that prevention is impractical.

Therefore, CMP is an essential component of an effective ERM system. A sometimes overlooked corollary is that a crisis management plan is most unlikely to be effective unless an effective ERM system already exists. A crisis management plan can only be as good as the organization's overall risk management system. By analogy, it is no good installing effective brakes on a car if the tyres are bald, the steering is defective and the lights do not work. This truism sometimes causes arguments when an organization hires external consultants to assist with CMP and cannot understand why the consultants insist on first examining in some depth the quality of the overall ERM system.

It would be inappropriate in this book, which is not a 'how to' book, to seek to provide any detailed guidance on CMP and for this the reader is referred to *PAS 200: 2011 Crisis Management: Guidance and Good Practice*. PAS 200 emphasizes many of the points above made by the author and notes also the need for treating CMP as a special risk management provision requiring special arrangements. For example, if a crisis arises it is no good simply expecting, say, the Group Risk Manager or the Chairman of the board risk committee to manage the crisis. Unambiguously identified individuals do indeed need to be assigned specific roles in the crisis management plan but it must be on the basis of the particular skills they personally bring to the crisis management task and not solely because of their job title or seniority, albeit that authority is needed as well as skill. The individual in overall command and control of a crisis requires a rare combination of skills and attributes, including strong analytical and decision-making skills, an innate toughness and knowing when standing instructions may have to be bypassed.

## Case 6.1   The Piper Alpha Disaster (Cullen 1990, Waring and Glendon 1998)

Piper Alpha was an offshore combined production and drilling installation owned by Occidental Petroleum (Caledonia) Ltd and operating in the North Sea. On 6 July 1988, owing to earlier procedural errors during plant modification, a flammable vapour cloud formed in the Gas Compression Module and ignited causing an initial explosion and fire, which knocked out the main power supplies and the installation control room. A number of critical emergency systems then failed (for example, fire water) and the fire from the initial explosion spread to the Oil Separation Module resulting in an enlarged conflagration. Within 20 minutes of the initial explosion, a second explosion occurred and the fire continued to intensify. During the early stages of the fire, a large proportion of the 226 persons on board (which included contractors) gathered in and near the canteen in the Accommodation Module to await further instruction. After the installation control room was knocked out by the initial explosion, the Offshore Installation Manager (OIM), the most senior official on board and the person supposedly in charge of the emergency, joined them to await rescue by helicopter or surface vessels. Unfortunately, the growing conflagration began to endanger the Accommodation Module. The OIM refused to recognize the threat and told the gathered crew to stay put and await rescue.

The official inquiry report by Lord Cullen (Cullen 1990, Waring and Glendon 1998) noted that: 'The system of control in the event of a major emergency was rendered almost entirely inoperative ... and little command or control was exercised over the movements of personnel.' Smoke and flames outside the Accommodation Module made evacuation by helicopter or lifeboat impossible. Divers who were on duty escaped to the sea. Some other personnel ignored instructions to go to the Accommodation Module and joined the divers to escape into the sea. Of the 61 survivors, 28 escaped to the sea by using their own initiative. Nevertheless, a large number of men (estimated by one eye witness to be about 100) assembled near the galley on the top level of the Accommodation Module. Cullen commented: 'There was no evidence that this was the result of any positive actions on the part of anyone in a position of authority.' Witnesses described the OIM as being unable to take command and reach a decision for them to evacuate the galley, although a number took their own initiative to escape and many of these survived. At least 81 stayed in the Accommodation Module and they all died. 'There was no systematic attempt to lead men to a means of escape.'

In his report, Lord Cullen noted that the disaster 'clearly demonstrates that conventional selection and training of OIMs is no guarantee of ability to cope if the man himself is not able in the end to take critical decisions and lead those under his command in a time of extreme stress'.

The Piper Alpha disaster remains the world's largest loss of life (167) in a single offshore oil and gas incident. The installation was totally destroyed.

Having clearly designated and carefully selected individuals trained for very specific key roles in a crisis is very important. The overall crisis controller has to be given the authority to do what is necessary, even if this may possibly upset superiors including directors or the board chairman. The controller must have sufficient strength of character to countermand unhelpful or even dangerous interventions by well-meaning board members or executives. The 'too many fingers in the pie' problem has been identified during the crisis management of a number of major hazard disasters where *post hoc* the author has been engaged as a consultant to review crisis management issues; for example, well-meaning but uninvited directors and senior executives entering the command-and-control centre to lend moral support to the crisis managers. Apart from being an unwelcome distraction at such a critical time, uninvited well-wishers may cause congestion in the room and there is always the temptation for them to offer 'concerned advice' or even try to pull rank.

The issue of clearly defined crisis roles also extends to external communications. The media are likely to report on a crisis as it unfolds and will be seeking statements and comment from the organization. Experience confirms that there should be only one designated and authorized individual of sufficient seniority (with a designated deputy in case of non-availability) to act as organization spokesperson to the outside world. Where complex technical or safety issues are involved, other individuals may also have to be authorized to communicate to external authorities but the protocols and criteria must be very clear. Failure to stick to this simple policy can result in the sort of debacle that arose during the Three Mile Island nuclear power station crisis at Harrisburg in 1979.

## Case 6.2   Three Mile Island (Bignell and Fortune 1984)

Three Mile Island is a US civilian nuclear power plant used for electricity generation. On 28 March 1979, a maintenance mistake led to a Loss of Coolant Accident (LOCA) which threatened the safety of the nuclear reactor. Although the LOCA should have been readily correctable, a series of systemic failures both technical and human created a developing crisis over the following few days as it looked more and more as if the reactor might blow and release radioactive material into the atmosphere. As the crisis unfolded, several external parties including the plant owners and managers (Metropolitan Edison and General Public Utilities Corporation), the Pennsylvania Emergency Management Agency, and the state governor were, unbeknown to the others, giving conflicting statements to other external parties and especially the media. Some of the information given out was also inaccurate or wrong. The result was a great deal of public confusion and alarm, especially when the possibility of a total evacuation of the population within a 20 mile radius leaked out. Fortunately, control of the reactor was regained, no radioactive material leaked out and no evacuation was necessary. However, although the crisis itself passed, the whole event had created a 'crisis of confidence' among the public, and not only in the US, about the safety of nuclear power. The public debate about whether nuclear power is too risky from a safety standpoint has continued and has been fuelled by the Chernobyl disaster in Ukraine (1986) and more recently the Fukushima Daiichi loss of containment accident in Japan in 2011.

In addition to the need for a well-rehearsed and robust crisis management plan, there will also be a need for an equally robust Business Continuity Plan (BCP). The BCP needs to start operation at the earliest sensible opportunity while the crisis is still running and then continue after the crisis for as long as is necessary to ensure that the organization's business continues as smoothly as possible. As with CMP, it is not the function of this book to provide any detailed guidance on BCP. For detailed guidance on BCP, the relevant standards include *BS 25999 Business Continuity Management* (now superseded by ISO 22301) which complements and dovetails with PAS 200. See also Elliott et al. (2002). However, in principle, before preparing a BCP a business process risk analysis is usually required so as to identify critical dependencies and potential 'show stopper' risks, if these have not already been identified as part of the CMP and routine ERM activities. Examples of the kinds of key BCP question that need to be answered in respect of a range of potential crises and threats are:

- Realistically, what is the range of potential threats and crises that we need to address? How far do we need to think globally about potential 'show stoppers' that might affect us directly or indirectly, for example pandemics, natural disasters, oil prices, regime changes and political risks, regional conflicts blocking oil and trade?
- How will our finances and cash flow be protected? If the crisis also affects our customers, will they be able to pay us and if so how? Do we need to secure turnkey emergency credit facilities now just in case? Do we need to clarify our insurance arrangements and how quickly the relevant policies would pay out?
- Which supplies are critical to the functioning of our organization? Are we vulnerable to supply interruptions because we operate a single-source policy? What can we do to alleviate this vulnerability?

- In the event that our key suppliers are also affected by the crisis and/or are unable to maintain supplies, what contingencies should be planned for activation if necessary?
- In the event of, for example, natural disaster, armed conflict, pandemic, which may prevent travel and transport of goods, what business survival contingencies do we require?
- How will we protect vital company information and computer data? What off-site data back-up and retrieval facilities do we need?
- How will we manage our staff during and after a crisis so that they can best assist with the continuity and recovery of the business? Who are critical persons essential for continuity and recovery? Which kinds of crisis might warrant temporary part-time employment or suspension and what salary arrangements could the organization bear? What kinds of crisis might warrant temporary home working?

In essence, crisis management and business continuity management, and the planning required for these, are all about ensuring survival of the business if and when a crisis or disaster of some kind befalls the organization. Experience shows that those organizations that make the effort to create robust crisis management and BCPs usually fare far better when a crisis arises than those that do not. While this statement may seem rather obvious, the low proportion of organizations which addresses these requirements at all suggests that they believe that a crisis will never befall them and, if one does, it will be easily survivable. History and experience contradict them.

## Further Cases

Owing to a wide-ranging variability, both in causation and how crises develop and end, the author felt it appropriate to include a number of further cases. The first two of these cases, 6.3 and 6.4, demonstrate the benefits of having an effective and well-rehearsed plan for dealing with crises. The remaining cases show variously how badly things can go wrong if risk management, including prior CMP and BCP, are deficient and also how complex and intractable some crises are.

### Case 6.3   PRUPIM Deals with Four Terrorist Bombings

PRUPIM is the real estate investment management arm of M&G Investments and one of the leading real estate investment managers in the UK. Over an eight-year period, a number of PRUPIM's assets in different parts of the UK suffered extensive damage from terrorist bomb attacks nearby. These include the bombings at:

Bishopsgate, London, 24 April 1993

Manchester City Centre, 15 June 1996

Omagh, Northern Ireland, 15 August 1998

Ealing Broadway, London, 3 August 2001

On each occasion, as a result of the company's well-rehearsed and sophisticated Crisis Management and Disaster Recovery Plan, the company was able to minimize the impact and disruption and to recover quickly. The plan included features such as safe evacuation of personnel; communication with staff, tenants, suppliers, the public and the media; containment and removal of any structural and other hazards caused by the explosions; if necessary, temporary transfer of operations to other sites; and coordination and cooperation with other businesses in the vicinity as well as with the police, emergency services and counter-terrorism agencies. This case shows how solid CMP and business continuity planning enabled PRUPIM to successfully manage not one but several terrorist bombings over a number of years. Consequently, not only were its personnel and assets protected but also its reputation as a solid and well-managed business was enhanced.

## Case 6.4   Singapore Airlines

In November 2000, Singapore International Airline (SIA) flight SQ006 from Taiwan to Los Angeles crashed on take-off during a typhoon after hitting construction equipment while on the wrong runway. It was and remains Singapore Airlines' only air crash. Eighty two of the 179 people on board died immediately and many more were injured.

The airline immediately admitted publicly what had happened and took full responsibility, even though some blame might have been attributable to airport ground conditions and radar systems. In addition, victims' families were immediately each offered compensation unconditionally at four to five times the level required under international law. SIA's reputation was not only protected but enhanced. Although SIA's share values fell 9 per cent in the first few days after the crash, they quickly recovered and SIA's profitability has been unaffected by the disaster.

## Case 6.5   News International Scandals and Ongoing Crises

If ever there were a high-profile example of (a) poor CMP, (b) bad crisis management, (c) seemingly non-existent ERM and (d) weak corporate governance, it is surely that of News Corp and the scandals surrounding illegal mobile phone hacking, e-mail hacking and alleged bribery of police officers and others by journalists and agents working for or hired by various newspapers in News International, News Corp's UK subsidiary.

Allegations of phone hacking first surfaced in 2005, when royal court officials alleged that the weekly *News of the World* (*NOTW*) had published a story about Prince William based on information that could have come only from interception of voicemail messages. Following a police inquiry, in 2006 the *NOTW*'s royal affairs editor Clive Goodman and a private investigator Glenn Mulcaire were arrested and charged with illegal mobile phone hacking and, in January 2007, Goodman was jailed for four months while Mulcaire received a six-month prison sentence. The *NOTW* editor Andy Coulson resigned over the affair but said that he had no prior knowledge of the wrongdoing. This claim was backed up by an investigation of e-mail archives by *NOTW*'s lawyers, which concluded that they could find no evidence that Coulson or other executives knew about Goodman's wrongdoing.

In July 2009, however, it emerged that during Coulson's editorship from 2003 to 2007 senior executives were aware that *NOTW* journalists were hacking into the mobile phone messages of politicians, sports stars, actors and other celebrities. It further emerged that the *NOTW*'s publisher News Group Newspapers, part of News International, had already paid out over £1 million in out-of-court settlements of claims by plaintiffs that otherwise would have exposed alleged involvement of *NOTW* journalists in phone hacking. However, over the next 18 months, despite continuing concern about the *NOTW* phone hacking scandal expressed by the House of Commons Culture, Media and Sports Committee and others, the momentum for further investigation appeared to peter out. In December 2009, the Crown Prosecution Service announced that owing to witnesses' refusal to cooperate with the police, no further charges would be brought in relation to the *NOTW* phone hacking scandal.

However, the crisis incubation period of the previous six years was about to end and what was to be an *annus horribilis* for News Corp's owner Rupert Murdoch was about to begin. From January 2011 onwards, the phone hacking crisis just kept escalating. In January 2011, the police opened a new investigation after the actress Sienna Miller, the Member of Parliament (MP) George Galloway and the trade union leader Bob Crow alleged that their phones had been hacked by *NOTW*. In February, the police announced that they had identified more potential victims and were now reviewing the files of the original case against Goodman and Mulcaire in 2006–2007. By March, allegations of hacking against more individuals emerged, as well as hacking into the e-mails of a former British Army intelligence officer.

In April, three *NOTW* individuals were arrested on suspicion of conspiracy to intercept mobile phone messages: the former Editor Ian Edmondson, Chief Reporter Neville Thurlbeck and Senior Journalist James Weatherup. For the first time, *NOTW* admitted that it had been involved in phone hacking and published an apology, while UK parent company News International announced a compensation scheme for 'justifiable claims'.

By May 2011, the growing list of alleged victims included the former Deputy Prime Minister Lord Prescott, the Labour MP Chris Bryant, the ex-Metropolitan Police Commander Brian Paddick, the journalist Brendan Montague, the professional footballer Ryan Giggs and the film actor Hugh Grant.

During June and July, the escalation of the scandal and crisis became much more intense, with almost daily revelations of new allegations and further official investigations, interspersed with admissions and apologies by *NOTW*. On 7 June 2011, News Group Newspapers (the *NOTW* publisher) issued a formal apology to phone hacking victim Sienna Miller and paid her a compensation settlement of £100,000 in damages and costs. On 9 June, the police confirmed that they were now also investigating computer hacking by *NOTW*. In early July, allegations emerged that *NOTW* had hacked into the mobile phones of murder victim Milly Dowler and her family, the family of the child Madeleine McCann who disappeared in Portugal, the parents of the Soham schoolgirls murdered in 2002 and victims of the London terrorist bombings of 7 July 2005. Other allegations were that the *NOTW* also hacked into the phones of relatives of British soldiers killed in Afghanistan and Iraq.

In the space of a couple of days, such was the upsurge of revulsion among the British public and the Government about the latest revelations about illegally spying on the families of murder victims and British soldiers killed in the line of duty that the *NOTW* had become synonymous with the unacceptable face of journalism and Rupert Murdoch had become 'public enemy number one'. Murdoch and the *NOTW* were pilloried mercilessly in Parliament and on television. Other newspapers' columnists and editors rushed to join the anti-Murdoch rhetoric and distance themselves from the *NOTW* practices. Major companies began cancelling their advertisements in *NOTW*.

The public and commercial backlash was so great that on 7 July 2011 News Corp announced that the weekly *NOTW* would be closed for good and that the 10 July 2011 edition would be the last. After 168 years, the *NOTW* ended in ignominy.

The next day, 8 July, the Prime Minister announced two official inquiries, one into the hacking scandal and the other into the need for tougher regulation of the press. The same day, former *NOTW* editor Andy Coulson was arrested on suspicion of conspiracy both to intercept communications and of corruption. The former *NOTW* royal affairs editor Clive Goodman was re-arrested regarding alleged payments to police officers by *NOTW* staff.

On 10 July, the final day of the *NOTW*'s existence, Rupert Murdoch flew to London ostensibly to take control of the crisis.

The next day, police confirmed that former Prime Minister Gordon Brown's name had been found on a target list of Glenn Mulcaire, the private investigator formerly contracted by *NOTW* and previously jailed in 2007 for hacking into phones of members of the royal household.

By 14 July, it was becoming clear that now the whole of News Corp's British operations under News International had been tainted by the affair. The former Prime Minister Gordon Brown described News International as having 'descended from the gutter to the sewers'. The same day, Murdoch withdrew his takeover bid for control of BSkyB, no doubt mindful that the competition regulator Ofcom would almost certainly take a very tough line on News Corp's and Murdoch's suitability given the current scandal. Shortly after, Murdoch went on a '*mea culpa*' public relations (PR) offensive, not on admission of his own failings but on those of his executives and journalists. He placed advertisements in national newspapers apologizing for 'serious wrongdoing' by *NOTW* and affirming that the *NOTW* management were both cooperating fully with the ongoing police investigation and committed to fundamental change in style and practices. Despite his PR efforts, when the news of the phone hacking scandal became widely publicized in the US and Australia, News Corp's share price fell 5 per cent in one day.

On 19 July, the Commons Culture, Media and Sports Committee began its televised hearings into the phone hacking scandal and key witnesses included both Rupert Murdoch and his son James who had become News Corp CEO. Rupert Murdoch denied any responsibility for the scandals and blamed *NOTW* staff. James Murdoch denied knowing that more than one journalist (Clive Goodman in the 2006–2007 case) had been engaged in phone hacking. Yet within days James Murdoch's testimony on this point was flatly contradicted by two former senior *NOTW* executives who asserted that he knew about the wider practice of phone hacking in 2008 because they had held a 15-minute meeting with him to discuss the implications of the extent of the problem as revealed in a particular e-mail which showed that three journalists other than

Goodman were involved. A lawyer at Farrer & Co, who was advising News International at that time, later confirmed their version of events, which also related to the *NOTW*'s liability to the plaintiff Gordon Taylor, Chairman of the Professional Footballers Association. James Murdoch, nevertheless, continued to refute the assertions.

Throughout August 2011, the crisis rumbled on with yet more allegations of *NOTW* phone hacking and further arrests of former senior *NOTW* editors. A copy of a damning letter from Clive Goodman to News International executives in 2007 became public. In it, Goodman claimed that former *NOTW* editor Andy Coulson backed the practice of phone hacking to the extent that it was often discussed during daily editorial meetings and conferences until Coulson banned explicit reference to it.

On 17 August, James Murdoch admitted that Gordon Taylor, Chairman of the Professional Footballers Association, had been paid £700,000 to settle his phone hacking compensation claim.

By this time, the public inquiry into the role of the press and police in the phone hacking scandal under the chairmanship of Lord Justice Leveson began to collect evidence and prepare for hearings to start in November 2011. The work of the Commons Culture, Media and Sports Committee on the scandal continued apace into September, with evidence from former senior *NOTW* executives that James Murdoch knew about the extent of phone hacking in 2008. Mr Murdoch was recalled by the Committee to examine his testimony further and ask whether he had misled them previously. The antipathy of Committee members towards Mr Murdoch was palpable. At one stage, Tom Watson MP suggested to Mr Murdoch that News International operated like the Mafia to which Mr Murdoch replied that this was both untrue and offensive. Mr Watson retorted to Mr Murdoch: 'You must be the first Mafia boss in history who didn't know he was running a criminal enterprise.' Evidence also emerged that News International had hired private detectives to spy on the lawyers representing phone hacking victims and even spy on Mr Watson himself.

As if all this was not enough of a crisis for News Corp, the *NOTW*'s sister daily tabloid *The Sun* was coming under pressure. On the one hand, *The Sun*'s circulation figures fell by 7 per cent in July 2011, the largest drop for a decade, as the British public began to generalize their disgust for anything associated with the Murdoch family. On the other hand, allegations of bribery of police officers by *Sun* journalists began to surface. On 4 November 2011, a *Sun* reporter was arrested in connection with such allegations.

By late January 2012, with the *NOTW* phone hacking crisis still ongoing, *The Sun* bribery scandal had blown into a second crisis with the potential to eclipse the first. Four senior *Sun* executives and journalists (some former, some current) were arrested on 28 January on suspicion of bribing police and public officials and former senior *NOTW* personnel were also questioned. By mid-February, the rest of the British press, including *The Times* which is also owned by News Corp, were writing a flood of articles and editorials against the illegal practices of News International journalists and the failure of News Corp's Management and Standards Committee itself to behave with probity.

In something of a bold move, Rupert Murdoch announced the launch of a new weekly newspaper *The Sun on Sunday* to replace the defunct *NOTW*. The first edition was published on 26 February 2011 and sold over 3 million copies, more than twice its nearest rival. The very next day, however, in her evidence to the Leveson Inquiry, the senior police officer leading the investigation of bribery and hacking at News International newspapers said that *The Sun* had established a network of corrupted officials and had created a culture of illegal payments. One public official had received £80,000 in alleged corrupt payments and one *Sun* journalist alone had paid out over £150,000 to various sources. She reported that her team was investigating substantial regular payments involving an internal system designed to disguise the illegal payments and who was being paid.

The Leveson Inquiry was further informed of evidence that both Andy Coulson, the former *NOTW* editor, and Rebekah Brooks, the former News International Chief Executive, knew in 2006 about the *NOTW* phone hacking, which contradicted their previous public statements and testimonies to the Commons Culture, Media and Sports Committee's investigation. By this stage, the number of alleged victims making compensation claims against News International had risen to over 200.

At the time of writing, the crises at News Corp had not subsided. On 13 March 2012, six people were arrested on suspicion of perverting the course of justice. These included Rebekah Brooks, the former News International Chief Executive, and her husband Charlie, Mark Hanna the former head of security at the company and three other former executives. On 15 May 2012, Rebekah Brooks was charged with three counts of conspiracy to obstruct the course of justice, which involved allegations that she hid documents and computers from the police and conspired to remove records from the newspaper's headquarters. On 24 July 2012, she was further charged along with a number of other former senior executives and journalists with conspiracy to hack into mobile phone messages of the murdered schoolgirl Milly Dowler. Additionally, Brooks and others were charged on 20 November 2012 with conspiracy to pay a Ministry of Defence (MoD) employee £100,000 for information. The ongoing various police investigations, arrests, prosecutions and official Government inquiries may not be complete until 2014. The prospect of further criminal prosecutions and civil actions cannot be ruled out and may even ensnare members of the Murdoch family. James Murdoch has already been forced to relinquish his position as News International Chief Executive and take a less high-profile job in a non-print media part of News Corp in the US. He is no longer deemed credible in the business world as a potential successor to his father to head the Murdoch empire.

In summary, it appears that the corporate culture within News International had long been one of 'What can we get away with?' (see Chapter 4) in which highly unethical practices, including blatantly illegal acts, had become not only commonplace but accepted as normal and justifiable. Equally acceptable in such a culture was the persistent use of evasion, denial and lies to avoid accountability when challenged about alleged wrongdoing, especially by outside authorities. Top management and senior journalists saw the end as justifying the means. They thought they could always brazen out any allegations, investigations or crisis and that they were untouchable and invincible. They saw no need for anything as tedious and inconvenient as good governance, a robust ERM system as outlined in Chapter 2 and CMP as outlined earlier in this chapter. The Management and Standards Committee singularly failed in its job and appeared to be window dressing. By the time the Murdochs belatedly tried to establish a modicum of governance and regain control of the situation, the overall crisis was way beyond their control. This saga is almost a parody of good governance, corporate risk management and crisis management.

## Case 6.6   The Iran Crisis

Iran has been the focus of world attention and indeed concern ever since the 1979 revolution and, within a year, the snuffing out of a fledgling all-party interim government and the takeover by Islamist ideologues led by Ayatollah Khomeini. Since then, the Islamic Republic of Iran has had a very uneasy and difficult relationship with the West, interspersed by a seemingly endless series of crises as seen from the perspective of Western and many other governments. Notable among the crises are:

- The storming of the American embassy in Tehran in 1979 by revolutionary elements and the taking of 52 diplomats as hostages.
- The abortive military mission by the US to free the embassy hostages.
- The attack on Iran by Iraq in 1980 and the subsequent Iran–Iraq war 1980–1988, which Iran regards as sponsored by the US and other Western powers which backed Iraq.
- The Salman Rushdie affair, when a fatwa was issued by Iranian clerics which resulted in death threats against him, years of police protection and a diplomatic rift with the UK.
- The shooting down by the USS Vincennes of an unarmed Iran Air airbus on a routine scheduled flight 655 from Shiraz to Dubai with the loss of 290 passengers and crew in July 1988. According to Ansari (2006), human error, poor training and panic among the Vincennes crew resulted in the airbus being mistaken for a threatening aircraft. See also Glendon et al. (2006, page 248). President Reagan awarded the Vincennes captain a distinguished service medal. The US Government paid compensation at local cost of living rate but refused to accept responsibility.
- Threats against Israel from President Ahmadinejad and the continuous war of nerves between the two governments.
- The ongoing crisis surrounding Iran's reluctance to be fully open about its nuclear development programme. Iran insists it is only for peaceful civil applications such as power generation and medicine but has declined to provide the United Nation's (UN) International Atomic Energy Agency with full access to all sites. Western and many other governments suspect that Iran is secretly developing nuclear weapons. UN and Western-led sanctions against Iran have caused widespread economic damage internally, including a 50 per cent drop in local currency value during 2011 and early 2012 and rocketing price inflation, but no sign of Iranian compliance.

Overall, 'the Iran crisis' is an immense subject worthy of a book on its own. Indeed, Dr Ali Ansari's 2006 book *Confronting Iran* fits that bill admirably. The author has therefore selected just one aspect, namely how the differing perceptions of the issues, on the one hand, by the Iranian Government and, on the other hand, Western and other countries, create differing definitions of the issues as well as of the component crises and how to handle them.

There can be no doubt that there are genuine and widely expressed concerns outside Iran that it is covertly developing nuclear weapons which it might then use against Israel and Western targets or to intimidate neighbouring Middle Eastern states. What is not known for sure is whether Iran really is developing such weapons and, if it is, how far it is away from having an actual deliverable nuclear weapon. Regardless of the unknown facts and speculation, there appears to be an element of bluff in the Iranian stance not that dissimilar to Saddam Hussein's failure to allow full access for independent inspection to prove that Iraq had no WMD (Weapons of Mass Destruction), thus generating a fear in the West that he really did possess them which gave the pretext for the second Iraq invasion and regime change. Keeping the UN and the West guessing while possibly buying time to accelerate nuclear weapons development is how the Iranian Government's behaviour is widely interpreted.

Since the Iran–Iraq War, the Iranian Government has followed a *de facto* policy of resurgent nationalism (Waring and Glendon 1998). Recovery of Iran's historical status as the primary regional power, while keeping the perceived bad intentions of the West at bay, is what drives Iran's political leaders. Their anti-Western rhetoric frequently has played to a regional audience in Arab states, although the outcomes thus far of the 'Arab Spring' revolutions of 2011 onwards have favoured a variety of putative democratic models rather than the Iranian model. Dr Ansari, a recognized authority on modern Iran, observes that the Iranian regime thrives on crises and paranoia (Ansari 2006). Keeping the crisis pot boiling suits the Iranian regime perfectly, as they can keep protesting their innocence, blame the West for all the tension and the ongoing crisis, tell the population that Iranian sovereignty is under threat from 'the Great Satan' (the US) and Israel and justify their policies and actions as simply protection of the nation. While at least half the population is keen for liberalization, a more democratic society and greatly improved diplomatic and trade relations with the West, and many would prefer a change of regime to achieve all this, many of that same group would undoubtedly immediately support the regime in the event of any external aggression, just as they did in 1980 when Saddam Hussein attacked Iran and started the Iran–Iraq War (see Waring 2006a).

But what of the West? It could be argued that they too have some vested interests in keeping the crisis pot boiling and playing up the anti-Iranian rhetoric. After all, presenting Iran as an increasing existential threat to regional stability and world peace, with that all-important accusation of covert development of nuclear weapons, provides Western defence ministries with another argument for strengthening defence capability and against cuts in defence budgets. The current tightening of UN and Western-led sanctions against Iran may not yield compliance or even containment of its nuclear ambitions. There are also many in the US who relish the prospect of armed conflict with Iran, which they hope will precipitate a regime change from within. Defence industries and infrastructure contractors always do well out of wars and post-conflict reconstruction, as Iraq and Afghanistan show.

Ansari's reference to crisis and paranoia within the Iranian regime is matched by his acerbic comments about the Americans being just as bad; he calls them mirror-images of each other. As far as Iran is concerned, the author, who has visited Iran many times over a 40-year period (see for example, chapter 13 in Waring and Glendon 1998), confirms that generally in the Iranian population there is always an underlying suspicion of Western motives and actions. This is especially true of how they see the British Government. There are good grounds historically for their attitude, when one considers that in 1953 the Anglo-Iranian Oil Company (now part of BP) was implicated with US and British intelligence agents in the overthrow of the democratically elected Iranian Prime Minister Dr Moussadegh because of his oil nationalization policy. This in no way provokes personal animosity towards Britons and, in the author's experience, Iranians are exceptionally civil and friendly towards all foreigners in their country. Perhaps the mood is best captured by a once very popular TV soap in Iran called *Uncle Napoleon*. The central character, Uncle Napoleon, was a middle-aged and rather cantankerous nationalist not dissimilar to the Alf Garnett character in a 1970s popular TV comedy series in the UK, which was then Americanized as Archie Bunker for the US market. For Uncle Napoleon, each day was a never-ending litany of problems, crises, rows and tussles with anybody and everybody but, in his mind, every single one was the fault of the British. If his milk went sour, it was the British who had sabotaged the milk supplies. If his car would not start, it was because the British were supplying dud components. And so on. His family tried but failed to reason with him – after all, in his mind anyone who disagreed with him must have been a British agent. To Britons, all this is quite comical but 'kar-e inglis hast' (it's the work of the British) is indeed a frequently heard reaction among Iranians whenever some misfortune befalls Iran. On several occasions in the past, Iranian officials have teased the author about his surname Waring by asking whether he has come to wage war on Iran. Harmless banter certainly but also indicative of a general expectation that Britain is always up to no good as far as Iran is concerned.

In summary, although the 'Iran Crisis' is in the realms of international conflicts, there are also lessons to be learned for how corporate organizations may need to approach crises where they are involved in disputes with another party. Differing perceptions of the issues by each party create differing definitions of the issues as well as how to handle them. Understanding the other party's world-view, including their perceptions and definitions, their motivations, expectations, outcome preferences and so on, can be invaluable in building bridges and resolving crises.

## Case 6.7    Preparing for Pandemic Crises in Asia

In 2003, the whole of the Far East was engulfed in the crisis caused by Severe Acute Respiratory Syndrome (SARS). Starting in Hong Kong in November 2002, the SARS virus epidemic resulted in 8,422 known cases of infection in 37 countries, including 916 deaths before finally subsiding after about nine months. It was a virtual pandemic, that is, an epidemic of an infectious disease spread across a wide geographical area, typically numbers of countries, entire continents or even globally.

Apart from the actual health impact on those infected, the SARS epidemic had a huge impact on the way the populations of countries in the Far East behaved day to day. For fear of infection, many people avoided public places and public transport. Schools were closed and conferences and business meetings were postponed or cancelled. Business travel dropped sharply. All of this behaviour change had an immediate negative impact on the retail, tourism and services sectors, with hotels, restaurants, bars and shopping malls bereft of customers and airlines carrying few passengers in the region. Unemployment shot up in Hong Kong and elsewhere. Fortunately, once the SARS crisis had passed, business recovery was fairly rapid but the bad experience is still vivid in the minds of those who were there at the time. For a relevant case study on how one organization in Singapore coped with SARS, see Arnold (2007).

Almost immediately, an epidemic of 'bird flu' caused by the H5N1 virus and spread largely by birds was moving rapidly across the Far East, Asia and into Europe and Africa. From 2003 to 2012, the World Health Organization (WHO) reported 594 cases including 349 deaths in 15 countries. Then, in 2009, a pandemic of 'swine flu' caused by the H1N1 virus arose and resulted in at least 18,000 deaths across more than 200 countries.

Throughout 2009 and 2010, the WHO and national health authorities disseminated a great deal of public information on suitable prevention and protection measures. Employers and organizations generally were encouraged to prepare themselves for the possibility that the epidemic could escalate into a full pandemic. In the experience of the author and many others who were involved in CMP at that time, few organizations in the Far East in fact took the issue seriously and did any kind of CMP and BCP for pandemics. A large part of the resistance stemmed from apathy and cynicism in boardrooms about the topic, coupled with the strong 'gambling' view of corporate risk management in Asian companies. The 'bird flu' and 'swine flu' epidemics were passing and few boards and corporate executives judged that a high-impact pandemic was a high probability. This attitude is all the more astonishing when one considers the fact that barely six years had passed since the relatively limited SARS epidemic and all its bad impact on businesses. In the author's opinion, most Asian businesses still remain unprepared for any such future crisis. For comparison, the so-called Spanish flu pandemic of 1918, also caused by the H1N1 virus, resulted worldwide in at least 20 million and possibly up to 100 million deaths.

However a crisis is defined, the emergence of a crisis is likely to be evidence that current ERM has not been totally effective. Crisis management and business continuity management, and the planning required for these, are essential components of an effective ERM system and are all about resilience and ensuring survival of the business if and when a crisis or disaster befalls the organization. Despite experience showing that without robust crisis management and BCPs organizations may be crippled or may not survive a crisis, many large organizations have yet to take this matter seriously.

# PART 2

# Corporate Due Diligence

# 7 *The Abuse of Trust*

The running of any enterprise and the entry by parties into any kind of business relationship, or investment arrangement, or master–servant employment or the purchase of goods or services, all involve an implied degree of trust between the parties involved. That trust encompasses a shared expectation that each party will act in good faith, will be honest in their dealings and will not do anything to the detriment of the other party or parties.

## Case 7.1  The Capital Investment Company

A well-established capital investment company, part of a global brand, had a large portfolio of technology-related investments in businesses in Asia. Some investments involved venture capital for start-ups whereas others related to expansion and development of existing companies. In at least two cases, principals of investment targets disappeared with the funds running into tens of US$millions. The company's due diligence checks on applicants amounted to little more than obtaining evidence of financial standing from a credit rating agency!

From the early days of the London Stock Exchange at the turn of the nineteenth century, 'my word is my bond' was then thought by many in City financial circles to be good enough to ensure that business dealings were above board and would be completed with integrity. Such was the implicit level of trust between parties that anything more formal as proof of honesty and integrity would have been frowned upon. As a young man, the author recalls in the 1960s a businessman from the City of London reciting to him the 'my word is my bond' phrase, while seeking to impress upon him the gravitas of trust and honour expected in business life.

Of course, over the past 200 years increasingly an expectation of implicit trust in oral warrants and oral agreements has been replaced by the need for documented contracts. Written contracts not only seek to pin down unambiguously the substance, terms and conditions of the agreement between parties but also to correct failing memories as well as counter future false assertions about what parties agreed to and intended when the contract was signed. One might argue that, in an ideal world, written contracts should be sufficient to minimize the risk of *post hoc* disagreements between parties. However, contractual disputes are legion. In some cases, allegations are made that one party not only breached the contractual terms and conditions but also may have broken a statutory duty or even committed a criminal offence.

Written contracts are clearly necessary as a risk control tool but it is self-evident from the myriad of cases where one or more parties have ignored both their implied and express contractual duties that such documents alone are not sufficient to control behaviour. For example, since the 1980s there have been numerous high-profile corporate scandals and/ or collapses involving breaches of trust to reflect upon, such as BCCI, MGN and Polly Peck through WorldCom, and Enron to more recently SIBL, Madoff, News Corp and many of the major banks. When gross breaches of trust, such as fraud and corruption, meet incompetence they create a particularly toxic brew. Shareholders, investors, employees, customers and suppliers may suffer major losses. Brands as well as individual, corporate and sometimes national reputations may lie in tatters. In extreme cases, members of the public have died, for example child victims of melamine contaminated milk products in China (see case 13.4 in Chapter 13), for which the convicted main supplier of the melamine formulations and another principal in the supply were executed in 2009 while others received long prison sentences, including the Sanlu Chairwoman who received a life sentence.

In order to overcome the apparent weaknesses of reliance on word of mouth and even written contracts to control corporate risk exposures emanating from breaches and abuse of trust, a 'due diligence' mechanism has evolved. The origin of the term due diligence is generally accepted as being section 11 of the Securities Act 1933 in the United States, which provided a potential defence for an individual accused of inadequate disclosure of material information to investors, if it could be shown that the individual had exercised due diligence in examining the probity of the company whose equity was being offered. Due diligence means that a party exercises and demonstrates an appropriate and adequate degree of searching examination of an individual or entity in seeking to establish their probity, truthfulness and *bona fides*, from which it may be reasonably deduced whether or not the party should go ahead with a proposed activity, dealing or transaction with that individual or entity.

## The Scope of Due Diligence

As due diligence originated in the world of investment and finance, it is perhaps not surprising that since then the application of due diligence has tended to be concentrated in finance and investment and dominated by legal, financial and accountancy thinking. This is particularly the case with due diligence examination prior to mergers, acquisitions and JVs, as discussed in more depth in Chapter 8. Some authors, such as Gilman (2010), do recognize the need for due diligence audits beyond those of a purely financial and legal nature, for example information systems and production, but even his list of nine different audit subjects omits a number of others that are growing in significance, such as corrupt relationships, money laundering, environmental and other major hazards, IP and immovable property/estate assets. Chapters 9–15 provide some graphic case examples of such risk exposures.

In the author's view, due diligence requires a much broader approach than much current practice, in order to protect shareholder, investor and other stakeholder value against all significant risk exposures and thus meet corporate governance requirements. In essence, as with corporate risk management overall (see earlier chapters), the scope of corporate due diligence should be unlimited and be responsive to all foreseeable risk exposures that are deemed significant. The following list should therefore be interpreted as just some of the subject areas that are likely to warrant a due diligence examination for a variety of purposes at different times:

- corporate finances;
- legal and contractual matters;
- business process;
- environmental contamination;
- other major hazards (including process major hazards, substance inventories, Major Accident Prevention Policy (MAPP) arrangements and so on);
- product safety;
- information systems and IT;
- HR and personnel;
- mergers, acquisitions and joint ventures (including integrity and financial probity of business partners and backers);
- capital projects;
- anti-money laundering provisions;
- political risks;
- IP and brands;
- immovable property;
- markets, marketing and commercial risks;
- R&D;
- production;
- external and foreign relationships (including corruption, human rights issues, money laundering);
- supply chains (including capacity, quality, redundancy, product safety, criminal enterprise).

The range and multiple overlapping nature of many of these categories implies that traditional due diligence that relies on audits covering financial, legal and perhaps also environmental contaminations will be inadequate in many cases to offer a level of protection that stakeholders are likely to expect. A more comprehensive and integrated approach is required. Further, individuals who typically carry out due diligence examinations in the financial and legal areas are unlikely to be sufficiently qualified to simply extend their scope to include the other areas. As many due diligence audits are commissioned by organizations from accountancy audit firms or law firms, to ensure a fully competent audit, such firms will need to sub-contract many of the topic areas to appropriate specialists. This will require a change of thinking within many audit firms as well as their clients. For further discussion, see Chapter 8.

## Background Checks

One area of due diligence that receives increasing attention is the background check on individual potential business partners, employees and suppliers. Despite the increasing use of background checks, in the author's experience large organizations vary widely in their attitudes and policies towards the requirement. Many employers do not carry out pre-employment checks at all and rely heavily on self-certification by the prospective employee plus perhaps references from previous employers. Sometimes employment agencies provide a so-called background check but, in the author's experience, these are usually perfunctory and may lull the employer into a false sense of security.

Background checks are essential for all prospective new employees, as experience shows that candidates are often economical with the truth about themselves in what they state in job application forms and at interviews. A survey by the Chartered Institute of Personnel and Development (CIPD) in the UK (CIPD 2008) found that in one year some 25 per cent of UK employers withdrew job offers after finding that candidates had lied or provided misleading information. A previous survey by CIPD showed that for similar reasons 23 per cent of employers questioned had dismissed someone already in post. These findings certainly square with the author's experience in recruiting job candidates over the past 35 years. Candidates for senior positions are among the worst offenders, perhaps because some of them have more experience than junior candidates at successful fibbing or perhaps because they believe that the rewards of getting the job are worth the risk of lying. False information typically includes such items as:

- inflated or invented formal qualifications;
- inflated salaries in current or previous posts;
- inflated descriptions of job title, or responsibilities or achievements relating to current or previous posts;
- falsifying employment dates for current or previous posts;
- glossing over or failing to reveal gaps in a CV;
- failing to mention a previous dismissal;
- failing to mention a significant absence from work, for example prison sentence, hospitalization, mental breakdown.

Typically, pre-employment and other similar due diligence background checks are carried out by independent vetting agencies that usually employ investigators with a professional background in the police, security or intelligence services. An identity check will be carried out with passport and immigration services to establish that the person is who they say they are. Claimed educational qualifications and memberships of professional bodies will be verified with the establishments and bodies concerned. Financial checks will be made with banks and credit reference agencies. Criminal records and court judgements will also be checked. A press and media search will be done to see if any articles by or about or with references to the candidate surface. Approaches will be made to former employers and colleagues for their evaluations and comments, and not only to those individuals put forward by the candidate as referees. In the author's experience, employer reference letters also cannot be relied upon implicitly as they tend to avoid negative statements, even though the latter may well be warranted and highly relevant.

All the above are fairly standard in Stage 1 of a typical background check and, should one or more 'red flags' be raised, the prospective employer can decide whether to stop the recruitment procedure or proceed to Stage 2. For example, evidence of a criminal conviction for dishonesty might be valid grounds for automatically not proceeding whereas discrepancies in previous employment dates could be raised at a subsequent interview.

## Case 7.2   Barings and Nick Leeson (BoBS 1995, Leeson 1996, Glendon and Waring 1997, Waring and Glendon 1998)

'Rogue trader' Mr Nick Leeson joined Barings Securities London (BSL) in 1989 as a settlements clerk. In 1992, when BSL applied to the Securities and Futures Authority for Leeson to be recognized as a registered representative, Leeson lied about not having any prior civil judgement against him for debt that had not been satisfied. There is no evidence that pre-employment or in-service due diligence checks were carried out that would probably have discovered this fact. Later, when he applied for SIMEX registration in Singapore, he lied again about not having an expunged civil judgement against him. While at Barings Securities Singapore (BSS), he forged a number of documents at different times to deflect scrutiny from superiors and external auditors that would have uncovered his unauthorized trades. Further, he was then promoted at BSS and given greater and greater latitude to 'run his own show' and all without any checks by his superiors or by any corporate integrity system as to whether he warranted such trust. As noted in case 3.5 in Chapter 3, referring to his C-level bosses, Leeson (1996) commented: 'The only good thing about hiding losses from these people was that it was so easy. They were always too busy and too self-important, and were always on the telephone. They had the attention span of a gnat. They could not make the time to work through a sheet of numbers and spot that it didn't add up.' Barings suffered the ultimate consequences of failed due diligence (in every respect of its risk management) when the whole bank collapsed on 26 February 1995 with cumulative losses of some £900 million.

It is important, however, that, where appropriate, a candidate should be given the opportunity to explain any apparent discrepancies rather than to assume a deliberate intent to deceive. Stage 1 is roughly equivalent to 'negative vetting' as applied by national security agencies for lower security classifications of personnel.

Stage 2 is a deeper check seeking, where warranted, to pursue red flags and to identify any significant facts or character flaws that had not surfaced previously. Stage 2 may also involve a personal face-to-face interview of the candidate by the independent investigator. Indeed, for many years the author's policy for Stage 2 has been to require such an interview in the candidate's own home. The reasoning is that experience has shown that whereas a person may be good at impression management in a variety of settings, including recruitment interviews, it is much more difficult to cover up the myriad of clues about the person's real character that their own home environment would reveal. Moreover, if the person is married or living with a partner then the home interview should also include them. The author is not suggesting that such interviews should ever be aggressive or intimidating or involve insulting questions and, on the contrary, a good investigator will be the epitome of good manners and make the questions all sound quite innocent and routine.

A Stage 2 is roughly equivalent to aspects of 'positive vetting' as applied by national security agencies for higher security classifications of personnel. Observation at the candidate's home may reveal clues about their character and habits, such as large quantities of empty alcoholic drink bottles, very expensive cars or even expensive yachts parked in the drive and perhaps irreconcilable with the candidate's known earnings, traces of illicit drugs carelessly left in a bathroom, and so on. Attitudes expressed by a candidate during the interview, for example rudeness towards their partner, racist comments or strongly held beliefs about politics, immigration, alcohol, or any number of potentially controversial topics may indicate a person whose intolerance of others or strong support for anti-social behaviour could pose a problem if they were to be employed. Local neighbours, shopkeepers, clubs and pubs will also be approached about the candidate's payment of bills, lifestyle, habits and proclivities. Mortgages, loans, debts and gambling habits will all be examined.

In addition to Stage 1 and Stage 2 checks, two other variants are the overt and covert background checks. With overt checks, the individual is advised in advance that the check will be carried out and usually a signed authorization is sought from the individual. This is common practice in recruitment and would be necessary, for example, if a home interview were to be included. Clearly, if the individual refuses to authorize the check, then a job offer may be forfeited. With covert checks, the target party is not informed in advance and may never be informed. Covert checks are usually restricted to major issues such as potential business deals with new and relatively unknown partners or where there is suspicion of impropriety or major wrongdoing.

Some people may regard such detailed investigation as unnecessarily intrusive, an invasion of privacy and possibly unethical. However, such concerns are of a similar nature to those raised about closed-circuit television coverage of streets, public places, buildings and so on, for security purposes. The author's view is that if the individual has nothing to hide, then he or she has nothing to fear.

In short, the question to be answered is 'Will this person be a liability to our organization?'

## Periodic In-Service Checks

Unfortunately, if only some organizations carry out pre-employment checks far fewer carry out any kind of in-service background check. An assumption appears to be made that a person who has passed a screening during recruitment will remain a person of integrity during their entire period of employment, which may last years and sometimes decades. While the basic character of most individuals is unlikely to change significantly, over a period of time some individuals may be subject to a variety of life events, stresses and temptations that are sufficient to compromise their integrity. For example, they may succumb to alcoholism, drug taking, gambling or other vices that render them vulnerable to unmanageable debt, personal risk-taking and possibly blackmail, coercion and extortion by third parties. They become a threat to their employer either because their work-related judgement, performance and general behaviour become faulty and unacceptable or because they decide or are persuaded to engage in fraud, theft, industrial espionage or some other abuse of trust.

### Case 7.3   Société Générale and Jerome Kerviel

At the end of 2007, how was Mr Jerome Kerviel, the young trader at Société Générale ('SocGen'), able to rack up €4.82 billion in unauthorized transactions that were bad? After all, some 12 years after the Barings collapse the finance sector had supposedly learned the lessons from Barings and other cases and risk management systems were claimed by the sector generally and SocGen specifically to be very robust. The reported signs and symptoms of his reckless gambles and his stressed-out behaviour patterns were eerily reminiscent of Nick Leeson. While not benefiting financially from their respective frauds, they both craved recognition and approval from colleagues and bosses. Both got hopelessly out of their depth and trapped with no way out yet were also driven by the intoxication of the process and the next 'one last trade' that might just cover their tracks. Both have admitted as much (see for example Leeson 1996). Yet, checks by Kerviel's superiors or by any corporate integrity/risk management system that might have spotted these aberrations and raised the alarm did not occur. Mr Kerviel was convicted and sentenced in June 2010 to three years' imprisonment and ordered to pay Société Générale €4.9 billion in damages.

## Case 7.4   Asia Pacific Breweries (Menon 2004)

On 20 January 1999, Mr Chia Teck Leng joined Asia Pacific Breweries (APB) as Finance Manager. Apparently, he had been a habitual gambler since at least 1994 in his previous capacity as a financial controller with Swire Pacific Offshore. Before joining ABP, he had already experienced wild swings of gambling fortune, from debts in 1996 of S$100,000 to winnings of S$1 million in 1997–1998. However, in August 1998 he suffered spectacular losses that wiped out all his accumulated winnings and put him back heavily in debt. Five days after joining ABP, he used his position to open an account with a S$500,000 credit facility using forged documents with Skandinavska Enskilda Banken in Singapore, in ABP's name but with himself as sole signatory. Between January 1999 and March 2003, he opened up other accounts with four other foreign banks. His fraud involved his forging board resolutions authorizing him to receive the banks' credit and loan facilities, to sign all transactions and to operate the accounts on ABP's behalf. The forgeries included the signatures of ABP directors, whose source he had found in internal documents and company annual reports. He juggled the fraudulently obtained monies between the accounts to maintain a semblance of being credit-worthy, while drawing off ever larger amounts to cover his burgeoning gambling stakes and losses. Typical single bets ranged from S$25,000 to S$78,000 (approximately €14,250 to €44,460) in casinos around the world. In Australia, he played for A$400,000 (approximately €300,000) a hand in one casino. He lived the lifestyle of an international playboy, flying in private jets, buying expensive status symbols, acquiring a young girlfriend half his age and showering money and gifts on friends.

Apparently, ABP were unaware of his fraudulent activities throughout. There is no evidence of any pre-employment or in-service background check. Following an investigation by the Singapore Commercial Affairs Department, he was arrested in September 2003. Before his arrest, he had racked up S$159 million (€90.6 million) in credit and loan facilities from the banks and had withdrawn S$117 million m (€66.7 million), of which only S$34.8 million (€19.8 million) was recovered. Convicted in 2004, aged 44, he was sentenced to 42 years in jail.

A significant promotion or transfer during an individual's career should also prompt a background check. For example, although Nick Leeson had been appointed in July 1989 by BSL without a proper background check, he was also subsequently promoted and sent out to Barings in Singapore despite his having no real trading experience (see Waring and Glendon 1998). A suitable in-service check then might have belatedly uncovered the fact of his prior dishonesty about his non-expunged civil judgement for debt. An in-service check during his work at BSS might have uncovered his increasingly stressed out and bizarre behaviour, such as binge drinking and binge eating of junk food, which were clues to his troubled existence and self-entrapment in a gigantic fraud. As he later admitted (Leeson 1996, page 145): 'I was drowning like an insect stuck in resin, clawing hopelessly but unable to pull myself out. I knew that the auditors were inching closer and closer ...' He also noted (Leeson 1996, page 148): 'My 88888 account was hanging round my neck like a string of rotten fish-heads...'

## Case 7.5   Business Media China (Anderlini 2009)

Mr Klaus Hilligardt, the creator of Business Media China (BMC), discovered too late and to his cost that highly trusted senior Chinese employees had been systematically defrauding the company. Mr Hilligardt placed a lot of trust and confidence in two individuals, one his personal secretary Miss Teresa Tu and the other a young senior executive Mr Li Yangyang whom he had appointed in Beijing. Before long, his secretary and the executive became romantically involved and got married.

BMC did well. By early 2008 and the approach of the Beijing Olympics, share values were over €20. Immediately after the Olympics, however, advertisement revenues fell sharply and far more than might have been expected. The revenue downturn continued throughout 2008 and income had virtually ceased by year end. By mid-2009 the share value was about €0.40.

The BMC main board in Germany lost confidence in the China operations and Mr Hilligardt and the senior executive Mr Yangyang were removed from the board. A new Swiss CEO was appointed who discovered that, despite the books showing no orders, in fact the BMC advertisement boards at prime sites were full of advertisements from BMC's clients. A separate company called BMC Heli using the same logo as BMC had been set up by the trusted senior executive Mr Yangyang and a number of current and former employees, including the trusted personal secretary Mrs Teresa Tu Yangyang. They were diverting all the advertisement business to the parallel company. BMC Heli was also invoicing BMC for all its operating costs. Arrests on charges of embezzlement were made.

The case is a salutary tale of allowing trust to take precedence over prudence. Trust is always an important ingredient in any business relationship but it cannot be extended to blind trust.

Evidence of trustworthiness is not simply furnished by lack of evidence of theft or fraud. Trust, and therefore trustworthiness, is based on a range of perseverant characteristics exhibited by an individual, including but not limited to the following:

*   integrity;
*   reliability;
*   honesty;
*   accepting responsibility for one's actions;
*   not succumbing to illicit temptations at the workplace such as theft, embezzlement or sexual opportunism, for example sexual harassment of subordinates or colleagues;
*   maintaining confidences and respecting confidential information;
*   protecting the interests of the employer.

Although an individual who meets such criteria may be accorded trustworthiness with greater confidence than one who does not, it does not mean that the individual is necessarily a paragon of rectitude or that they will never become untrustworthy. Also, some employers have been known to deliberately place temptation in the way of an individual to see how they will react. In the author's opinion, whatever the person's behavioural response to such a covert test, nothing can be inferred safely about their trustworthiness. Failure to be tempted in such a test does not, of itself, confirm trustworthiness any more than succumbing to the artificial temptation confirms untrustworthiness. In short, there is really no sure way to classify someone as trustworthy.

How to develop trust and trustworthy individuals is beyond the scope of this book. Approaches and techniques that are likely to be beneficial have much in common with, and in many ways are integral to, forging a culture of responsible risk-taking as set out in Chapter 4. For more detailed discussion, see Pearce (2000).

## Pre-Investment Due Diligence

What about when investors do consult independent advisers about the probity and trustworthiness of an investment opportunity? A number of companies who provided risk advice to investors in SIBL have been sued by some of the investors. SIBL's controlling owner Sir Allen Stanford was under arrest in the US from June 2009 accused of operating a US$7 billion 'Ponzi' fraud scheme with investors' money over a 20-year period until his conviction on 13 counts out of 14 in March 2012 (US Department of Justice 2012). On 14 June 2012, he was sentenced to a 110-year jail term. As the following two cases summarize, these investors claimed that they only entrusted SIBL with their investments after seeking the advice of trusted brokers and being assured that all was OK:

### Case 7.6  Kroll Inc and Stanford International

An SIBL investor alleged in 2009 that Kroll Inc, a leading corporate security consultancy and part of the Marsh & McLennan insurance broker group, carried out a due diligence check on the bank's soundness and presented a favourable risk report which the investor relied upon. It was also alleged that a senior SIBL employee was a former Kroll executive, which created a conflict of interest. Whatever the truth of the matter, one clue that something was not right was the reported statement by Kroll that they had only ever been commissioned to carry out limited due diligence checks for a US$15,000 fee. If accurate, the report would indicate that the client was being very unrealistic in expecting a comprehensive due diligence risk evaluation for a paltry US$15,000! When $millions are being invested or are at stake, the scale and tailoring of any independent due diligence work (and therefore the cost) has to be in proportion to the financial – and reputation – risk. Corner-cutting is asking for trouble. The case was settled out of court.

### Case 7.7   Willis and Stanford International

In July 2009, a group of 97 SIBL investors filed suit in the Federal Court in Dallas against another global insurance broker, Willis Group Holdings, alleging that they had suffered large losses after relying on assurances from Willis that SIBL was safe and secure. This was followed quickly by another Federal law suit in Miami by a Venezuelan investor, who alleged that Willis were 'instrumental' in enabling SIBL and related companies to carry out a $multi-billion fraud against investors. He alleged that Willis provided Stanford agents with letters falsely certifying that SIBL's staff were first-class business people and that SIBL had undergone a stringent Risk Management Review by an independent audit firm. In November 2010, a further group of seven investors laid a lawsuit against Willis based on substantially the same allegations as in the previous lawsuits.

These two cases (7.6 and 7.7) highlight the need for clients to ask probing questions of potential consultants or agents offering to carry out a due diligence examination of an investment target. They need to satisfy themselves that the examination will be sufficiently thorough, for example obtain a detailed schedule of the checks to be made, that no conflicts of interest arise and that a written report will be delivered containing both a clear analysis referencing the detailed schedule and a clear conclusion. Clients should apply common sense and expect to pay realistic fees in proportion to the investment risk.

## Partnership Due Diligence

The same basic principles of background checks apply to forming partnerships as they do to recruiting employees, in-service and pre-investment checks. Large-scale partnerships such as JVs are discussed further in Chapter 8.

### Case 7.8   The Oil Refinery Investment Swindle

A privately-owned company with plans to build two oil refineries in an Asian country formed a partnership with a small American company, whose primary role was to help raise the initial US$8 billion finance for the first project. Unbeknown to the Asian principals, who had failed to carry out a due diligence check, the CEO and main shareholder of the American company was the subject of an official investigation in the US for fraud. He was accused by the US SEC of raising US$14.5 million from over 900 investors through the fraudulent and unregistered sale of securities, which were based on a false claim that he owned valuable licences for constructing the refinery. He promised investors returns of as much as 1,000 per cent and assured them that funding to start construction was imminent. According to the official court papers, he cited to investors the following sources of funding: 'a financial windfall from letters-of-credit or other bank instruments provided by a wealthy contact; a vault filled with gold bullion and guarded by tribal elders; and the largesse of the Saudi royal family.' In fact, his claims were completely baseless. Predictably, the promised financing never materialized. Moreover, he 'used $millions of investors' funds to pay his personal expenses and support his lavish international lifestyle'. The SEC obtained an interlocutory judgement against him, whereby he agreed to the case and judgement against him being made public and had to compensate victims and to cease any further fraud. In return, he was not prosecuted and not convicted in a court of law.

In the course of his work as a consultant to the principals, the author met the American partner who came across as a rather slick talker and a tad flamboyant. On one occasion, the partner turned up late to a business meeting chaired by the principals' CEO and blamed his lateness on a last minute telephone call from a major Middle Eastern oil company whom he claimed were interested in investing in the project. The author was immediately suspicious about his claim that the oil company had telephoned him as it was inconsistent with their way of doing such business. During the meeting, skating over any potential conflicts of interest, he asked if anyone present who was not already an investor, including the author, was interested in investing now was their golden opportunity. After an hour or so, he excused himself from the meeting so that he could get to the airport as he was, he claimed, going to Geneva to meet a director of one of the world's largest computer companies who had expressed an interest in investing US$500 million in the project. In the author's opinion at the time, this was yet more flim-flam. None of these potential investments ever materialized.

## Case 7.9   The Official Representative

The author was approached by a highly plausible Australian gentleman who stated in writing and in numerous discussions that, as part of his business consultancy work, he was the official Eastern Mediterranean representative of a large and well-known European company. His large suite of offices was also adorned with framed photos of himself in the presence of world leaders and state presidents. He name-dropped shamelessly and spoke authoritatively about the latest developments in a wide range of 'blue chip' companies. Eventually, a potential partnership with the author was discussed.

As a matter of routine, the author arranged for a due diligence background check on him to verify that he was who he said he was and that his CV, his claimed business experience and his credentials were all accurate and complete. Also, were there any instances in his background or behaviour that reflected badly on his integrity and honesty? It transpired that much of his legend, including being the official regional representative of the well-known European company, was bogus. His array of photos in the presence of presidents and other dignitaries became explicable once the author spotted his propensity for attending charitable and other public events where such persons were guests of honour and went round shaking just about everyone's hand and providing photo opportunities. Certainly, the appointed due diligence agency had been unable to find any trace in national intelligence files of his name or any known meeting with these presidents. They also noted that among the 'red flags' there were significant gaps in his CV and he was completely untraceable for long periods of time, commenting that there were usually three possible reasons for this:

- he was in a witness protection programme;
- he was a member of the security or intelligence services;
- he had made strenuous efforts not to be traceable.

Attempts by the author to get him to explain these discrepancies and gaps proved fruitless as he became defensive and, unsurprisingly, their relationship ceased.

## A Note of Caution

The background check market has become highly competitive in recent years. A Stage 1 pre-employment check on a single individual that typically might have cost US$5,000 in the period 2004–2006 was commanding only US$3,000–4,000 by 2009. Moreover, a number of vetting agencies began offering to do them for as little as US$2,000 or even much less than this. They are able to do such low-cost checks because they rely almost exclusively on online computer database searches, frequently carried out not by experienced investigators but by junior office staff. This commoditized approach may be attractive on cost grounds to a naïve client but clearly it is likely to be a false economy if corners are being cut.

There is ample anecdotal evidence that a cost-driven commoditized service approach has also been imposed by some of the larger accounting audit firms on the vetting agencies to whom they sub-contract background checks. Senior personnel from such agencies have reported to the author that they have been forced to accept fees slashed to US$2,000 or less per check by accounting firms acting on behalf of major banks who wish to take on a significant number of new employees. As a director of one such agency complained, it should be self-evident that at rock bottom fees the check cannot be expected to be thorough as the time needed for a thorough check is not being paid for. It is unlikely that the client organization is even remotely aware of this issue. In view of the deception perpetrated by the audit firm on the client, one might reasonably argue that the deception is in itself a breach of trust. The breach is compounded, given the fact that each background check is supposed to help prevent an undesirable person from gaining employment with the client.

Clients need to ensure that background checks have sufficient breadth and depth. A full service description should be obtained in advance and probing questions should be directed at the provider. If the fee structure looks too good to be true then it probably is. Clients need to recognize that they have a responsibility to appoint competent vetting agencies and have realistic expectations of what they should expect for the fees charged.

However, it should be noted that whereas a skimped due diligence background check is more likely to fail to spot undesirable characters, even the most rigorous check cannot guarantee that a rogue will not slip through the net. Some individuals are so skilled at deception that they can hide character defects even from background checks and multiple interviews by experienced investigators and recruiters. The author has recruited senior individuals having glowing references from large high-reputation previous employers and who passed both Stage 1 and Stage 2 background checks, only to discover too late that they were either devious and dishonest or 'employees from hell'. This is not a justification for dispensing with background checks but a recognition that such checks cannot guarantee to identify every rogue. Finally, due diligence background checks are only one part of an integrated risk management system and cannot substitute for the rest of that system.

# 8 *Mergers, Acquisitions and Joint Ventures*

Any M&A, or JV, or venture capital investment represents a major opportunity for the two primary parties to make significant long-term gains. At the same time, there are huge potential risks involved. One might imagine therefore that both parties, and especially any party putting in a large amount of money and other commitments, would automatically undertake a rigorous pre-contract due diligence exercise. Surprisingly, this is often not the case. To be sure, some due diligence is likely to be done and any financiers involved will normally insist upon it. Nevertheless, the extent and quality of such due diligence often has a lot to be desired.

## Case 8.1 'Fawlty Towers' Risk-Taking

A global hotel chain routinely entered into JVs with local partners who fund and run one or more hotels but under the hotel group's name, brand, livery, standards and so on. Sometimes the local partners would also contribute to or run hotel refurbishment and upgrade projects. In a number of cases, local partners failed to complete such projects on time or to budget or to quality – or at all. In others, local partners failed to run the business competently and profitably. The hotel chain has suffered significant losses, both financially and to reputation. It emerged that the hotel group had no discernible due diligence evaluation system before entering into such JVs, other than routine financial and legal checks.

The very strength of having external legal and financial advisers can also become the very weakness of traditional pre-contract due diligence exercises. Not surprisingly, law firms tend to focus on what they know about, that is legal and contractual risk exposures, whereas accountants and bankers tend to address such topics as balance sheets, liquidity and credit risk exposures. Whereas such matters are clearly important and a necessary part of any due diligence scope, the fact remains that there are a number of other critical areas of risk exposure in such transactions which are often overlooked or ignored. For example:

- contaminated land;
- major hazards;
- criminal elements;
- inflated or worn out assets and exaggerated capabilities;
- supply and value chain risks;
- mismatched cultures;
- mismatched systems and processes.

The scope for the due diligence exercise will be determined largely by whoever is in overall charge of it. Sometimes, they will require, for example, an environmental due diligence audit where industrial assets are involved and this is usually commissioned from specialists on a sub-contract basis. However, beyond that, it is abnormal for any of the other 'extras' to be addressed. The net result of such limited scope is that 'elephant in the room' risks such as mismatched cultures are allowed to lie dormant until after the contracts are signed and executive implementation is underway, when their damaging effect becomes all too real and apparent.

Why are pre-contract due diligence assessments for M&As, JVs and venture capital injections so deficient? In the author's opinion, based on his professional experience of such matters, the answer comes down to two primary reasons: (a) due diligence fees are usually considerable if lawyers or accountants are controlling the overall task, and (b) many lawyers and accounting auditors wrongly imagine themselves to be all-knowing and often regard other risks as relatively trivial compared to legal and finance risks. These two reasons are then combined with a self-sealing justification put forward by various parties, including lazy or ignorant client directors and their due diligence contractors, for why it is practically impossible to do more than the traditional limited scope. That justification asserts that once the two parties are interested in the possibility of a transaction they will, necessarily, wish to proceed with all haste and there just is not enough time for a thorough due diligence with a broad scope. Such an assertion is manifest nonsense. There are usually many months and sometimes more than a year of pre-contract discussions and negotiations, which give more than enough time for a proper due diligence evaluation. If only a limited due diligence is carried out, the parties involved can blame only themselves if post-contract the venture performs badly or even disastrously.

## Contaminated Land

Contaminated land has a number of characteristics which make it a costly risk that everyone wishes to avoid. Contamination may be unnoticeable to the naked eye and may have been occurring over a long period of years or even decades. Industrial chemicals and substances that are toxic may have contaminated the ground surface of a site and also soaked into the ground below the surface. Toxic substances used in processes may have been washed to effluent instead of being properly contained for specialist waste disposal off-site. Containers of substances may be poorly maintained or leaky and unused materials may simply have been abandoned. Once a site is contaminated significantly, it can be very costly to clean it up in addition to potential litigation from affected parties.

### Case 8.2   Purchase of Airline Ground Facilities

The author once undertook an environmental due diligence audit on the UK ground assets of a US-based airline which was scheduled for purchase by another US-based airline. The latter's legal counsel commissioned the acquisition audit so as to provide evidence that the ground assets did not contain any residual environmental liabilities such as contaminated land or proximity to environmental contamination from neighbouring or nearby property situated in or around London Heathrow and London Gatwick airports. The list of potential contamination sources that were examined included underground fuel storage tanks and fuelling areas, vehicle repair workshops, aircraft hangars and maintenance facilities, drains and sumps, waste handling and waste disposal.

# Major Hazards

In some instances, environmental hazards and contaminated land may be on such a scale as to represent a major hazard. A major hazard is one which presents in a single incident a risk of death or injury to a large number of people and/or major damage to the environment and/or major damage to property. Major hazards include significant quantities of such things as highly flammable, explosive or toxic substances in a single location. The vast majority of major hazards relevant to M&As and JVs will be man-made and therefore amenable to prevention and control (see Chapter 14) and a due diligence audit should take a close look at the quality of the major hazards risk management of the target organization and the target site(s). In developed countries, there are also usually major hazards regulations requiring minimum standards to be met and risk assessment reports to be maintained.

## Case 8.3   A Small Petrochemical Company

A small petrochemical company in the UK operated two production sites, both in remote rural locations near the sea. The processes did not involve any chemical reactors and were relatively simple admixing operations. Nevertheless, the total inventory of hazardous materials on each site (in their case, highly flammable liquids) amounted to some 80,000 tonnes and thus constituted a major hazard as defined by the Control of Major Accident Hazards Regulations (COMAH). These regulations (see Chapter 14) required the site operator to undertake a technical risk assessment, take any remedial action necessitated by the risk assessment, establish an effective SMS and a MAPP, prepare and revise as necessary a COMAH report and prepare an environmental impact assessment. All of these elements were reviewed on a regular basis by the company's management. This good management proved invaluable when after a few years the company was up for sale and potential buyers were seeking due diligence evidence that major hazard risks were well controlled.

## Case 8.4   Capital Investment in the Former Soviet Union

A major investment bank based in the West provided capital injection for industrial companies across the Former Soviet Union (FSU) and Warsaw Pact countries. A single investment could range from £20 million to over £200 million. Typically, during perestroika the task had been to enable such industrial companies to replace antiquated and inefficient equipment and systems with modern, high-performance technology. Bankers from headquarters, in conjunction with their local resident staff, would evaluate each application on its merits and usually this included a site visit by the case banker. In the early years, the due diligence element of the evaluation was limited to legal and financial matters. On advice from the author, the due diligence scope was extended to include specific examination of major hazard exposures, since a single incident could jeopardize the bank's entire investment in that company.

## Criminal Elements

Chapter 7 has already introduced a number of cases of underhand and even unlawful activity by untrustworthy individuals in a range of circumstances, including capital investments. Case 7.1, for example, highlighted the case of the capital investment company that was defrauded of US$millions by applicants who disappeared with the money, simply because the investment company had no proper due diligence system to identify potential crooks.

In addition to fraud as exemplified in the previous paragraph, investment companies approached for funds can also become victims of attempts to extort the funds and, in some cases, investment executives have been threatened and even jailed abroad as a result of failed applicants filing fictitious complaints to the local police.

### Case 8.5 Your Money or Your Life (Dickerson 2011, O'Hare 2011)

Joseph Dickerson was a UK-based investment consultant/broker who sought appropriate venture capital funds for selected applicants. In 1994, he and a colleague flew to Cyprus to meet two Cypriot brothers who had applied for £3 million to buy a hotel plus a further £2 million for its renovation. Before any application could be submitted to venture capitalists, the consultants carried out a due diligence check on the probity of the applicants and their application. This revealed that the purchase price which they had quoted for the hotel had been inflated by £2 million from the actual asking price.

When the consultants sought an explanation from the applicants, the latter became very defensive and apparently threatened that unless the money was forthcoming the consultants would not leave the island alive. The consultants took the threats seriously and decided to fly out that night. However, before they could do so, they were visited at their hotel by plain clothes police officers, handcuffed and transported to Limassol police station without any explanation. Eventually, they were informed that they had been arrested for fraud, apparently because the well-connected applicants had falsely accused them of accepting payment for flights and accommodation while having no intention of brokering the provision of venture capital. According to Mr Dickerson, the consultants spent several weeks in jail before the efforts of his MP and the British High Commissioner succeeded in securing their release without charge.

## Poor Assets and Exaggerated Capabilities

For an MNC to increase its production capacity, in some regions it may seek to purchase existing production facilities from local companies or alternatively enter into partnerships. Such an investment can result in significant cost savings on production and distribution. However, how does the multi-national know that the asset which it is buying or accessing is not a pig-in-a-poke?

## Case 8.6   Buying a Pharmaceutical Production Unit in China

AX Pharmaceuticals Inc. (not its real name) based in Germany was seeking to expand its bio-production capacity in China and learned that the Tsui Wah Pharma Co. (not its real name) was potentially interested in selling its factory. On paper, the Tsui Wah assets and prospectus looked well suited to the AX requirements. They claimed to have maintained a consistent output of high-quality bio-pharmaceutical products for several years and quoted their output tonnage and sales figures to back this up. Their biochemists and other technically qualified staff were identified.

AX decided that the scope of the due diligence examination of the Tsui Wah company and production facility would have to include not only legal and financial matters but also (a) the background and probity of its owners, directors and managers, (b) the age, quality and output capacity of its production plant, (c) environmental and safety risks, and (d) the quality of the personnel, their adherence to good manufacturing practice (GMP) standards and likely harmony with AX values and culture. The probity check (a) was deemed necessary as it is not unknown in China for production companies to operate parallel production lines, some overt and with output and sales on the books whereas the others are covert with output and sales off the books. In some cases, the local management of foreign-owned factories have been caught selling the illicit products in competition with the valid products and pocketing the illicit proceeds.

Check (b) was necessary to ensure that the production plant was reasonably up to date and efficient, so as to be competitive with other manufacturers and also to avoid the possibility of a costly plant replacement within a short period after purchase. At the same time, the claimed production capacity could be checked. AX took a two-pronged approach to the due diligence, whereby various external third parties were commissioned for the legal, financial and safety and environment checks, while checks (b) and (d) were undertaken by a highly experienced former production director of AX who was able to evaluate these matters expertly and efficiently.

# Supply Chain Risks

Suppose that in case 8.6 Tsui Wah had come through with flying colours on the AX due diligence evaluation. Were the due diligence checks as outlined sufficient to ensure minimized risk for AX? The short answer is No. For example, how would AX know that a unit somewhere in the supply chain was not using unsafe materials or ingredients, or supplying counterfeits as originals, or being run or controlled by criminal gangs? This potential threat is not as far-fetched as it may seem. For example, Chapter 13 includes cases where contractors in the supply chain in China were supplying counterfeit drugs or contaminated blood products or contaminated food products, which severely damaged the reputations of the Western-based multi-national corporations they were supplying through these corporations' China operations.

## Mismatched Cultures

The vital importance of corporate culture in successful risk management was highlighted in Chapter 4. Developing a culture of responsible risk-taking in one's own organization is difficult enough but what if significant numbers of people in the target of an M&A have quite different views on the business, its future and how it should be run compared to those of the purchaser? Any such disparities need to be identified well before deciding on whether or not to go ahead with the merger or acquisition, otherwise it could (and regrettably often does) end up as a marriage made in hell. Harding and Rouse (2007) assert that cultural evaluation in the vast majority of pre-M&A due diligence exercises 'is at best cursory and at worst non-existent'. Only a proper due diligence examination will tease out significant culture clash issues; reassuring noises or 'it will be alright on the night' assumptions expressed by either board just will not do as many of the individuals at that level simply will not be aware of potential issues and culture clashes.

### Case 8.7   Production Engineering Culture versus Consultancy Culture

The author once worked for a consulting firm specialising in major hazards and environmental risks, including assessment, evaluation and mitigation of such risks and acting as expert witnesses in legal proceedings, public inquiries and so on. The firm had built up an awesome reputation for its expertise and frequently acted as consultants to the government in major accident inquiries. After several decades, the founding partners sold out to a much larger environmental consulting firm but this acquisition lasted barely two years and it was sold on again, this time to a well-known publicly listed engineering company with a global reach.

Although the consulting firm was allowed to retain its existing management, within days of the completed takeover, the new owners sent in their own executives to check on management policies, systems and procedures as well as to inform the staff in a series of pep talks on what was expected of them and what the 'new culture' was going to be. The latter amounted to adopting the engineering company's approach to just about everything. Everything was now orientated towards how an engineering firm operated, including the language of production lines, production schedules, cost efficiency and so on. Cynics among the consultants joked about the new owners trying to convert them into 'widget bashers'. The overbearing attitude of the new owners even went so far as to declare that a strict 'clear desk' policy for the end of each day would now be enforced. The author himself was actually ticked off on this topic by a rather unpleasant director of the new owners who decided that he would pay an unannounced 'enforcement' visit.

What the new owners had failed to realize, much less accept, was that in general a consulting firm is usually very different in its ethos and methods compared to an engineering company that manufactures tangible products. For a start, consultancies tend to employ a very high concentration of highly qualified personnel who often work together in loose teams on a collegiate basis, project by project. They neither need nor will accept being regimented into a production line environment having a 'clear desk' policy, which would be totally unsuited to their work requirements, such as desktop arrays of multiple 'work-in-progress' client files and documents that would be badly disrupted if they had to be closed up at the end of each day and then resurrected the next day. A clear desk policy not only interferes with the consultant's workflow and efficiency but paradoxically such 'tidiness' also creates a preposterous illusion of efficiency. Also, although clear desks can certainly help with information security up to a point, they are hardly likely on their own to stop any determined attempt to steal confidential information.

Further, fully professional consultancies tend to charge their fees on a mixture of (a) time spent on the client's particular job and (b) a fee rate that reflects the complexity of issues addressed, the seniority and experience of the consultants applied and the perceived value to the client. This is quite different to the cost and pricing model that an engineering company would use to sell its 'widgets'.

The new owners had expected, somewhat naïvely, to turn the consulting firm rapidly into a highly efficient production cash-cow and then sweat it for profits. Too late, they realized that the culture and realities of the consulting firm would never be in harmony with such a crude conversion and that, as a result, the consultants had become increasingly antagonistic towards the new owners and many were quitting the company. Within two years, it had been sold on to a consulting group, where it fitted in much better.

## Case 8.8   Acquisition of First Chicago by Bank One (Khurana 2007, Harding and Rouse 2007)

The merger–acquisition of the First Chicago Bank by the Bank One Corporation of Chicago in 1999 demonstrates how much damage a culture clash can cause. The merger created the USA's eighth largest bank yet it was, by all accounts, a disaster, with almost continuous in-fighting among executives from the two merged banks and deterioration of financial performance for several years from an already poor performance at the time of the M&A. By 2002, not a single senior executive of the top 16 appointed to run the merged organization remained in post. This case reflects case 8.7, where highly qualified and experienced personnel simply would not tolerate being 'kicked around' by a new owner. It is vital that, as a company's greatest asset, key skill groups and individuals and their values and expectations are identified as part of the pre-M&A due diligence and then adequate steps taken to ensure their retention post-M&A.

## Case 8.9   Mergers and Aquisitions Culture Clash

The US$multi-million merger–takeover of a manufacturer by another larger company in the same line of business in the same region nearly ended in disaster. The management of the acquiring company had views, traditions and expectations rooted in the strong religious values of its founders, whereas the target's management were of a different religion. This religious difference *per se* should not have caused a clash but unfortunately the senior management of the acquiring company adopted an arrogant and disrespectful attitude towards their new colleagues, who took the attitude to be based on an assumed religious superiority. This resulted in the latter becoming increasingly disdainful of and uncooperative towards the management from the acquiring company. Company efficiency and marketplace reputation started to fall and the group board of the acquiring company began to receive concerns expressed by both aggrieved executives and worried customers. In the nick of time, a troubleshooting director was sent in to take charge of the crisis. He quickly replaced the offending directors and managers with individuals of the right quality to ensure that a harmonious culture prevailed and company performance soon started to improve.

## Mismatched Systems

It would be very convenient if all IT systems and software packages were fully compatible and similarly factory production lines and tooling. In reality, they rarely are and when a merger or acquisition occurs there is likely to be a requirement for work to be done to rationalize or harmonize the technical systems of the two parties. This is particularly relevant to a merger. How big the incompatibilities are and how critical the systems are to the functioning and output of the post-merger organization will determine how much time, work, effort and capital investment may be needed to ensure a relatively trouble-free transition. A due diligence evaluation should therefore identify each party's systems, any significant incompatibilities between them, the practical options for rationalizing or harmonizing the systems and the cost–risk–benefit implications of each option.

# PART 3

# *Fraud, Corruption and Organized Crime*

# 9 *The Nature and Scope of Corruption*

Many people think of fraud and corruption as being essentially one-and-the-same. This is perhaps unsurprising since fraud and corruption are frequently found co-habiting and many of the cases featured in this book involve both. However, despite their links, fraud and corruption are logically distinct. Neither necessarily causes, includes, or is dependent on the other. For this reason, they warrant separate chapters. Corporate fraud is dealt with in Chapter 10 and immovable property fraud is covered in Chapter 11.

## What is Corruption?

Corruption scandals feature almost every day in newspaper and other media reports. With such frequent media coverage, it is easy for the public to suffer from 'attention fatigue' and relegate the latest corruption exposé to the 'just another bit of bad behaviour' category. After all, although someone may have gained unlawful advantage via corruption, the perpetrators are often remote from the everyday experience of the public and indeed most businesses. Corruption thus often appears to be a 'victimless' crime. Nothing could be further from the truth.

The UN Convention Against Corruption (UNCAC 2004) has become the primary reference on anti-corruption policy and how countries should view the problem of corruption and its eradication. The working definition of corruption adopted by the UN is 'an abuse of (public) power for private gain that hampers the public interest'. This gain may be direct or indirect. Mostly, corruption entails a confusion of the private with the public sphere, or an illicit exchange between the two spheres. In essence, in this view of corruption, corrupt practices involve public officials acting in the best interest of private concerns (their own or those of others) regardless of, or against, the public interest. The EU Civil Law Convention on Corruption describes corruption as:

> Requesting, offering, giving or accepting, directly or indirectly, a bribe or any other undue advantage (to any public official), or prospect thereof, which distorts the proper performance of any duty or behaviour required of the recipient of the bribe.

However, in a number of countries the scope of definition is extended to include *any* abuse of relationships in the private sector that threatens the public interest. For example, in Hong Kong, the ICAC, under Section 9 of the Prevention of Bribery Ordinance, will also investigate corrupt practices between private companies and/or private individuals.

Fundamentally, corruption is an abuse of power whereby those who in some way control access to, or the decision to grant, such valued items as contracts, resources, jobs, goods, finance, licences, permissions, penalty waivers or official documentation deny, block or delay such access or decision unless the applicant is a friend or relative or is prepared to offer a bribe. The particular vulnerability of procurement processes to corruption is well recognized and the UN has published further guidance on this problem (UNCAC 2008).

For those in the UK under the age of 40, it may appear from increasing media attention that corruption has only become a major problem in recent years and that it is very much a 'foreign' problem. While it may be true that corruption is now less of a problem in the UK Government and the public sector (if only because of strict monitoring and audit regimes and the almost certainty of being caught), case 9.1 shows that it was very much alive and kicking in the UK in the 1960s and early 1970s. The Poulson scandal is a classic tale of corruption of public officials.

## Case 9.1   The Poulson Corruption Scandal

John Poulson had his own architectural practice which he started in the 1930s. In the 1950s and 1960s, he had expanded and had built a reputation for pioneering ideas for making the design and build process more cost-efficient. His business became one of the largest in Europe and, in addition to several offices in UK cities, he had offices in Nigeria and Lebanon.

Well-connected in local and national political circles, Poulson developed a close business relationship with T. Dan Smith, the leader of Newcastle-upon-Tyne city council in the North East. Smith had great ambitions for the redevelopment of Newcastle and Poulson's organization was a ready vehicle to facilitate his plans. Smith was appointed as a consultant to Poulson's company Ropergate Services Ltd. He introduced Poulson to numerous contacts in other local authorities in the region and some of these also became Poulson consultants. Smith's Labour Party connections also led Poulson to establish a relationship with Andrew Cunningham, a senior figure in the Labour Party in the North East and the General and Municipal Workers' Union. Soon, Poulson was being awarded contracts to build large public housing projects in Cunningham's home town in County Durham.

Poulson also won contracts from the nationalized industries as a result of his long-standing connections with civil servants involved. Years earlier, when these civil servants had been quite junior, Poulson had given them gifts and he was now asking for the favours to be returned. For example, during the Second World War, he had met a railway employee named Graham Tunbridge, who went on to become the estates surveyor for British Railways Eastern Region. Poulson received several contracts from Tunbridge and then, when the latter was promoted to estates and rating surveyor for British Railways Southern Region, he gave Poulson further contracts relating to mainline terminus stations at Waterloo and Cannon Street as well as East Croydon Station. For his services, Pouslon paid Tunbridge £25 per week (approximately £500 per week in 2012 terms) plus the loan of an up-market car.

Another civil servant suborned by Poulson was George Pottinger in the Government's Scottish Office. Over a six-year period, Poulson gave Pottinger more than £30,000 in gifts (a huge sum in the 1960s) for which Pottinger gave Poulson the lead architect contract for the £3 million redevelopment of Aviemore as a winter sports complex.

Various MPs and senior national officials of all the major political parties (Labour, Conservative and Liberal) also became enticed by Poulson's consultancy and grace-and-favour web, both within the UK and overseas. Perhaps the most high-profile and damaging political relationship Poulson had was with the Shadow Commonwealth Secretary Reginald Maudling. Poulson was looking for a 'big name' to be Chairman of one of his companies and Maudling was looking to boost his income. In 1966, Maudling took up the chairmanship at a remuneration of £5,000 per year and Maudling's son also got a job with Poulson. Unfortunately, Maudling helped Poulson by using his ministerial position to pressure the Maltese Government to award Poulson a £1.5 million contract to build the new Victoria Hospital in Gozo. In Parliament, he vigorously opposed the Government's plans to reduce British troop and defence spending in Malta and altered his own (Conservative) Party's policy so as to give Malta a much more generous benefit. When the Poulson corruption scandal surfaced in 1972 and police began a serious fraud investigation, Maudling, who was by then Home Secretary, was forced to resign. Other MPs who also fell owing to their close connections with Poulson were John Cordle and Albert Roberts.

At its high point, Poulson's business had an annual turnover of £1 million. However, his undoing was his business model, which involved a large amount of up-front expenses for business, marketing and other items whereas actual contract revenue receipts were on a longer timescale. To cover this gap and get more contracts in, Poulson resorted to yet more corruption and bribery of public officials and, on his own estimate, he paid out some £500,000 in such illicit payments in the last few years of the business. In today's money, that is about £5 million.

As part of his promotional activities, he even managed to get himself appointed as a local Commissioner of Taxes. It is indeed some irony that he himself had serious tax debts which culminated in the Inland Revenue obtaining judgement against him in 1968 for £211,639.

Poulson was formally removed from control of his group of companies in 1969 and he declared himself bankrupt in November 1971. His bankruptcy hearing revealed a lot of details about his business activities, including his payments and gifts to individuals, and in July 1972 the police began a fraud investigation. He was arrested in June 1973 and charged with corruption in connection with the award of building contracts. Convicted of fraud in February 1974, he was sentenced to five years in jail, later increased to seven years. The judge described Poulson as an 'incalculably evil man'. Fellow defendants also found guilty were T. Dan Smith, jailed for six years, George Pottinger, jailed for five years and Andrew Cunningham, also jailed for five years but reduced to three years on appeal.

Corrupt and fraudulent payments may not always be made for the direct benefit of the individual payer, as case 6.5 (News International) illustrated. The following case 9.2 involved alleged false payments on a large scale over many years by the Japanese Olympus group, apparently primarily for the purpose of hiding mammoth corporate losses that had arisen from risky investments. The underlying motive appeared to be to try to avoid accountability and humiliation for the Olympus board.

## Case 9.2 Olympus and a Board Whistleblower

Olympus became a global brand in the 1980s, instantly recognizable for its easy to use pocket cameras. However, it soon diversified into specialist medical cameras and other equipment. In the mid-1980s, Olympus had bought into the British company Key Med and in 1987 bought the company outright. With the purchase of Key Med came its star salesman, its young Managing Director Michael Woodford. Soon Woodford started to rise within the Olympus group in Europe but it was their domination of the medical endoscopic camera market that was making the big money while their retail camera revenues were sluggish.

He became a protégé of the Olympus Chairman Tsuyoshi Kikukawa and by 2011 Woodford took over the President and Chief Operating Officer's (COO) position at Olympus in Tokyo. Japan is a very conservative country where age is revered and foreigners are not generally trusted and no less so in corporate life, so for Woodford in his forties to be given such a position was a considerable achievement and endorsement of his skills.

Olympus share values rose as the market anticipated the impact Woodford's appointment would have on revenue performance, on which he had built his reputation. At the Olympus AGM in June 2011, Woodford received the most votes of endorsement among the directors. However, within weeks he was alerted to an article in a Japanese business magazine named Facta (Gwyther and Anderson 2012, Bovingdon 2012) which made detailed damaging allegations about alleged corporate malfeasance at Olympus involving very large sums of money. These allegations in summary were:

- Olympus had bought three small companies with modest turnovers (a mail-order cosmetics business, a microwave antennae manufacturer and a waste recycling company) for which it paid in total some US$900 million. It was alleged that this excessive expenditure was to hide massive losses that Olympus had made on unwise investments in securities.
- In 2008, Olympus had bought a British company Gyrus, which made gynaecology equipment, for an inexplicably huge US$2 billion price when its pre-tax profits were only £10 million.
- Olympus paid a massive US$687 million consultancy fee for advice on the Gyrus acquisition, with the cash being transferred to a Caymans Island account which was closed soon after the transaction.

Woodford, who was in Germany at the time, went immediately to Tokyo to take charge of an investigation into the allegations. He reported that he was surprised to find that the Olympus board and executives appeared to be unconcerned and relaxed about the allegations (Gwyther and Anderson 2012). As the weeks and months progressed, Woodford reported that he felt that the rest of the board were working against his investigation and being deliberately evasive and uncooperative. The Chairman Kikukawa and the Vice-President Hisashi Mori seemed to him to becoming increasingly defensive and antagonistic towards him, he reported. Woodford then commissioned PricewaterhouseCoopers to investigate and report on the payments to the Cayman Islands and Woodford said that their negative report provoked even greater hostility towards him from the Chairman. Apparently, Kikukawa accused Woodford of disloyalty while Woodford told Kikukawa that he should resign.

The final showdown came at a board meeting on 14 October 2011 at which the board fell in behind Kikukawa and voted for Woodford's immediate dismissal on the grounds of gross misconduct. Kikukawa later justified this accusation on the grounds that Woodford had ignored the company's organizational structure and had adopted a management style that differed from that of the rest of the management team.

Kikukawa and the board may have imagined that Woodford would just go quietly and that there would be no more investigation into the allegations made in the original Facta article. If so, their expectations were very quickly proven disastrously wrong. Within minutes of Woodford having been bundled out of the Olympus headquarters with all his company privileges revoked or blocked, he had revealed the whole saga in detail to the *Financial Times* (*FT*), which ran an article. As a high-profile global newspaper for the business world, the revelations in the *FT* article quickly led to more and more damning evidence against Olympus becoming public. Olympus was forced to admit that over a 13-year period its senior executives had run a corrupt and fraudulent scheme to hide over US$1.5 billion losses on risky investments in securities, very much as the Facta article had suggested. Police fraud investigations of Olympus began in Japan, US and the UK and Kikukawa and other individuals were arrested in connection with the investigation in Japan. Unanswered questions addressed by investigators included:

- Who were the consultants to Olympus who were paid US$687 million? Investigative journalists have cited a former Japanese banker working for a small US investment firm as being the consultant. He was reported to have had a relationship with Olympus for over 30 years and became a specialist in the now banned practice of moving large losses from a parent company onto a subsidiary so as to hide losses from investors and the markets.
- Who was the true beneficiary of the Cayman Islands payments?
- Were the payments fictitious, that is, did they never leave Olympus or were they redirected straight back to Olympus?

As for Olympus, its share values dropped drastically (by at least 60 per cent) after the scandal broke, before making some recovery, but by spring 2012 the company's market capitalization was less than half its pre-scandal level of US$4.5 billion. Kikukawa was sacked as Chairman, although remaining a director, and Mori was also sacked. The company was restructured with large redundancies. Angry shareholders sued the Olympus board members to compensate for their losses.

Woodford himself also sued Olympus for a reported £60 million. That legal action was concluded on 29 May 2012 with an out-of-court settlement of £10 million. His interpretation of what happened and why (Gwyther and Anderson 2012) is that he was catapaulted by Kikukawa into the top position because of his known 'rainmaker' reputation when they desperately needed more sales and revenue, Kikukawa's belief that he and the board could keep the prior losses and cover-up secret from Woodford, and once Woodford had done his job as rainmaker, they could engineer his departure. The underlying motive, according to Woodford, was the board's abject fear of the truth about the losses getting out and their loss of face and humiliation as a result. In this respect, their behaviour appears not vastly different to that of rogue trader Nick Leeson at Barings Singapore and Jerome Kerviel at Soc Gen. None of them appeared to perpetrate their frauds for personal financial gain but rather for reasons of inadequacy, pride and ego. Naïvely, they all thought they could hide whacking great losses and cover their tracks by 'robbing Peter to pay Paul' fraudulent means.

This case has also highlighted the fact that the boards of large corporations in Japan are still largely dominated by conservative traditions which directly challenge the transparency, ethics and robust risk management principles of good corporate governance.

Two main categories of corruption are recognized in the UN model. Petty corruption involves individuals or small groups acting on their own initiative. Grand corruption, however, exists when public policy making, its design and implementation are compromised by corrupt practices. At a strategic level, if a policy decision on which option to choose for a particular programme or project appears to ignore independent objective expert advice and appears to favour particular parties, then unsurprisingly questions of corruption may arise. For example, press reports may allege that a particular decision taken by a government is corrupt. Such reports often seem to suggest some odd goings-on, but to what extent are they 'flakey' behaviour and incompetence rather than actual corruption? As a senior ICAC official once said to the author, one can observe obvious conflicts of interest in many relationships and often monumental incompetence but that does not necessarily entail, much less prove, corruption. The implication is that care needs to be taken in making specific allegations of corruption so as not to confuse and conflate it with incompetence (even though both corruption and incompetence may be involved in some instances).

At a more mundane level, hypothetically what if all driving test examiners, for example, were encouraged by their superiors to fail as many test applicants as possible, even when they have met the test standard, so as to boost the department's revenues from re-test fees, keep the department fully occupied and keep driving schools fully employed? Is this grand corruption as defined? It is certainly against the public interest and it certainly favours particular parties who gain unfairly. There is an element of official direction and government procedures have certainly been compromised. The purpose of driving tests is to ensure that drivers meet prescribed standards of safe driving, not to perpetuate jobs for civil servants or driving instructors! On top of this, the 'test failure culture' may engender an additional level of petty corruption, whereby examiners accept bribes from candidates to ensure a test pass. One can imagine many such hypothetical examples and in some instances in some countries they do actually occur.

## Who are the Victims?

Ultimately, each citizen suffers from corruption. This may be indirectly because favours bestowed corruptly on a small number of people result in magnified outcomes that damage the public good. For example, if a major government contract is awarded corruptly to a mediocre or the worst bidder, the works may be finished late, probably with a budget over-run, and the 'product' may be shoddy or even permanently blighted. The cost over-runs and the remedies get loaded onto the taxpayer. Any project, even those run by the best companies, can get into difficulty. However, it is much more likely that a corruptly awarded contract will run aground because corruption and incompetence usually go hand-in-hand. After all, competent companies do not need to win their work through corruption. Fraud and corruption also often go hand-in-hand. Here again, the costs of fraud may get loaded onto taxpayers as a whole.

Citizens may also suffer more directly as individuals. For example, if a property developer corruptly influences local planning authorities into letting him build an apartment block having more than the statutory maximum number of floors or letting him build up against a neighbour's home, the amenity of neighbours such as blocked natural lighting and access may be blighted.

If the best candidate for a particular job or promotion is passed over because it has been awarded instead to a less-qualified candidate who is a friend or a relative of the boss, not only does the individual suffer but also the company. The aggrieved best candidate will almost certainly leave; the company will be left with the lesser candidate and all the consequences of that. The best talent always flows to high-reputation companies. A poor-reputation company is a victim of its own mediocrity and incompetence, which may well involve petty corruption such as nepotism.

Corruption destroys trust, which is the basis of all transactions. Fraud and corruption within a company may damage the company's financial stability and share values, thereby adversely affecting not only employees and shareholders but also damaging the reputation of the industry sector and the country. Inward foreign investment relies on having a reputation overseas for being a safe and secure place for investment and that includes foreign investors not seeing TV documentaries and a litany of newspaper reports on fraud and corruption in your country (see Chapter 11, for example).

## Corruption of the Spirit

However, regardless of the scale of actual conventional corruption, the author believes that 'corruption of the spirit' in a number of countries is overwhelming. This kind of corruption does not feature as such in the UN Convention or the Groupe d'Etats Contre la Corruption (GRECO) reports yet arguably it constitutes the most pernicious, corrosive and debilitating of all. Corruption of the spirit refers to a culture in which officials lack the will or the encouragement to act professionally, ethically and efficiently. No one individual is to blame for this state of affairs arising and perpetuating but 'the system' and operating environment in which they function are so suffocating, pedestrian and timeless that collectively officials feel that have little choice but to keep plodding on with little prospect of radical improvement. A corrupted spirit may be readily identified in a number of countries where a pervasive *laissez-faire* attitude to life exists, where patronage, cronyism and nepotism prevail and where change that would benefit society as a whole is strongly resisted by vested interests. See Chapters 11 and 15 for current examples.

The UN Convention (UNCAC 2004) identifies 13 key factors that encourage corruption. Four are also particularly relevant to corruption of the spirit in many countries:

- Excessive red tape and procedural complexities at all levels of government, which may also encourage corrupt 'speed payments' to officials to bypass the bottlenecks.
- The abuse of discretion and uncertainty in the application and interpretation of regulations and laws within the administrative public sector domain.
- Poor motivation among public sector personnel due to the lack of a merit-based system used to hire, promote and remove employees at the local and central levels of government.
- The absence of results-based management in public service delivery.

## Sovereign Corruption

While examining the subject of corruption over recent years, the author found that the UN categories of petty and grand corruption are not entirely adequate in that their definitions when considered together do not cover all forms of corruption. Apart from the 'corruption of the spirit' issue not being covered, there also remain instances in some countries where the scale of state-inspired corruption and its tentacles is so vast and all-pervasive as to go way beyond the definition of grand corruption. A corrupt decision in the awarding of a major government contract that favours particular interested parties may be an example of grand corruption but it is discrete. Even if such corrupt decisions occur on a regular basis, there is a measure of limited scope involved. However, what if petty and grand corruption were occurring not just on an opportunistic case-by-case basis but in a much more endemic and systemic way top-down throughout the entire government apparatus, legislature, law enforcement and judiciary and thereby infecting all aspects of business, industry, commerce and civil society? Allegations are frequently made which suggest that some countries in Asia, Africa and the Middle East fall into this category but it should not be assumed that, therefore, it is a phenomenon which only appears in developing or third-world countries. Prospective candidates also exist within the EU (see Chapters 11 and 15). In a particular country, widespread collusion between, on the one hand, unethical companies (for example, those engaged in wholesale cheating of customers and the taxpayer) and, on the other hand, administrations of successive governments may occur over a long period of time, to the detriment of the public interest in general and particular classes of person or corporate entity in particular. If the government fails to radically correct the system and the collusion, it creates an impression of it having become an accepted and institutionalized fact, that is an instrument of state policy. That is sovereign corruption.

## Corruption League Table

The annual Corruption Perceptions Index (CPI) published by Transparency International ranks more than 180 countries according to the degree of corruption perceived to exist among public officials and politicians. Scores range from 10.0 (highly clean) to 0 (highly corrupt). For example, in 2011, New Zealand with a score of 9.5 was ranked as the least corrupt country whereas Somalia with a score of 1.0 was ranked the most corrupt (CPI 2011). Fourteen of the top 25 (least corrupt) countries having a score of 7.0 or more are in northern Europe. Eighteen Southern European and 'new entrant' EU member states range from Estonia at 6.4 down to Bulgaria at 3.3.

By comparing the annual index reports, it is possible to gauge whether a country over time is perceived as becoming more or less corrupt. It should be borne in mind that the CPI reports are based on reported perceptions of corruption, whether or not those perceptions are accurate. In the investment world, perceptions mostly over-ride facts in decision-making. Not surprisingly, therefore, countries are sensitive to their ranking in the CPI reports. In the 2011 CPI report, India ranked 95 with a score of 3.1. Anecdotally, India has long been perceived as inherently corrupt despite its strong democracy and burgeoning economy. The following case 9.3 set in India is particularly interesting as it involves not only classical bribery on a grand scale but also international money laundering, political intrigue and significant damage to the Indian economy.

# Case 9.3 The 'Rajagate' Indian Telecoms Scandal

In one of the biggest fraud and corruption scandals to hit India in recent years, the Indian Government's Central Bureau of Investigation (CBI) and Enforcement Directorate (ED) investigated the laundering of a 'huge sum of money' through Cyprus, under the Prevention of Money Laundering Act and the Foreign Exchange Management Act.

*The Times of India* reported that the investigation, stretching back to 2009, related to allegations that the former Telecommunications Minister Mr A. Raja received some Rs30,000 crores (approx €479 million) in bribes for favouring particular telecom companies bidding for 2G mobile frequency spectrum allocations. The overall scam may have caused the Indian Government Rs45,000–50,000 crores (€7.18–7.98 billion) in revenue losses, although it was reported that a Government auditor estimated that the losses may reach US$39 billion (€27.3 billion). Some press articles dubbed the scandal as 'Rajagate'.

The ED investigated jointly with CBI the flow of foreign funds in the telecom sector, as well as whether money was sent abroad by suspects in the 'Rajagate' scandal. Following initial soundings abroad in October 2009 by the CBI, the ED then sent Letters Rogatory to up to ten countries where illicit money appears to have been invested in little known companies and then routed back or elsewhere, either as bribe pay offs or as foreign direct investment.

Among allegations against Raja are that he used his wife's bank accounts in Mauritius and Seychelles to deposit part of the bribes he received. One unnamed senior official involved in the investigation is quoted as saying that they had a 'strong suspicion' that most of the money was routed to Cyprus and Mauritius. Livemint.com reported that documents in the possession of ED reportedly showed that a 'huge sum of money' had been routed to a network of 22 Cyprus-registered dummy companies, all subsidiaries of Unitech Telecom, one of the telecom companies alleged to have bribed Raja, all registered at the same Cyprus address in Strovolos, and all with subsidiaries in Mauritius.

The CBI informed the Supreme Court on 29 March 2011 of its intention to file an 80,000-page charges sheet against Raja, four former officials of his Telecommunications ministry and two companies alleged to have participated in and benefited from bribery for favouring particular telecom companies bidding for 2G mobile frequency spectrum allocations. Bribes were alleged to have been taken from firms that are now the Indian operations of Telenor and Etisalat.

Early July 2011 saw the arrival in Cyprus of a team of investigators from the Indian ED who were following a substantial money laundering trail in the alleged bribery and corruption case against Mr Raja. On July 25, Mr Raja began a spirited defence against the prosecution's framing of charges, to which had now been added fabricating false evidence and perjury. The Indian Income Tax Department had also now begun an investigation into Mr Raja in connection with his family income.

At the time of writing in early 2013, the case against Raja was still proceeding in the courts.

## The Groupe d'Etats Contre la Corruption Reports

The Council of Europe's GRECO carries out high-level evaluations of the anti-corruption policies and programmes of most countries in Europe and even further afield, for example the Caucasus. The majority have already been subject to three such evaluations. These include 'new entrant' EU members (2004–2006) such as Malta, Cyprus, Romania and Bulgaria.

The second evaluation report on Bulgaria, for example, noted that the country had been establishing a permanent Anti-Corruption Commission which appeared to meet the UN/GRECO criteria, that is, is active rather than window dressing, yet corruption of senior state officials in Bulgaria has been so rampant (for example, major government civil engineering contracts given to family members of ministers) that the EU withheld major state funds as a punishment.

Cyprus seems to be some way behind with an Anti-Corruption Advisory 'Talk Shop' and a general denial by the Government in its evidence to GRECO (second report 2005) that corruption exists at all in Cyprus, especially as the population is relatively small. Yet, the former Finance Minister (2008–2011) Charilaos Stavrakis flatly contradicted this official denial in his book *Economy in Politics and Politics in the Economy* (Stavrakis 2012). The Second Evaluation Report from GRECO was positive overall about Cyprus's potential and capacity to combat corruption but was critical of some aspects, particularly attitude and motivation to take corruption seriously.

The GRECO team 'was not convinced that a small population in itself is a deterrent to corruption. One can argue that in a small country in which people to a large extent know each other, the willingness to report activities such as corruption may be less than in a larger and more anonymous society'. The Cyprus Government's Co-ordinating Body Against Corruption which 'appeared to be an advisory body without any targeted mandate and clear mission, could provide a good platform for development of a consolidated anti-corruption strategy'. Perhaps GRECO had in mind something along the lines of Hong Kong's ICAC, which has become a model for many countries. The GRECO team was 'surprised to hear' that the Ombudsman had never received any complaints concerning corruption and recommended that the Ombudsman's mandate should be clarified 'to the effect that he/she has the ability to investigate corruption in public administration and to raise the public's awareness' of this. The third evaluation report (2010) observed that Cyprus was still using old anti-corruption legislation instead of that required to be fully compliant with the Criminal Law Convention on Corruption. Cyprus had said that it had ratified the Convention yet had not done so properly or implemented it. Moreover, although adequate penalties exist in Cyprus law for criminal offences including corruption, the report noted that very few cases had ever been brought to court over many years (for example, four connected cases in 2006, two cases in 2007 and two cases in 2008) and that actual penalties imposed were light.

Chrysafis (2010) refers to the corruption *status quo* in Cyprus as 'negligently passive'. He points up the circularity and snowball effect of sovereign corruption:

> *Unfortunately, laws have also become victims of corruption. They are forever being broken and abused by corrupt officials under the very noses of the authorities, and yet, those responsible to uphold the law frequently refuse to take positive action on prosecuting the offenders. The reason for this is a simple one: nepotism and corruption!*

The above examples illustrate the very limited power of GRECO, which is really a high-level consultant to governments and whose role is educative and persuasive. It has neither the remit nor the resources to find out about the real extent of corruption in a country or to enforce any recommendations that it makes in its reports. In this respect, GRECO is rather like the EU Commission, which has no remit, resources or mechanism to monitor and audit compliance with EU Directives in member states. National governments are left to comply 'on their honour' and many have shown a propensity for evasion, dissimulation and downright lies in their responses to such supra-national bodies. GRECO recommendations are largely ignored, evaded, diluted or delayed by recalcitrant governments. Even where it may have some scope for imposition of limited penalties, the EU Commission has shown itself to be very reluctant and slow to do so. To that extent, by being unwilling or unable to 'get their hands dirty' with compliance and with specific cases of non-compliance, both GRECO and the EU Commission have tarnished their images and reputations and engendered widespread contempt among populations who, not unreasonably, expect such bodies to offer them real protection and not act like paper tigers.

## Extra-Territorial Jurisdiction

In the UK, after several years of preparation, the Bribery Act 2010 came into force on 1 July 2011. The Bribery Act, in a similar fashion to its US counterpart the Foreign Corrupt Practices Act, places strict obligations on British companies not only to desist from making corrupt payments anywhere in the world but also to establish and maintain active systems designed to prevent such payments and monitor, audit and control all payments. This would include systems to carry out adequate due diligence checks on partners, agents and suppliers and recipients of fees and commissions. A number of high-profile cases have involved corruption that pre-dated the Bribery Act and a sample of these (cases 9.4 to 9.6) follows:

### Case 9.4   BAE Systems

The British company BAE Systems is Europe's largest supplier of defence systems as well as being a major supplier to the US, Saudi Arabia and many other countries. For several years, the company was at the centre of a number of scandals alleging corrupt payments to overseas governments and middlemen. In 2007, the company was accused publicly (Leigh and Evans 2007) of paying at least £1.2 billion over 10 years or more to Prince Bandar of Saudi Arabia, as facilitation for the Saudi Government continuing to buy from BAE Systems. Further, it was alleged that successive British Governments, including the then Blair Government, had given the MoD full authorization to do so, that is, it was a case of alleged grand corruption. The SFO had already begun an investigation into the £43 billion Al-Yamamah arms deal signed in 1985, which involved Prince Bandar (whose nickname was Al-Yamamah). However, in December 2006, the Attorney General on instruction from the Prime Minister Tony Blair ordered the investigation to stop, arguing that cessation was in the UK's national interest and there was little prospect of obtaining convictions. It later emerged that the real reason behind the 'stop order' was much more likely to have been that the allegations and investigations had created a huge diplomatic row with Saudi Arabia with the threat of long-term damage to British defence and other exports to that country, and that complicity of the British Government's Defence Export Services Organisation in the bribery and corruption inevitably would be revealed.

BAE Systems again came under the spotlight of bribery and corruption allegations when in 2010 they were prosecuted by the SFO for an accounting offence in relation to the sale of £28 million worth of radar equipment to Tanzania in 2002. The company pleaded guilty to this single offence after a plea bargain to avoid them pleading guilty to corruption. In fining BAE Systems £500,000 plus the £225,000 legal costs of the SFO, the judge in the case, Mr Justice Bean, said that he was astonished at claims by the defence that BAE had not acted corruptly when its executives had made illegal payments to a Tanzanian middleman Sailesh Vithlani to secure the contract. The payments to Vithlani amounted to £8 million over five years or nearly a third of the contract value. The judge rejected the suggestion by BAE that Vithlani was merely an expensive lobbyist and even considered the idea of calling expert witnesses to verify or not whether a commission or fee of 30 per cent of a contract was 'the going rate' for a legitimate lobbyist. In addition to the fine and costs, BAE also agreed to pay an *ex gratia* sum of £29.5 million to the Tanzanian Government as recompense for its citizens who had been the ultimate victims of this corrupt way of doing business.

By the end of 2010, BAE Systems had paid fines totalling US$450 million in the UK and the US following the long-running corruption investigations and prosecutions into its defence contracts with Saudi Arabia, Tanzania, Hungary and the Czech Republic. In May 2011, the company agreed to pay the US Government fines totalling a further US$79 million (£48.7 million) following its admission that it had submitted false statements on its sale of fighter aircraft overseas.

## Case 9.5    Willis and the Former Soviet Union

Willis Limited, one of the world's largest insurance brokers, was fined £6.895 million by the UK FSA for failings in its anti-bribery and anti-corruption systems and controls. This action on 21 July 2011 was only three weeks after the Bribery Act came into force and was brought under pre-existing legislation, including the Financial Services and Markets Act 2000. In 2009, a fine of £5.25 million for similar failings was made against Aon Limited, another global insurance broker,

In the Willis case, between January 2005 and December 2009 the company made payments to overseas third parties who assisted in winning and retaining business from overseas clients, especially in high-risk jurisdictions. These payments totalled £27 million. The FSA found that up to August 2008 Willis failed to:

- ensure that it established and recorded an adequate commercial rationale to support its payments to overseas third parties;
- ensure that adequate due diligence checks were carried out on overseas third parties to evaluate the risk involved in doing business with them;
- adequately review its relationships on a regular basis to confirm whether it was still necessary and appropriate for Willis Limited to continue with the relationship.

The FSA report said that these failures contributed to a weak control environment surrounding payments to overseas third parties and gave rise to an unacceptable risk that these payments could be used for corrupt purposes, including bribery. Further, although Willis improved its policies in August 2008, it continued to fail to monitor and ensure that its staff recorded an adequate commercial rationale and carried out sufficient due diligence throughout the period from January 2005 and up to May 2009.

The FSA identified a number of suspicious payments in respect of business carried out by third parties in Russia and Egypt and these were reported by the FSA to the Serious Organized Crime Agency. Willis cooperated with the FSA investigation and as a result received a discount on the fine, which otherwise would have been £9.85 million.

## Case 9.6  Macmillan Publishers in Africa

On 22 July 2011, the SFO in the UK settled a civil recovery enforcement action against Macmillan Publishers Ltd for sums which the company had allegedly received as a result of bribery to sell its educational books in Africa. The company was subject to a High Court order under the Proceeds of Crime Act 2002 to pay £11.3 million.

Following an initial investigation by the World Bank into allegations of corruption in Sudan by Macmillan, the company was blacklisted for three years by the World Bank. This led to a much wider joint investigation and action by the SFO, the World Bank and the City of London Police into Macmillan's activities in Rwanda, Zambia and Uganda. The company agreed to carry out an internal review and upgrade of its accounting function and procedures so as to identify corruption-related risks and institute adequate controls. Further, the company voluntarily ceased current and future public tenders by its Education Division in East and West Africa.

# Organized Crime

Organized criminal gangs are known to infiltrate and, in some cases, gain effective control of legitimate businesses. More often, however, they establish corrupt relationships with bankers, police officers, members of the judiciary, public officials and indeed anyone who could further their aims. Those criminals who operate cross-border are especially interested in facilitation, favours and 'blind eyes' for their illegal activities such as money laundering and the trafficking of drugs, counterfeit goods trafficking, arms and people. Legitimate companies from first-world countries who are new to operating in areas such as the FSU, Asia, Far East and Africa are particularly vulnerable not just to extortion by corrupt officials or middlemen but also to the attentions of organized criminals. Thinly veiled protection rackets are not uncommon.

The subject of organized crime and the business world warrants a book by itself and cannot be considered adequately here. However, as a sample vignette of the problem, the entertainment, leisure and gaming industry has proven to be particularly attractive to organized crime. Casinos especially are like a honeypot for legitimate operators and criminals alike because of the huge sums of cash in takings. In 2008, for example, Macau's casinos pulled in US$13 billion in earnings, twice as much as those in Las Vegas. In whichever country, casinos relieve the punters of large sums of money and the government coffers gain from licence fees and taxation. Hotels, restaurants and other local businesses also get a lot of spin-off from the influx of such visitors.

By owning or controlling a casino, a criminal enterprise can do double book-keeping and declare false low earnings thereby paying far less tax and siphoning off the undeclared money. In addition, casinos provide an ideal vehicle for laundering 'dirty' money from other criminal activity. Casinos also provide a hub for other criminal activity, especially trafficking of drugs and people, often involving prostitution. The bigger the casino opportunity, the more likely that the criminals attracted to it will be 'big fish' from outside the country. The international gangs are better organized, more sophisticated, better funded and far more ruthless than any local criminals and quickly take over or eliminate any local criminal control of casinos. Once embedded, they are notoriously difficult to root out.

Even countries having strong government regulation of gambling are fighting a never-ending battle to keep organized criminals out of control and influence in the sector. In Hong Kong, for example, casinos are barred and only gambling (horse racing and betting shops) operated by a single licensee, The Hong Kong Jockey Club (HKJC) is legal. The HKJC has a major permanent Integrity and Security department dedicated not only to general safety of racing events but also to eliminating race fixing, bet fixing, fraud and infiltration of Club membership by undesirable elements. Working closely with the ICAC and organized crime and anti-corruption units of the police in Hong Kong and other countries, the HKJC has successfully prevented sustained efforts over many years by criminals and undesirables in the Macau casino industry from gaining undue influence or even control of the Club.

Corruption, whether petty, grand, sovereign or spiritual, is not a victimless crime. Fraud and corruption frequently cohabit and increasingly governments are showing a determination to stage high-profile prosecutions of corporations that have broken the very clear laws on either fraud and/or corruption. Companies who fail to live up to the high standards of governance in this area are likely to pay dearly in terms of fines, damage to share values and long-term reputational damage.

# CHAPTER 10 *Corporate Fraud*

Many of the cases of inadequate risk management and poor governance in previous chapters have involved, to varying degrees, fraud by or against organizations. Typically, instances of such corporate fraud fall into a relatively small number of categories. The UK SFO cites four main categories:

- fraudulent trading;
- asset stripping;
- share ramping;
- publishing false information.

The author prefers a broader list which cuts across and/or exemplifies these four categories:

- Ponzi investment schemes (promises of high returns on investments which are actually weak or non-existent, coupled with robbing-Peter-to-pay-Paul money movements, false accounting and false investment statements);
- grossly inflated and excessively optimistic claims for investment opportunities and returns;
- false descriptions of products, services and benefits so as to deceive;
- intentional non-delivery of items that have been paid for;
- false stock sales between related companies having the same owner so as to inflate share values ('share ramping');
- deliberate masking or hiding of investment losses so as to deceive;
- use of forged or otherwise worthless documents and financial instruments;
- dummy company set up by rogue employees of a legitimate company; issuing false invoices from the dummy company for operational expenses to siphon off money from the legitimate one; trading in direct competition – see case 7.5;
- illicit payments from company funds to directors, executives or external parties;
- impersonation and misrepresentation of ownership, background, experience, qualifications, assets or other attributes of key persons.

The ingenuity of fraudsters to come up with new variations on these basic themes seems to know no bounds. This chapter examines the characteristics of corporate fraud, the range of motivations for fraud and why corporate fraud often goes undetected for long periods. A number of further cases are provided.

## The Characteristics of Corporate Fraud

There is no universal definition of fraud in law and definitions and scope of what constitutes fraud vary from one jurisdiction to another. The UK SFO classifies fraud as a type of criminal activity defined as 'the abuse of position, or false representation, or prejudicing someone's rights for personal gain'. All fraud involves one or more acts of deception intended for personal gain, or corporate gain or to cause loss to another party. Corporate fraud involves deception either by or on behalf of an organization or against an organization.

Sometimes corporate fraud involves deception by one organization or its senior personnel against another organization. In relation to the Fraud Act 2006, the SFO uses a narrower definition of corporate fraud as noted above but there is no dispute about the serious adverse impact that such corporate deception has on many parties likely to be affected.

In most countries, fraud is classified as primarily a criminal offence but also with the possibility of civil offences being involved. In England and Wales and those countries which follow English law and precedents, the standards of evidence and proof differ between civil and criminal law. In civil actions, the standard of proof is 'on the balance of probabilities', whereas for criminal actions it is the higher standard of 'beyond reasonable doubt'. Fraud cases may therefore involve both kinds of legal proceedings against alleged fraudsters. If convicted in a criminal action, the fraudster may suffer penalties such as a fine, imprisonment, forfeiture, being barred from company directorships or any or all of these. In a civil action, if the court finds for the plaintiff, the fraudster as defendant may have to pay financial compensation and/or restitution or hand back assets and may be ordered to complete specified transactions or obligations by a certain date.

In some jurisdictions, for a criminal conviction for fraud to succeed the prosecution would have to prove only that a fraudulent act was committed by the accused. In other jurisdictions, however, a much higher standard is demanded to prove that not only the fraudulent act occurred and that someone suffered loss or damage as a result but also that the defendant perpetrated the fraudulent act knowingly and with intent to permanently deprive someone of assets, finance and so on. A similar variability in standards of proof occurs between different jurisdictions regarding civil actions for fraud. Oversight and unintentional mistake may be defences in some fraud cases but usually court proceedings are only brought where such a defence is highly suspect on the evidence.

The position of immovable property fraud involves further complexity in that in English law the tendency is for courts to expect a civil action first to decide on ownership and any civil penalties before considering possible criminal charges. However, there is an important *caveat* in that where the issues are clear and the offences serious it may be in the public interest to proceed with criminal prosecution regardless. This issue is considered further in Chapter 11.

The following case 10.1 is a classic example of business-to-business corporate fraud in which a number of major insurance brokers were engaged in systematically defrauding corporate clients over a number of years, in relation to both selection of insurers and insurance premium payments as well as receiving corrupt 'kickbacks' from the favoured insurers.

## Case 10.1 Contingent Payment Scandals

In 2004 Eliot Spitzer, the Attorney General for the State of New York, uncovered a vast system of fraud inside Marsh & McLennan ('Marsh'), the world's largest insurance brokers. Apparently, for many years Marsh had been receiving massive hidden payments from certain insurance companies in return for promoting their policies to clients against those of their competitors. These payments went under the innocent sounding terms of 'contingent fees' in the UK or 'market services agreements' in the US – or 'kickbacks' to ordinary mortals. In 2003 alone, it was reported that Marsh received US$800 million from contingent fees and in 2004 Marsh's contingent fees represented some 80 per cent of their operating profits.

Brokers are entitled to receive commissions but both brokers and insurers must operate above board. A broker is meant to offer his clients independent and impartial advice on which insurers to use and not rigged advice for the financial benefit of the broker and the particular insurer at the client's expense. A broker is not entitled to coach favoured insurers in submitting fictitious and non-competitive bids while discarding competitive bids from non-favoured insurers. Bid rigging and price fixing is illegal. As Spitzer noted, 'There was craven disregard for ethics and the law at some of our nation's largest companies ... Not only was it wrong, it was harmful to the economy.' Further, he claimed that the firm had 'corrupted the marketplace'.

Marsh was forced to set up a US$850 million fund to repay defrauded clients. Other fall-out costs to Marsh included a sharp fall in their share prices from US$46 to US$32 in late 2004 and a further decline to US$28 by September 2005 when indictments of eight former senior executives were announced. In addition, the impact on their business resulted in at least 5,000 redundancies. As a result of all this, Marsh's corporate credibility and reputation were severely damaged. After all, Marsh had prided itself as a risk management specialist. How could clients now possibly trust Marsh to advise them on risk management when it had failed so spectacularly to manage its own risks?! Marsh's market position and stock values have recovered but it will take a long time to shake off the stigma of this scandal.

While Marsh was the high-profile broker to be prosecuted, it was not the only company in the insurance market that was engaged in such dodgy dealings. Several other large insurers were also implicated in the Marsh case. Contingent fees had been common practice in the insurance world for a long time but perhaps not on such a grand scale as in the Marsh case.

# Motivations for Fraud

It is usually assumed that greed, envy and power lie behind the activities of fraudsters and, indeed, the vast majority of fraud cases do involve these base human motivations, for example Madoff, Refco (case 3.4), SIBL (case 7.7), Business Media China (case 7.5). Some cases also involve gambling addiction and an attempt to clear massive personal debts, as in Asia Pacific Breweries (case 7.4). Although undoubtedly in the Marsh case 10.1 senior executives benefitted personally from the fraud via receiving bigger sales bonuses and other benefits, the primary motivation seemed to be to make sure that Marsh won business via unfair and illegal methods in a competitive market, that is, a culture of the end justifying the means. Other cases (10.2 to 10.4) where greed was the primary motivator follow.

## Case 10.2   The Enron Scandal

The collapse of Enron, one of the world's largest energy corporations, in 2001 revealed a massive fraud by the company's senior executives. Complex money movements, 'special purpose entities', 'mark-to-market' accounting and opaque financial reporting were used deliberately to try to ramp up share prices while hiding large losses. While special purpose entities and mark-to-market accounting are not, of themselves, illegal or fraudulent, ultimately they proved themselves to be inappropriate to Enron's risk exposures and undoubtedly encouraged the fraudulent activities that led to the company's collapse.

The three top Enron executives involved in the fraud were: Kenneth Lay, Enron's founder and variously its CEO and Chairman; Jeffery Skilling, initially its COO and then CEO; and Andrew Fastow, its CFO. However, where the Enron fraud differed from so many other corporate frauds, for example MGN (case 10.3) and the rogue trading cases such as Barings and Soc Gen (case 10.6), was that instead of either a single person or very small number of people being involved, a considerable number of Enron staff were knowingly involved and even the firm's independent auditors Arthur Andersen were corrupted and drawn into it.

For most of the 1990s, Enron grew at a phenomenal rate in operational size, geographical footprint, turnover and market capitalization. By the end of 2000, the company's share price had risen to US$83, its revenues to US$100.8 billion and its market capitalization to over US$60 billion. The stock market saw it as a great future performer. It was greatly admired by business and market analysts, commentators and the media and won many plaudits for its innovative style. However, beneath the attractive froth lay a toxic brew of highly misleading performance and accounting data, high-risk activities and highly dubious methods, all validated by a dysfunctional corporate culture focussed on short-term earnings and share ramping emanating from Lay and Skillings' mantra of the stock price being king. The dominant focus on earnings was further fuelled by executives' knowledge that their own large cash bonuses and share options were based on them, thus leading to careless and less than scrupulous executive behaviour of the 'end justifying the means' variety. Both Lay and Skilling as Enron directors each owned shares worth hundreds of millions of US$. The top 200 highest-paid employees at the end of 2000 were paid on average US$7 million per annum, based on Maclean and Elkind (2004). In this respect, the Enron greed culture was no different to that of the Barings senior executives and Barings Singapore traders (see case 3.5 and Waring and Glendon 1998).

By 2001, the company had set up hundreds of 'special purpose entities' or shell companies created by sponsors but funded by independent equity investors and debt financing. Some of these debt financing mechanisms went by the delightful name of 'Raptors', implying high-speed predatory behaviour and ripping into victims' flesh! Competent hedging reduces risk exposure but at Enron derivatives were involved in faulty hedging, which eventually resulted in huge value losses, as much as 50 per cent. Not only were these special entities used to deliberately bypass accounting rules but also to hide the fact that large losses had been suffered. Shareholders were unaware that these special entities were in effect gambling against themselves by using the company's own shares and financial guarantees to finance the faulty hedging. Enron's balance sheet overstated its earnings and equity while understating its liabilities.

Another dubious practice employed by Enron was to borrow from the finance sector an accounting method called mark-to-market. In essence, this method provides for a discounted cash flow application on the estimated Present Value (PV) of the future cash flow arising from a client contract. In 'normal' accounting, revenues are accounted for on hard data on an invoice issued/payment received basis. However, with mark-to-market the true future cash flow may bear only a weak relationship with the earlier forward accounting estimate because actual invoicing, receipts and costs can only be estimated. The likelihood is that actual cash flows will be less than predicted, which proved to be seriously the case with Enron. This led to very misleading financial reports in which cash flows were over-optimistic and investors and shareholders were duped. Moreover, the company had to keep finding new, extra sources of revenue to maintain the momentum of the snowball model. A number of failed business deals that Enron signed were reported to fall into this category.

The robust assertions by the senior Enron executives that all was well, coupled with their share ramping attempts and the deliberate hiding of high-risk activities and losses, were not unlike how Nick Leeson managed for a time to bamboozle anyone too inquisitive and rely on his infamous 88888 error account which he used to hide his fraudulent activities; the fraud was just more extensive and intricate in Enron's case. On a number of occasions, in an attempt to boost market confidence and share price, Skilling even temporarily moved employees from other departments into the offices of a department that external analysts were going to visit, so as to create an impression of a bustling business that had so much revenue-generating work it could barely keep up. For a time, the smoke-and-mirrors worked but eventually, like all frauds, the awful truth began to emerge as external market analysts and financial journalists began to ask persistent questions such as how was it possible for Enron to maintain such a high share price which was trading at more than 50 times its earnings, why were cash flows so erratic and why was Enron using unusual accounting methods? Such questions were brushed aside with contempt by Skilling and Fastow.

Market confidence began to collapse during August 2001 but Lay kept up the pretence that all was well. By 22 October 2001, when the SEC announced an investigation into a number of opaque and suspicious transactions by Enron, the share price had fallen to US$20.65 which was a far cry from the US$83 value only ten months earlier. Skilling had resigned in August and Fastow was forced out on 25 October, with the Enron share price then at only US$16. The company's credit rating dropped significantly amid rumours that it was seeking between US$1 billion and 2 billion re-financing. A proposed rescue buyout by rival Dynergy failed to gel as Dynergy began to learn just how big Enron's debts and debt obligations were (US$9 billion within 12 months) compared to what they had said originally. On 28 November 2001, with Enron's cash flow position critical and its credit rating at junk level, Dynergy pulled out of the potential takeover.

On 30 November 2001, the European operations of Enron filed for bankruptcy and sought Chapter 11 protection within a couple of days. Nearly 4,000 employees lost their jobs and a large proportion also had their retirement plans based on Enron shares which were now almost worthless. Enron shareholders lost US$74 billion in the four years leading up to the bankruptcy, of which over half was attributable to the fraud.

Lay and Skilling were prosecuted for a range of financial crimes including insider trading, bank fraud, securities fraud, wire fraud, making false declarations to banks and auditors, money laundering and conspiracy. Skilling was convicted on 19 out of 28 charges and was sentenced to 24 years and four months imprisonment. Lay, who pleaded not guilty to 11 charges and blamed Fastow, was convicted on six counts of wire fraud and was likely to be sentenced to up to 45 years imprisonment with the SEC also seeking over US$90 million in civil damages. However, he died before he could be sentenced or pursued for damages. In total, 21 individuals were prosecuted, found guilty and received a variety of sentences.

Enron's auditors Arthur Andersen were also prosecuted and in 2002 found guilty of obstruction of justice for destroying evidence of its audits at Enron. Prior to the Enron collapse, Arthur Andersen employed some 85,000 staff worldwide. Andersen ceased its accounting and audit work, although retaining a small staff of 200 to handle ongoing litigation. So far as can be ascertained, the company is still registered and not bankrupt. In 2005, the US Supreme Court overturned the Andersen conviction of 2002 but this came too late to save either the company's reputation or business.

That such a massive fraud could have arisen and carried on for so long illustrates just how superficial and ineffective Enron's much vaunted risk management system really was. The senior executives encouraged a 'What can we get away with?' culture, internal controls were conspicuously absent, the audit firm was working in cahoots with the fraudsters and the Enron audit committee was incompetent. Corporate governance and ethical conduct were not in the Enron lexicon.

## Case 10.3   Maxwell and Mirror Group Newspapers

The gigantic corporate fraud perpetrated by the former British MP Robert Maxwell, when he was the controlling owner of MGN in the 1980s, is legendary. This fraud, along with other corporate cases around the late 1980s and early 1990s such as the collapse of Asil Nadir's Polly Peck group and the BCCI, provoked the investigation and report by Sir Adrian Cadbury and eventually the London Stock Exchange and accounting profession formulating the first issue of the Combined Code on Corporate Governance (Turnbull 1999).

Noted for his large girth and his even larger than life personality and flamboyance, the Czech-born entrepreneur acquired the unflattering nicknames 'The Fat Fraudster' and 'The Bouncing Czech', which alluded to his dodgy business proclivities. His large size, menacing and baleful stare and deep, gravelly voice fitted well with his reputation as a bully. Part of his fraud involved share ramping by buying and selling stock between his large network of companies. The need for such transactions was solely to artificially increase the share prices in a merry-go-round fashion. In fact, his corporation overall was short of liquidity and this was a way of inflating its value to impress and convince the banks and other outsiders that the business was strong when it was not. Another string to his fraudulent bow was to 'borrow' large amounts from the company's pension fund, some £460 million in total, to pump into his web of companies. Some 30,000 MGN pensioners lost most of their pensions as a result. Maxwell's behaviour had all the hallmarks of a 'What can we get away with?' boardroom culture (see Chapter 4). He died in 1991 before he could be prosecuted, although two of his sons Kevin and Ian were prosecuted for their alleged part in the fraud but were acquitted. Although much has been done subsequently in the UK to prevent such pension fund frauds, the same cannot be said for all countries, as case 10.4 illustrates.

## Case 10.4   The Missing Pension Funds

The Electricity Authority of an EU member state contracted out the management of its staff pension fund to a company specializing in securities and financial services. However, the owner of the pension fund management company began siphoning money from the fund to an amount thought to total over €16 million before the fraud was uncovered by an internal audit at the Authority in December 2004. The fraudster was arrested in March 2005 and charged with unauthorized removal of money from the Electricity Authority's pension fund, false accounting and intentionally issuing cheques from his client's account for unauthorized purposes including his own expenses. In October 2007, the Fund Manager was found guilty of stealing €8.34 million from the pension fund (there was insufficient evidence to convict on the rest of the missing money). He was also found guilty of presenting false accounts which undervalued the stock portfolio as a means to cover his theft. He was further found guilty of issuing cheques from the fund account for his own expenses. He was sentenced to seven years imprisonment.

The case raised great public concerns about corporate governance at the Authority, especially as the fund was not covered by a bank guarantee. How had the pension fund manager been appointed and why did three Electricity Authority officials sign a power of attorney (PoA) giving the Fund Manager unlimited authority over the fund? One Electricity Authority official was suspended after evidence emerged that the Fund Manager had secured him a personal loan.

Meanwhile, an internal audit at another semi-government organization whose pension fund had been passed to the same pension fund manager had discovered large discrepancies, also not covered by any bank guarantee. On top of this, the same Fund Manager was implicated in defrauding the pilots' provident fund of the country's flag-carrier airline of over €2.5 million. In 2012, in a civil action against the Fund Manager and his company, they were found to have defrauded €784,000 from the pilots' provident fund and were ordered to repay €800,000. The judgement held them guilty of fraud, negligence, breach of fiduciary and statutory duties, and conspiracy.

In addition to these various frauds on client pension funds, the same Fund Manager had previously been charged in 2004 with forgery of property title deeds and circulation of forged deeds in connection with a mortgage application for some €3.4 million. All these cases beg the question: what due diligence checks on the Fund Manager did any of the client organizations carry out before appointing him?

However, despite all the above cases, as the following cases (10.5 and 10.6) illustrate, greed and accumulation of personal wealth are not always the primary motivators for fraud. More complex motivations are sometimes involved.

## Case 10.5   The Generous Finance Director (FSA 2012)

The Royal Liver is one of the UK's longest established insurance companies and the Royal Liver Building still dominates the business district waterfront in Liverpool. In 2009, James Stuart-Smith, who had been Head of Investments at Royal Liver from 2005 until his resignation at the end of 2008, left to set up his own Utility Capital Management group. The Finance Director at that time, George McGregor, apparently felt that Mr Stuart-Smith's severance package should be a generous one and, to ensure that it was, he awarded two consulting contracts to Mr Stuart-Smith's new group. Under the terms of the contracts, Mr Stuart-Smith's companies were to provide investment management services to Royal Liver to be compensated by fees of 0.06 per cent of a portfolio valued at £2.5 billion.

Mr McGregor later said that he intended the compensation fee to be 0.006 per cent and not 0.06 per cent and made a simple error in the contract wording but, whatever the case, when he received the first of two invoices from the Utility Capital companies for £1.8 million he knew that he would be in trouble. For a start, any invoice for over £500,000 would require to be approved and signed by the Chief Executive. As the latter and the board knew nothing of the terms of the two contracts, not only would the approval be unlikely but also the very instruments that McGregor had organized would be investigated thoroughly. To cover this up, McGregor decided to forge the Chief Executive's signature approving the invoice. No evidence has come forward that Mr Stuart-Smith and his companies either knew of or were involved in McGregor's 'mistake' and fraud. The contractual liabilities to Royal Liver on this issue may be as much as £18 million. However, Royal Liver's new owners (the Royal London Group from July 2011) stated that they may seek to recover from Mr Stuart-Smith the £3.6 million already paid to his companies.

Although McGregor was investigated by the Merseyside Police, charges were never brought, on advice from the Crown Prosecution Service. However, he admitted his wrongful conduct. On 8 March 2012, the FSA described his misconduct as 'dishonest, deliberate and sustained' and declared him not to be a fit and proper person to work in financial services (FSA 2012). The FSA banned him from working in financial services and fined him £109,000 for failing to act with honesty and integrity as required from a person in his position. The FSA had considered fining him £1 million but reduced the fine in view of his financial hardship.

## Case 10.6   Rogue Traders

Much has been written about the 'original' rogue trader Nick Leeson whose fraud brought about the ignominious collapse of Barings Bank (see Waring and Glendon 1998 and cases 3.5 and 7.2). As noted earlier in this book, although Leeson clearly enjoyed the lifestyle of a highly rewarded executive, greed and personal financial gain did not appear to be his primary motivation in the fraud he committed. His own book (Leeson 1996) and other studies such as Glendon and Waring (1997) suggested that, whereas he gave an external impression of great self-confidence, most of the time he was out of his depth in terms of trading and financial expertise and got by through bluff and 'winging it'. His main motivation appeared to be to become recognized as a 'big shot' trader and gain the respect of his peers and superiors. He wanted a big bonus to impress them rather than for what it could buy him. When his reckless gambling on derivatives started to go wrong, he ventured into fraud as a means to cover up his costly mistakes and with a naïve expectation that his fraud would buy his way out of the mounting losses. In many ways, the motivation for the fraud committed by Kerviel at Soc Gen (case 7.3) was very similar to that of Leeson: to make big earnings that would boost his standing in the eyes of peers and superiors at the company.

However, the motivations in other alleged rogue trading cases may be quite different. For example, Kweku Adaboli, the former Senior Funds Trader at UBS's London office, was charged with two counts of fraud and two of false accounting. He was accused of dishonestly using his position to make a personal gain, exposing the bank to the risk of losses up to £7.4 billion (US$12 billion) and causing UBS actual losses of £1.4 billion. However, he pleaded not guilty. In November 2012, he was convicted of the two counts of fraud but cleared of the counts of false accounting. Sentencing him to seven years in jail, the judge Mr Justice Keith told Adaboli 'There is a strong streak of the gambler in you. You were arrogant to think that the bank's rules did not apply to you'. Prosecutors attributed his motives to seeking to increase his bonus, status and job prospects.

In essence, combatting corporate fraud requires good detection, deterrence and prevention and these rely on a combination of all the elements of a robust risk management system as described and exemplified in previous chapters. Internal and external audits are vital weapons in the anti-fraud armoury and should be used as the routine long-stop checks to identify fraud that has slipped undetected through the preventive framework. The audit committee in particular should be supervising fraud prevention policy and practice and ensuring that robust anti-fraud mechanisms are in place. Corporate governance will have failed if, as in the case of Enron, board committees adopt a *laissez-faire* attitude or allow themselves to be manipulated or swayed by external auditors who have failed to report flagrant fraud. Failure to challenge dubious practices and a 'What can we get away with?' culture almost always ends in damage to corporate reputation and market performance and, frequently, in disaster.

# 11 *Immovable Property Fraud*

In different parts of the world, land and buildings are referred to either as real estate or immovable property. In the English speaking world, land and buildings are often called simply 'property' by the general public, but of course there are other kinds of property (see Chapter 12, for example). To avoid potential confusion, in this chapter the terms 'immovable property' and 'property' meaning land and buildings are used interchangeably. This chapter also focusses on purchase of residential property overseas as opposed to commercial property, as overseas residential property has proven to be the sector which has experienced the most problems and controversy over fraud.

The property sector is a significant contributor to the economy of most countries and, for some, it is a key contributor. When any major problem (of whatever kind) strikes the property sector in a particular country, it usually has wider negative repercussions for the national economy, for example, the sub-prime mortgages scandal in the US and the toxic mortgage debt bubble in Ireland. If and when property fraud arises on a significant scale in a particular country, it too can have devastating consequences for many parties, corporate as well as individuals and, indeed, national economies may suffer. Without doubt, as part of their due diligence, foreign companies and corporate investors in whatever sector need to be on the lookout for evidence of widespread property fraud, as this may be a valuable proxy indicator of general unscrupulousness in the country's business community and a potential red flag as far as investor trust and confidence are concerned.

Those organizations (whether commercial, construction, banks, real estate agencies, law firms or government functions) that engage in immovable property fraud thereby expose themselves to huge and real risks to their own finances, corporate reputations and even survival. Some of the cases in this chapter illustrate these risks, as well as the financial and other losses incurred by corporate buyers and investors, as well as by individual home buyers, as a result of such fraud. In addition, the 'risk bubble' of toxic debt entangled with fraud may expand to such an extent in a particular country that it threatens the stability and survival of the whole property sector and the whole banking sector as well as the government's financial position. In 2012, Spain and Cyprus were brought to the brink of national disaster (that is, potential bankruptcy of major banks and the government itself) whereby property debt bubbles inflated by fraud played a significant role.

Despite the obvious importance of immovable property fraud to corporate risk management, there are few risk management books that cover this topic in any detail or at all. Persuaded by a number of senior risk management professionals who were concerned at this gap, the author has sought in this chapter to provide an introduction to the topic, albeit a limited one.

## Caveat Emptor

*Caveat emptor* or 'buyer beware' remains the first guiding principle of property buying. This implies that it is the primary responsibility of the buyer to conduct their own research to satisfy themselves that the vendor's offer is honest and that their intended purchase will be 'safe'. Nevertheless, national and EU legislators and the courts have long recognized that, over and above *caveat emptor*, the public needs additional legal protection and safeguards in most areas of consumer transactions. For example, the Unfair Commercial Practices Directive 2005/29/EC places strict requirements, limitations and conditions on any vendor or their agents in an EU member state in what they do in relation to the sale of immovable property. On misleading omissions, the Directive states:

> *A commercial practice shall be regarded as misleading if, in its factual context, taking account of all its features and circumstances and the limitations of the communication medium, it omits material information that the average consumer needs, according to the context, to take an informed transactional decision and thereby causes or is likely to cause the average consumer to take a transactional decision that he would not have taken otherwise.*

Vendors or their agents must not in any way mislead or present false information so as to induce a prospective buyer to sign a contract of sale. Failing to disclose the existence of encumbrances on the title deeds would constitute one such example.

Despite the existence of such legal safeguards, experience has shown that many parties on whom the legal duties fall have been slow to recognize and implement the requirements upon them. In some cases, unscrupulous vendors of overseas property in the EU continue to ignore the Directive. Worse still, in at least one member state the government itself failed to implement the Directive for at least four years and has still to do so in any meaningful sense, despite being 'outed' in the international media.

With such a negative environment in some countries, the expectation that prospective foreign buyers of property will have sufficient time, knowledge and skills or indeed money to undertake adequate 'due diligence' checks on a prospective purchase is, frankly, unrealistic. Moreover, whereas in their home country the norm may be to rely on the honesty, integrity and competence of their own lawyer for much of the due diligence, in the target country such reliance is often wholly misplaced. In most jurisdictions, a lawyer is not allowed to act for both parties, but in some jurisdictions it is only a good practice expectation and is not enforced. Simply accepting a single joint lawyer, however charming he or she may be, nominated by the vendor is asking for trouble, as it is more than likely that they will be working 100 per cent in the vendor's interests. Indeed, there are many cases where overseas lawyers who appear to be paragons of integrity and virtue have turned out to be utterly unscrupulous, even to the extent of failing to disclose a business relationship with the vendor and conspiring with the vendor to defraud the lawyer's own client. In such environments, the limitations of *caveat emptor* become apparent and a purchaser may have to rely on finding an upright lawyer through recommendations by trusted contacts or 'approved' lawyers listed by embassies, although even the latter is no guarantee that every lawyer listed is scrupulous.

Experience shows that property fraud against foreign buyers flourishes successfully for the fraudsters in any particular country for a limited period only. As word spreads, buyers become more wary and, if the country's property fraud reputation is especially bad, new buyers simply stop coming or place demanding pre-conditions on any purchase. For example, the title deeds fraud scandal in Cyprus, which had been flourishing since the 1970s and especially since 2000, eventually became so well known around the world that by 2009–2010 a property without a title deed was virtually unsellable in Cyprus. Those involved in some way in perpetrating or enabling these frauds had failed to realize the impact on potential new foreign buyers of international media attention, 'holiday homes from hell' documentaries on television, public protests, lobbying campaigns by action groups, and high-profile court cases. Attempts by the fraudsters and their supporters to rally some kind of defence of the indefensible were simply obliterated by a relentless tide of outraged blogs from the public on the Internet.

Persistent bad publicity about property fraud in a country also acts as a warning signal to foreign companies thinking of operating in or investing in that country, whether in the property sector or other sectors. If fraud and bad practices are so bad in the property market, it is likely that they will also be bad in all sectors, especially if there is suspicion of state-sponsored entanglements in the wrongdoing.

## Types of Immovable Property Fraud

The common immovable property frauds by vendors, developers, agents, lawyers and banks against buyers typically fall into one or more of the following categories in Table 11.1:

**Table 11.1  Common frauds on buyers of immovable property**

| Category of Fraud | Fraud Mechanism |
| --- | --- |
| Impersonation; vendor is not real owner | The fraudster typically befriends a potential buyer and pretends to own a property for sale. The fraudster shows the buyer the property and persuades them to pay cash for a cut-price quick sale. Once the buyer has paid the fraudster, the 'owner' promptly disappears. |
| Developer does not own the land | The developer may have simply squatted on someone else's land. |
| Double selling | The fraudster (typically, a developer working in concert with corrupt agents and lawyers) agrees to sell a property to the buyer and receives down payment or even the bulk or full amount. Meanwhile, the fraudster sells the same property again to another buyer but pockets the first buyer's money. Sometimes, the same property will be sold to several buyers and all the monies pocketed. The fraud may not become evident to the various buyers for a considerable time after their transactions, especially if they normally live abroad. |

**Table 11.1 continued  Common frauds on buyers of immovable property**

| Category of Fraud | Fraud Mechanism |
|---|---|
| Hidden mortgages on land | A developer may have taken out a mortgage on the land prior to selling the house or apartments built on it. The existence of such a mortgage will prevent the buyer from obtaining a title deed until and unless the mortgage is cleared but only the lender can compel the borrower to discharge the mortgage. If the developer becomes a delinquent borrower, the bank may force a liquidation of the asset with the buyer relegated to lesser creditor status and suffering great loss. Despite the requirements of the EU Unfair Commercial Practices Directive, developers with the collusion of corrupt lawyers supposedly acting for the buyer have continued to hide pre-existing mortgages from buyers until after contract signature. |
| Off-plan deceptions | The buyer purchases off-plan but the as-built dwelling differs significantly in size and layout from the original plans and may contravene planning regulations. The developer may also submit additional invoices for unsolicited 'extras' beyond the agreed specification and price. |
| Failure to complete construction | The buyer signs an off-plan contract to pay for the property in stages as it is built. The developer and/or agents send the overseas buyer regular updates with photos of the developing project. The buyer sends stage payments accordingly. At some point, but often not until the supposed completion, the buyer discovers that either the progress is way behind the statements and photos sent by the developer, or that building work has ceased or that building had never started. In some instances, the developer has already disappeared with all the monies paid by various buyers, who may number hundreds on large apartment complexes. |
| Retention of title deeds | In most countries, the title deed as absolute proof of ownership must be handed over on the day of delivery (or shortly thereafter), either to the purchaser or to their lender. However, in a few countries, delays (sometimes up to 15 years or more) are caused by bureaucratic incompetence in the issuance process, exacerbated by fraud variously by developers, lawyers and banks. |
| Power of attorney abuses | For convenience, foreign buyers who may travel infrequently to the country of purchase may be persuaded to sign a PoA to their local lawyer. In some instances, crooked lawyers have abused the arrangements so as to tie the buyer to inappropriate and/or expensive commitments. Some lawyers have used legally void POAs and some have even forged PoAs from buyers. |
| Inflated/ expensive/ misleading mortgage arranged by vendor | Developers have persuaded buyers to buy with a 'preferential' mortgage that they will arrange with a friendly bank. Mortgage interest rates and terms are agreed orally. Later, the buyer discovers that the interest rate is several percentage points higher than quoted and the repayment period is much longer. Worse, the mortgage may be in an unsuitable currency, for example Swiss francs and unfavourable trends in currency exchange may have resulted in a huge increase in the mortgage repayments. |
| Misleading or deceptive advertisements, sales literature or sales contracts | Developers are often very economical with the truth in their advertisements, literature and contracts, contrary to the EU Unfair Commercial Practices Directive. For example, assertions aimed at persuading potential British buyers may state wrongly that the country's laws are identical to those of the UK when in fact they are quite different for property. Sales pitches may state that title deeds will be available in a matter of months when in fact it may take years. |

**Table 11.1 continued  Common frauds on buyers of immovable property**

| Category of Fraud | Fraud Mechanism |
|---|---|
| Selling a pig-in-a-poke property | For example, the developer knowingly builds on unsuitable land prone to flooding or subsidence, fails to build in adequate engineering safeguards and fails to advise the buyer of the hazards and defects. The property becomes dangerous and uninhabitable owing to subsidence or landslip. |
| Immovable Property Tax (IPT) fraud | Where a developer has been responsible for payment of IPT up the point of transfer of title deeds and can then reclaim the payments from the buyer, some developers have inflated their bill to the buyer by as much as 1,000 per cent. |

In addition to the above frauds perpetrated by individuals or entities selling property and/or those providing services to vendors or buyers, in some countries there is strong evidence that organs and officials of the state are also engaged in corrupt practices which defraud property buyers. Such practices include:

- Revaluation of registered contract prices by the land registry under, for example, 'discretionary powers' for taxation purposes, implying but without any cogent evidence that the vendor and purchaser agreed to artificially lower the sale price in the contract so as to lessen their respective taxation liabilities. With a false revaluation, the buyer has to pay higher transfer tax to the government. This type of deviant practice is currently prevalent in Cyprus.
- 'Land grab' orders without compensation by local authorities which allow the compulsory acquisition of private property by developers seeking land for new projects. This type of fraud has been prevalent in Spain.
- Planning authorities knowingly allowing buildings to be erected by developers without planning permits and/or allowing occupancy without the required certificate and/or refusing as-built planning certificates on dubious or minor grounds, presumably to induce illicit payments to clear the infringements (real or invented) or to obtain extra fees from planning amnesty applications. This type of disreputable practice is currently prevalent in Cyprus.

Where such state-sponsored fraud occurs on a systematic and widespread scale as opposed to isolated or rare instances, it may be classed as sovereign corruption (see Chapter 9). The particular state appears knowingly and deliberately to operate a system of fraud which unfairly benefits the state's taxation coffers and/or developers, at the expense of purchasers and all against the public interest. The alternative explanation for such a phenomenon would be that all the many instances merely arise spontaneously without any direction or purposeful input by state organs; they are but administrative errors and oversights. The problem with the 'entirely innocent' argument is that it not only frequently flies in the face of the evidence but also implies incompetence and negligence, if not the turning of blind eyes by senior officials, in relation to their departments' self-evident 'errors and oversights'.

## Cross-Border Property Buying in Europe

The property sector is characterized by a boom–bust model, which typically tracks the economic fortunes of the country. In the UK, the property slump from 1991 to 1996 was followed by a phenomenal rebound from 1996 to 2001. The market then slowed somewhat to 2004, followed by another upward trend before the global financial crisis hit in 2009. Since then, UK property prices have fallen significantly overall, although 'hot spots' remain in exclusive areas. Other countries, including the US, have had a similar experience. Those countries whose property markets rely heavily on foreign buyers from countries such as the UK and other northern European economies affected by recession or quasi-recession have also felt the pinch as individual buyers tend to protect their main residence and finances in their home country first and avoid new discretionary purchases of property overseas.

Since 1995, and particularly since 2000, the overseas 'holiday homes' market has mushroomed. This is especially so in Europe, with the large numbers of 'baby boomers' born after the Second World War in the industrialized major economies of northern Europe seeking a holiday or retirement home in the southern European countries bordering the Mediterranean. The author himself declares a personal interest as someone who entered the fray nearly a decade ago.

Let us be clear. Wherever there are people and property transactions, there is likely to be a proportion that is subject to fraud. In the developed countries of northern Europe, typically frauds are perpetrated by buyers deliberately making false mortgage applications or by crooked solicitors who pocket clients' money. The audit and anti-fraud systems employed by banks and building societies usually spot such frauds and action is taken. Such fraudsters are usually prosecuted, fined and often jailed. The Law Society in the UK publicizes all cases, including fraud, where members have been caught and struck off.

In southern Europe, however, property frauds are usually perpetrated against buyers (whether individual home buyers, individual investors or corporate investors) by unscrupulous property developers from whom they have bought and, frequently in such cases, the purchaser's local lawyer may be a co-conspirator with the developer against the buyer. Local estate agents could also well be involved and there is now abundant evidence that local banks have also been widely engaged in highly reprehensible activities which many people would describe as property fraud against buyers. Worse still, there is evidence that in some countries government departments and the judiciary have been encouraging and backing such frauds through a combination of incompetence, negligence and corrupt relationships and practices.

There have been some attempts at the European level to combat the worst excesses but, thus far, success has been limited. A number of Members of the European Parliament (MEPs) have been proactive in seeking to help constituents who allege they are victims of property fraud or attempted fraud in an EU member state, usually involving the buyers (as victims) from one EU country and the alleged fraud being perpetrated against them in another EU country. A large part of the difficulty in getting any kind of tough action and justice from the EU Commission centres on the fact that complainants must first exhaust all local legal remedies available within the member state where the alleged fraud occurred before any action will be considered by the EU itself. Legal actions within some member states can often take years and, in those states that are essentially antagonistic towards protecting the rights of foreign buyers, experience has shown (for example, CPAG

2007, 2011 and Howarth 2011) that plaintiffs are unlikely to be treated sympathetically or to receive redress from the courts. The attitude of the EU Commission, however, is that if a semblance of a legal redress system exists in the member state it is up to plaintiffs to use it; if they fail to get the result they want, that is not the EU's concern as, in the Commission's eyes, justice has been served.

There is evidence that some member state governments submit flagrantly misleading statements (some people call them outright lies) to the EU Commission to the effect that the member state has an efficient and effective system of legal protection and remedies for all alleged victims of property fraud, including foreigners. The EU Commission then compounds the problem by tamely accepting the false self-certification from the member state, presumably on the basis that every member state government must be assumed *a priori* to be scrupulously honest and incapable of lying to the Commission to serve its own ends. Moreover, as mentioned in Chapter 9, the tough wording of EU Directives is not backed up at EU level by any kind of monitoring, audit and control function, and implementation of the Directives is left to each member state 'on its honour'. As cases within this chapter show, some member states have been extremely lax in implementing EU Directives in so far as immovable property is concerned, both in the letter and the intended purpose of protecting EU citizens. For example, it has only been as a result of sustained pressure on the EU Commission by local self-help action groups representing aggrieved property buyers, mainly foreigners, in particular EU member states that the Commission has been forced to re-visit its previous brush-off declarations that all is well in these states. Only when the Commissioners have been confronted by overwhelming and compelling evidence from such groups which contradicts the member state government's blandishments have they conceded that a re-examination was warranted. For example, in one instance, for several years the member state (Cyprus) failed to publicize the existence of EU Directive 2005/29/EC Unfair Commercial Practices or that it had been adopted into local legislation (CPAG 2011). When found out, the Government continued to exercise only perfunctory implementation of the Directive and continued to deny, despite the explicit and unambiguous wording of the Directive, that the Directive applies to the selling of all immovable property.

The flaws and weaknesses in the protection of cross-border property buyers in Europe prompted Diana Wallis MEP to compile a report 'European Property Rights and Wrongs' (Wallis and Allanson 2011), which seeks to lay out the nature of the problems and a way forward for the EU to do and achieve far more to protect EU citizens' fundamental human rights. Contributors to the book advocate a European Land Law. According to Wallis, EU Justice Commissioner Viviane Reding has proposed 2013 as the 'European Year of Citizens' during which 'the Commission will need to demonstrate a European system of justice that has the capability to link, overlay or check national legal systems in a way that can produce some sort of coherent whole as citizens go about their daily lives'. Unfortunately, such fine rhetoric is likely to sound hollow and meaningless to the thousands of aggrieved victims who remain unprotected, without redress and deeply cynical and mistrustful of the EU and its Commission. They will not be expecting that Commissioner Reding will wave a magic wand in 2013 and deliver even a scintilla of protection and justice for them any time soon.

Two countries, Spain and Cyprus, top the list of EU member states having bad, if not appalling, reputations for frauds against property buyers. These two countries are cited in Diana Wallis's report (Wallis and Allanson 2011), with Spain being given the most attention. Spain and Cyprus not only lie at opposite ends of the Mediterranean but they are also opposites in terms of land mass, population, GDP, economic diversity and numbers of foreign buyers of property. Spain is big on all these measures whereas Cyprus is tiny. Nevertheless, recent Government census data (CySTAT 2012) show that 21.4 per cent of Cyprus's 840,000 population is now foreign, the majority from Greece, UK, Romania and Bulgaria. Between 2003 and 2011, the percentage of overseas property buyers in Cyprus was 34.13 per cent of the 129,848 properties sold over that period (DoLS 2012), the majority being sold to buyers from the UK.

The Cyprus property market has a disproportionately high dependency on foreign buyers and also has one of the highest incidences in the EU of alleged fraud and wrongdoing against buyers. What happens in this market in a country such as Cyprus is a very good barometer for risk exposures in other sectors and aspects of the economy. The imperative need for any company considering operating in or investing in any foreign country to undertake a rigorous due diligence exercise beforehand should be self-evident. The following section outlines the nature and extent of the problem in Cyprus as a somewhat extreme example of how things can go badly wrong.

## The Cyprus Property Scandal

Many property buyers in Cyprus have been hit by fraud and thousands still cannot obtain their title deeds. Despite much vaunted Government plans to rectify the property mess, business leaders agree that even if these work it could well take up to two generations for the global stigma and its marketplace consequences to fade. Since 2004, the main complaint by Cyprus property buyers, particularly foreigners, has been non-issuance of title deeds, sometimes intertwined with fraud allegations. Typically, the developer has taken a prior mortgage on the land, which was either not disclosed or deliberately hidden but, in any event, not revealed because of non-existent or negligent searches by the purchaser's local lawyer. Non-discharged mortgages add to developer foot dragging and outrageously long bureaucratic delays. Some 130,000 properties were still in 2012 awaiting their title deeds, typically for seven to 15 years or more as noted above. Some 40,000 of these properties have been bought by non-Cypriots, primarily from the UK. Indeed, despite new legislation in 2011 aimed at breaking the log-jam, the number of outstanding title deeds for properties bought by foreigners actually increased from 29,949 in October 2008 to 40,170 by the end of November 2011. Since the year 2000 to the end of December 2011, of 51,500 properties purchased by foreigners less than 11,500 had received transfer of their title deeds. As Professor Andonis Vassiliades has noted (Vassiliades 2009), a title deed is nothing more than a certified receipt by the government that Party A has bought a property from Party B and is now the full legal owner of the property. In Cyprus, however, right of ownership as affirmed by the issuance of a title deed has become entangled with and dependent on compliance with planning regulations which have nothing to do with and no bearing on that right. The fact that successive governments over the 25 years up to the end of 2012 failed to introduce the simple 'on day of completion' issuance procedure adopted by all other developed countries led inevitably to accusations that powerful vested interests, such as developers and banks, had corruptly influenced ministers and Parliament against such a change.

The consequences for a buyer not receiving title deeds can be very serious if the developer has not discharged any of his prior mortgages on the land, as the lender (usually a Cyprus bank) has first charge on the property. At best, the innocent buyer who has already paid in full or the bulk of the contract price has only a registered financial interest in the property whereas the bank can, in principle, seek liquidation of the asset if the borrower (the developer) defaults on the mortgage or goes bust. Since 2007, there have been a number of significant developer collapses in Cyprus, including A&G Froiber, SNK Venus/SNK Exclusive and Liasides, as well as the large UK-based property broker Parador Properties. As the following cases 11.1 and 11.2 illustrate, banks have not been shy in seeking to liquidate and pursue the buyers for the developer's bad debts rather than pursue the developer personally and his guarantors.

## Case 11.1   The A&G Froiber Collapse

On 18 September 2009, A&G Property Wise Development Ltd operating under the Froiber brand collapsed and went into liquidation. The liquidation had been prompted by the Government's Social Security Fund on the grounds that the company had persistently failed to pay its social insurance obligations to employees over several years and appeared unable to pay all the arrears. Even in 2003, figures show that the company's liabilities were €15 million and it was verging on insolvency. However, a large number of property buyers who had already paid A&G Froiber for their property had not received their title deeds prior to the company's collapse. Many then found themselves in conflict with the banks which had issued mortgages to A&G on the same properties.

Over the succeeding months, it was reported that such buyers received letters from the banks which threatened the buyers that they would not receive their title deeds unless and until they contributed a 'symbolic' amount of €8,000 per apartment towards the outstanding debt of the liquidated developer. In addition, the letters demanded a larger sum to help pay off the developer's tax liabilities to the Inland Revenue. The outcome is as yet unclear but at one stage a bank spokesman was unequivocal that liquidation could well result in buyers losing their property and, at best, receiving only a percentage of the liquidation money.

Allegations also emerged that in some instances the banks, after the individual apartments had been bought and unbeknown to the buyers, had issued loans to the developer with charges against these properties as collateral. In December 2008, the developer had received the title deeds of nine apartments in his name and the buyers all then insisted on transfer to them. However, it was reported that the developer demanded that they first pay him the outstanding Immovable Property Taxes, other expenses and the Transfer Tax (normally the Transfer Tax is paid directly by the purchaser at the Land Registry and not to the developer). Reluctantly agreeing, they paid up on 2 February 2009 and the developer gave them a written undertaking that he would transfer the deeds within three weeks. On that basis, the buyers' lawyer obtained a court order to be executed on 3 April 2009. However, the developer failed to attend the Land Registry as directed by the court and instead issued the buyers with a further demand for outstanding taxes. A buyer then issued a writ for non-performance but the court date was far later than the liquidation date. It was also reported that the developer had failed to pay any of the taxes he had collected from the buyers.

The final outcome is not yet known. However, questions that have been raised in public debate include how the banks could have issued further loans to the developer against properties that had already been sold and without informing the buyers or obtaining their prior agreement.

## Case 11.2   Liasides Bankruptcy and Alpha Bank

In December 2011, Alpha Bank sought permission from the Land Registry to auction eight plots of land it had repossessed from the bankrupt developer Yiannis Liasides. The land included some 70 homes (over 100 residents) which had been bought and paid for from Liasides before he went bankrupt. When he ceased trading in 2007, some 250 people across 14 sites had bought properties from him but had not received their title deeds.

Evidence has emerged that the developer took out mortgages on a number of the properties just before buyers signed their contracts and unbeknown to them. It is unclear whether or not the buyers' lawyers were aware of the mortgages prior to contract but, if they were, they failed to tell their clients or advise them against signing their contracts.

Victims of the Liasides/Alpha Bank debacle are among a number of cases of alleged contravention by Cyprus of the EU Unfair Commercial Practices Directive now lodged with the European Court of Human Rights (ECHR).

Not all the cases involving apparent moral delinquency and financial mismanagement by Cyprus banks centre on actual bankruptcy of developers and liquidation by the banks of dwellings already bought and paid for by innocent buyers. A far greater number of cases involve reckless lending by the banks over the past decade to developers who were never likely to be able to pay off the loans. A common assumption frequently voiced privately within the business community is that the banks have lent out a huge amount of money to Cyprus developers who number at least 1,200 and possibly as many as 3,500. The popular reason cited for why the banks do not seem to be pursuing non-performing loans (NPLs) after the standard 90-day default, contrary to Basel II and Central Bank instructions, is that (a) it would cause a collapse of the property sector, the banks and the national economy, (b) bank officials are alleged to often have nepotistic or otherwise corrupt relationships with particular developer borrowers, (c) the banks are alleged to hide NPLs to developers by each time either switching the borrowing account to a new file just before it would become an NPL or, alternatively, (d) justifying a non-NPL classification on the grounds that the loan is backed by collateral (such as title deeds, including those relating to some of the 130,000 transfer backlog referred to above), even though such practices are considered highly improper in the normal banking world. The fact that the two main Cyprus banks, Bank of Cyprus and Marfin Laiki Bank (now Cyprus Popular Bank), were relegated to junk status by the global credit agencies in the first quarter of 2012, primarily owing to their high exposure to the debts and bonds of the mainland Greek banks and the Greek economy, hardly inspired confidence that their exposure to local developer debt was under control. International Monetary Fund data (IMF 2011) show that Cyprus banks had assets (and potential liabilities) totalling €152 billion or some eight and a half times the country's GDP of approximately €17.5 billion.

Market analysts Stockwatch (2009) commented on Cyprus developer risk exposures from unsold properties and put their total borrowings at €5.9 billion, based on official data, but by 2013 it was thought to be significantly higher and possibly as high as €10 billion. Bohdjalian (2012) states that, as Spanish banks were forced to do, Cyprus banks urgently needed to offload €billions of property left on their books by developers who technically were bankrupt but protected by the banks' corrupt policies. On 26 June 2012, Cyprus formally requested bailout assistance from the EU, first estimated by the Troika (EU, European Central Bank and the IMF) to be some €17.5 billion or 100 per cent of GDP to cover both bank and government debts. The Troika identified that while exposure to Greece's debt problems had been instrumental in the crisis for Cyprus banks, many of the latters' problems were home grown and related to over-expansion in the property sector as a consequence of the banks' poor risk management. The Cyprus Central Bank governor Mr Panicos Demetriades went further and accused the banks not just of poor risk management but also of 'casino banking'. On the 130,000 title deeds backlog, the Troika specifically required the government by quarter 4 of 2014 to 'eliminate the title deeds issuance backlog to less than 2,000 cases' that remained pending for more than 1 year. It remains to be seen whether this requirement will be met.

After much wrangling, a €10 billion bailout deal was reached on 25 March 2013, barely 24 hours before withdrawal of €9 billion in European Emergency Protection(EMP) from the Laiki Popular Bank. As part of stringent conditions imposed on Cyprus, Laiki Popular was to be dismantled and its EMP debt transferred to the Bank of Cyprus.

The following case 11.3 illustrates one way in which the banks have been reckless and thereby have encouraged, or have been complicit in, fraud against purchasers.

## Case 11.3  Tiny Developer, Massive Borrowings

A small developer who started around 2000 built modest developments in and around his home village. Over a ten-year period, he built only a few such developments of apartments. One business investor who had bought several apartments decided in 2011 to pursue his title deeds but found the developer difficult to contact and unresponsive. He then decided to do a search on the developer at the Registrar of Companies, which among other things lists every mortgage and loan taken out by a company, the date started, the bank and whether the particular borrowing is still open or discharged. To his consternation, he discovered that over a ten-year period his developer had borrowed from several different banks nearly €40 million in total and none of the loans or mortgages had been discharged. To the buyer's knowledge, the developer had not built anything since 2008, had no new projects being planned and had no known source of significant income. The non-discharged mortgages probably explained why the developer could not, and did not want to, obtain and release the title deeds to this buyer. How was the developer servicing these massive loans? Even if he could, would he ever be able to pay them off. If this case typifies the lax lending of the banks, even if on average they had lent out only €5 million to each of 2,000 developers, the outstanding developer debt burdening the banks would amount to €10 billion. It is rumoured that some of the larger developers have debts ranging from €100 million to over €400 million each. The proportion of this that is toxic and virtually non-recoverable increased as the property market remained stubbornly flat since 2008–2009 and developers were unable to service their loans and mortgages.

However, in addition to hidden mortgages, some cases have also involved alleged 'double selling' fraud whereby the developer sells a property to Party A, fails to lodge the contract with the Land Registry and then sells it again to Party B (possibly for a higher price) but fails to reimburse Party A. There are also alleged variants of this scam. In a number of cases, it has been alleged that developers have sold the same property several times over and inexplicably in some cases all the contracts of sale appear to have been lodged with the Land Registry. Since the Government through the Attorney General has determined that most cases of this kind are civil wrongs and not criminal offences, the police will not accept information laid before them and will not proceed with a criminal investigation. One suggested reason is that the Attorney General has imposed a very high hurdle list of five criteria, all of which must be met before a criminal case will be considered. One criterion is particularly onerous, namely that the fraud complainant must have suffered actual and significant pecuniary loss. Foreign companies and investors need to be aware that a fraudulent act, however flagrant and damaging, does not in itself constitute a crime in Cyprus, unlike in many other countries. So, if for example, an attempted fraud is discovered and defeated before it succeeds, the perpetrator is not pursued by the police. If the significant pecuniary loss is clearly evident from the perpetrator's actions but not yet actually materialized, the police will not act. Perhaps it is also felt that there are so many potential property fraud cases that to accept one as warranting criminal investigation would open the floodgates to hundreds, if not thousands of others, that would both swamp the police and add to international embarrassment. However, an official blanket denial that property fraud is a crime may not be effective in quelling angry buyers, investment boycotts or international reaction. It may, in colloquial parlance, simply throw fuel on the fire.

For many years, the standard claim by the Cyprus Government, developers, lawyers and estate agents has been that a buyer of immovable property is absolutely protected once his or her sales contract is lodged with the Cyprus Land Registry. This claim, supported by a precedent Supreme Court ruling, has been their main counter to the avalanche of allegations, criticism, anger and demands for justice from property buyers, largely from foreigners and their MEPs.

In line with this claim, on 22 July 2009 the then Minister of the Interior, Mr Neoclis Sylikiotis, issued a lengthy official statement about the title deeds scandal, noting that 'those allegations are entirely unsustainable'. He further clarified that 'the current system and the existing legislation protects buyers and their ownership status'. He went on: '... the ownership status of a buyer–owner of immovable property in Cyprus is definitely secured and cannot be challenged, as long as the buyer–owner has submitted the buying-contract to the Department of Lands and Surveys.' Finally, he emphasized that: '... there is something that one must not forget. Nobody and no Authority anywhere can ever challenge the property rights or ownership status of buyers of immovable property within the territory which is under the control of the Republic of Cyprus.' A few days earlier, in a letter to Sir Graham Watson MEP, Mr Sylikiotis's aide had stated: '... buyers of immovable property are protected, once they deposit the Contract of Sale at the appropriate District Office of the Department of Lands and Surveys according to the Sale of Lands (Specific Performance) Law, Cap 232.'

What possibly could be doubted from such emphatic statements from the Minister himself, backed up a Supreme Court ruling? Well, the judge in the private criminal prosecution brought by Conor O'Dwyer clearly thought otherwise.

# Case 11.4   The Conor O'Dwyer versus Karayiannas Scandal

Mr O'Dwyer alleged that he paid Cyp£66,000 towards an off-plan property in Frenaros from the developers Karayiannas. Midway through construction, O'Dwyer raised some concerns about the build work. The developers then accused O'Dwyer of missing a stage payment, which he denies, and they commenced civil litigation against him for breach of contract. However, he alleged that the developers then immediately sold his property again to another buyer at a higher price and also failed to return his money. He alleged that this happened without his knowledge or permission and despite his contract having been deposited at the Land Registry for specific performance. As the Attorney General views such issues as civil and not criminal, Mr O'Dwyer felt obliged to take out a private prosecution for fraud under section 303A of the penal code against both the developers and the second buyer (who now occupies the property).

The defendants were found not guilty of 'double selling' fraud. Apparently, the judge decided that the prosecution had failed to prove, as required under criminal law, that the defendants had committed fraud 'beyond all reasonable doubt'.

In the author's opinion as a non-lawyer, the prosecution would have had to prove a deliberate intention to permanently deprive the rightful owner of his property. The judge acknowledged that O'Dwyer was the rightful owner and that he had lodged his sales contract at the Land Registry. She further acknowledged that he had made stage payments as per contract and that the developers had not returned his money, despite having re-sold the property to another person. The fact that the developers apparently have never offered or made any reimbursement of his money appears to demonstrate a deliberate intention to permanently deprive him of the property. Under civil law, *res ipsa loquitur* (the thing speaks for itself) and 'on the balance of probabilities' would apply. However, this was a criminal case and the judge felt that intent was not proven beyond all reasonable doubt.

One might reasonably ask what other logical reason could be put forward for what they did. It cannot have been just an error or forgetfulness, as the matter was brought swiftly to their attention. By eliminating other potential defences such as insanity and intoxication, that just leaves 'lack of intent' but the purposefulness with which they went about it strongly suggests intent. After all these years and no hint of a repayment, the intent also looks pretty permanent.

However, just as disturbing, and contrary to the precedent Supreme Court ruling, the judge also stated that lodging of a sales contract at the Land Registry does not automatically confer protection against 'double selling': 'The fact they (plaintiffs) submitted a sales contract to the Land Registry did not mean they automatically and in perpetuity have become the 'owners' (as they mean it) of the residence.' This judgement thus appeared to cancel the standard claim by government, developers, lawyers and agents that buyers are absolutely protected. An appeal ruling was still pending at the time of writing.

In September 2012, regarding the double selling issue, O'Dwyer received a civil judgement in his favour over the allegation that the developers unlawfully and unilaterally terminated his original contract of sale without refunding him the money he had paid. The developers were ordered to pay him €141,000 plus interest. However, the court also found him guilty of running an Internet website www.lyingbuilder.com that defamed the developers and ordered him to pay them some €60,000 plus interest.

O'Dwyer brought a number of other legal actions against the developers. While collecting video evidence of the property in question, Mr O'Dwyer alleged that senior representatives of the developer arrived and assaulted him (see also Howarth 2012 for similar case). In his absence, a criminal case of assault was dropped but later the developers (father and son) were found guilty in the civil court and ordered to pay damages. On O'Dwyer's next trip to Cyprus, a further assault took place and this time his injuries were serious enough to keep him in hospital for a week. For this second assault, the father and son were sentenced to suspended jail terms of ten months each. A third defendant was fined €3,000. An appeal of this sentencing and a civil claim for damages against them were pending at the time of writing.

The following cases 11.5 and 11.6 are further examples involving 'double selling'.

## Case 11.5   K&M Famagusta

K&M Famagusta Developers and Construction Ltd was established in 2005 by Kypros Kyprianou, who was not a newcomer to property development in Cyprus. During the 1980s, he ran Kyprianou Estates until he was prosecuted for double selling fraud, fled to Germany, was extradited back to Cyprus and then spent most of the 1990s in jail for fraud offences. Released in 2000, he later set up K&M Famagusta Developers.

In August 2010, the police announced that they were pursuing K&M over eight complaints filed since 2007 involving alleged forgery, obtaining money and property under false pretences and usurping property belonging to another person (Psyllides 2010a and b). Specifically, double selling was cited in at least one of the cases in which a buyer bought the property off-plan in 2007 for €131,000. He arranged his own mortgage and kept up all his stage payments to the developer. However, when the building work was nearly finished and the buyer had already handed over €120,000, apparently he discovered that another buyer was also laying claim to the property. Owing to an 'error' by the Land Registry, when he had lodged his contract of sale with the Land Registry, they failed to notice or inform that there was a prior contract lodged by an earlier buyer which should have prompted them to reject his contract. He was therefore lulled into a false sense of security, had taken out a personal mortgage for the purchase and, while the property was being built, had handed over €120,000 to the developer. When asked by the aggrieved buyer for the return of his money, it was alleged that the developer issued him with a dud cheque twice.

The police also announced that Kyprianou had been arrested in January 2010 and had admitted some of the charges. Immediately following the police announcement in August, the developer issued vehement public denials that he had done anything wrong or that his company was anything but in the pink of financial strength and probity.

It emerged that K&M had been struck off the registry of the Contractor Registration and

Oversight Council in May 2009 and thereafter had been unlicensed. On 6 August 2010, Kyprianou was put on the 'stop list' so that he could not leave the island. At the time of writing, the outcome of the various criminal cases and charges against him has not yet emerged.

One puzzling aspect of the whole K&M Famagusta/Kyprianou affair is why, of the many cases of alleged property fraud involving broadly similar allegations, the Attorney General decided to authorize a police criminal investigation in this one. It remains a very rare exception to the normal rule from his office that such cases are civil matters. Some have suggested that he needed to make a gesture to an increasingly sceptical public and critical international press and show that he was prepared to treat some instances as criminal cases.

## Case 11.6    Lane Homes

In 2009, a court issued a judgement in favour of the plaintiffs in a flagrant case of double selling fraud which had nearly resulted in their complete loss of the property they had paid for (Christou 2009). A British couple bought a property from developers Lane Homes for a price of £Cyp400,000 as a rental investment. They paid for the property off-plan, that is in stages but, as they were not satisfied that the developer had fulfilled all his contractual obligations, they withheld the final £Cyp23,000 and instead gave it to their Cypriot lawyers to hold in trust until the work had been finally completed satisfactorily and they could take possession.

By chance, they discovered in March 2009 that the locks on house had been tampered with and that other people were in process of buying the property. Further, unbeknown to them, the developers had gone to court alleging that the couple had defaulted on their stage payments, despite knowing that the final payment was in escrow. The couple's lawyer failed to inform them of the developers' action against them. The case went ahead and, in their absence, the developer obtained a court order for repossession and the couple were ordered to remove their contract of sale from the Land Registry within seven days. The court made no order for return of the £Cyp377,000 the couple had already paid.

Fortunately, the couple quickly appointed a new lawyer (Yiannos Georgiades) who acted immediately to get the judgement set aside as there was clear evidence of an abuse of judicial process. Mr Georgiades then discovered that the developers were using none other than the couple's first lawyers and possibly in violation of the Cyprus Bar Association's (CBA) conflict of interest rules. Evidence backed up by technical experts from the couple's Internet Service Provider also showed that the developers had submitted false evidence to the court in the form of concocted e-mails purportedly showing that the couple had been informed of the initial court case.

The couple narrowly escaped losing their entire investment and were granted possession of the house. However, as Georgiades noted, the developer had sold the same house to new buyers for £Cyp550,000 (£Cyp150,000 more than the first couple). This double selling had now been reported as a criminal offence. Moreover, the new buyers had now become exposed legally. So far as is known, the couple's original lawyer has not been disciplined by the CBA and the Disciplinary Board, has not been prosecuted and is still operating unfettered.

It should be noted that there are highly reputable, honest and competent lawyers in Cyprus. Regrettably, there are also negligent and/or corrupt lawyers who feature in a number of cases. Ostensibly, the CBA is the professional body for lawyers and to practise as a lawyer in court in Cyprus requires CBA membership. The CBA supposedly sets professional standards and a Disciplinary Board of Advocates (DBA) exists. However, owing to a lack of transparency which is an essential requirement of good governance, evidence available to the public that these bodies take their respective licensing and disciplinary roles seriously is sparse.

The DBA does not appear to actively pursue allegations of member misconduct in a way that would automatically engender greater public trust and confidence in Cyprus lawyers and the courts. For example, the Bar Association could change its policy and openly publish statements on its property conveyance standards and on its response to all allegations of misconduct against named members. A published summary of disciplinary cases and disbarment statistics would also be both illuminating and a sign of the CBA's integrity. On the contrary, the CBA is highly secretive and refuses point-blank any suggestion that it should become more transparent and ethical, in the public interest and for the good reputation of its members as a whole.

With such a growing number of allegations of professional misconduct, including fraud, against CBA members, especially in property-related cases, it is germane to consider the purpose, function and duties of a professional body. A professional body exists primarily to protect the public from the activities of rogues, quacks and charlatans and should never allow itself to fall into the trap of becoming a trade union protecting the interests of its members at the expense of its duties to the public. One would therefore expect any professional body to act swiftly – and publicly – at the merest hint of impropriety.

In English law, it is standard for civil cases to await the outcome of related criminal cases so that a higher standard of proof ('beyond reasonable doubt') has been tested, although in property cases it may sometimes be preferable to deal with any civil proceedings first. Cyprus law references, for example Neocleous (2000), state that in determining whether actions are fraudulent, the authorities 'must concentrate on the acts committed and determine whether the taking was deliberate and intentional'. The general 'lack of intent' exemption from criminal liability therefore does not normally apply if there is *prima facie* evidence that, for example, a developer has both received payment from one buyer, kept the money and then sold it again to a second buyer (or, in some cases, more than two!) and refused or failed to return the first buyer's money. The UK's SFO also makes it clear that in English law property fraud is a criminal offence and that, although running a civil case first before a criminal case may sometimes be preferable, the seriousness of the case and the public interest may warrant a criminal case at the earliest opportunity.

However, as the Cyprus Attorney General appears to have repudiated all this in relation to property offences, the police cannot act. It is puzzling why property crime has been singled out for this special dispensation. Why not also for murder, rape, robbery or blackmail? Why are long-winded civil cases forced on property victims before a criminal investigation is allowed, even when strong *prima facie* evidence of a crime exists? A perverse parody of English law appears to be acted out.

Foreign corporate and business investors, as well as individuals, have also been among the victims of what might be termed property 'mis-selling', although the author considers it to be simply a type of fraud. A number of corporate and business investors have consulted the author on aspects of their risk exposures relating to Cyprus. Typically,

Cypriot developers and their agents have sold investors up to ten or more units each off-plan in large coastal developments such as golfing and leisure complexes, with promises of all-year-round rental income at high rates. The reality is that many developers got into financial difficulty and some developments for which investors had already paid some or all of the money, many via bank mortgages, were not completed. Of those that were completed, many if not most have sat idle as rent generators because sufficient numbers of tenants did not come forward owing to the downturn in the tourist market and the often absurdly high rents demanded on the basis of the developers' unwarranted statements during mis-selling. Also, there are distinct seasonal variations in rental demand. Banks then sought repossession. As one example, in June 2012 a group of UK investors successfully obtained a ruling by the High Court in London that their civil case for damages against the Cypriot developer Alpha Panareti and its agents could be heard under UK jurisdiction rather than in Cyprus, where doubts existed about judicial impartiality and efficiency. They alleged that the company and its sales agents in the UK had engaged in negligent misrepresentation and the company was in breach of contract. Previously, the MEP Mr David Alton had raised in the European Parliament a question regarding an alleged fraudulent off-plan property scheme operated by the company and BBC Inside Out had also broadcast an investigation into a dubious £500 million property scheme run by the company. At the time of writing, the civil case had not been concluded and it was reported that British police were still investigating.

The following case 11.7 illustrates further some of the problems faced by aggrieved property buyers when seeking legal redress in Cyprus. Although the plaintiffs were private home buyers, there is every reason to believe that a business or corporate investor might have faced similar problems. Dissatisfaction with lawyers' conduct has been frequently cited to the author by aggrieved buyers, both corporate and individual.

## Case 11.7   The McClays versus Lemoniati Case

In October 2005, Mr and Mrs McClay from Scotland appointed Emily Lemoniati as their local lawyer to assist in the conveyancing to purchase a property from Paschalis Holdings Ltd. The McClays gave Miss Lemoniati a conditional PoA requiring her to obtain their faxed authority on any occasion that she wished to use it The contract of sale was signed on 25 October 2005. On 2 June 2006, the McClays e-mailed Miss Lemoniati requesting confirmation that their contract had been deposited with the Land Registry and she replied by e-mail that this was correct.

The McClays paid for the property in full and took possession in December 2006. Over the next 18 months, disputes arose between the McClays and the developer over snagging issues and, in October 2008, they advised Paschalis Holdings that they were changing lawyers in order to pursue the outstanding repairs. When in May 2009, the McClays appointed new lawyers Andreas Neocleous and Co, Miss Lemoniati was formally notified that her PoA was revoked and she was asked to hand over their file to their new lawyers.

On conducting a search at the Land Registry, the new lawyers discovered that the McClays' contract had not been lodged until 21 October 2008 and not in 2005 as Miss Lemoniati had stated in her e-mail in June 2006. Furthermore, the McLays denied all knowledge of a second contract, apparently signed by them and dated 10 October 2008, which she submitted to the Land Registry on 21 October 2008. In addition to the apparent unauthorized inclusion of their signatures, the McClays reported that there were other glaring errors, inconsistencies and contradictions throughout the document. To make matters worse, the Land Registry search also revealed that on 1 March 2006 (two months after the legal cut-off date for the deposit of their actual contract dated 25 October 2005) a mortgage of €598,010.50 with Hellenic Bank had been registered against their property and nine others. This mortgage was removed in December 2009 and replaced by four others totalling €951,930.

The McClays filed a complaint with the police about Miss Lemoniati's actions but she sought to deflect the allegations by accusing them of demanding €100,000 from her with menaces. With the police investigation stalled, in July 2009 the McClays also filed a complaint about her with the CBA. After much delay, the case was heard by the DBA and during a lengthy series of hearings the strength of the McClays' submission and evidence became increasingly clear. Apparently, the defendant admitted during the proceedings that the second contract had been created by her and submitted to the Land Registry three years too late to prevent the developer raising a mortgage on the plaintiffs' property.

In March 2012, the Disciplinary Board issued its decision finding for the McClays on two counts of 'dishonourable or uncompromising (sic) conduct to the advocate's profession'. However, the Disciplinary Board felt it appropriate only to fine her €1,000 and give her an admonishment rather than removal of her practising licence. According to media reports, Miss Lemoniati refused to apologize to the Board or to the McClays for her unprofessional conduct.

With such a welter of bad cases, a false impression could be gained that the small country of Cyprus is awash with fraudsters. The fact is that the vast majority of the population are law-abiding and do not go around defrauding people. The country has, however, become cursed by the activities of a hard-core minority sub-culture of greedy and unscrupulous developers, property agents, lawyers and bankers who, individually, severally and in concert, have succeeded in destroying a once buoyant market and a good reputation. Their adverse impact is out of all proportion to their small numbers. Not all lawyers and developers are crooks, any more than all developers are, but the good get tarred with the same brush as the bad. Regrettably, the supine attitude of the CBA and other relevant representative bodies in the property industry on these matters indicates that they do not want to clean up the bad practices for which, through inaction, they bear a major responsibility. They could and should have done it years ago. The active and passive engagement of departments and functions in successive governments, from the very top downwards, in perpetuating this state of affairs, is also virtually a seal of official approval and so invites the accusation of sovereign corruption.

Persistent bad publicity about property fraud in a country, especially if there is suspicion of state-sponsored entanglements or sovereign corruption in the wrongdoing, also acts as a warning to foreign companies thinking of operating in or investing in that country in any sector. Investment decisions require that the investor has a large measure of trust and confidence in the target country and awareness of a stream of media and Internet reports on property fraud allegations will almost certainly dampen the investor's enthusiasm. Due diligence checks and investigations by foreign companies therefore have to be that much more rigorous and penetrating before investment commitments and decisions are made.

# 12 *Combatting Intellectual Property Threats*

Who has not at least been tempted to buy those dirt-cheap 'global branded' DVDs, CDs, computer games, T-shirts, perfumes or trainers from the car boot sale or street hawker? It is easy to imagine that buying cheap fakes is harmless but counterfeit goods sales are not a victimless crime. Brands are damaged, company profits and jobs are lost, whole economies suffer and people are sometimes injured or killed by unsafe products, whether counterfeit or legitimate. These issues and other theft of IP feature prominently in trade concerns raised by Western governments against China in particular and other Asian countries.

The US Government Trade Representative's Office produces annual statistics regarding copyright industry losses (USTR 2007 and 2008). For the Asia Pacific Region, for the two years 2005 and 2006 the total estimated trade losses were just over US$6 billion in each year. The US Government's so-called 301 List of countries that would be penalized for failing to impose effective IP controls placed India, PRC and Thailand in the Priority Watch List. Others on the Watch List were Indonesia, Malaysia, Pakistan, Philippines, South Korea, Taiwan and Vietnam and many of these remain on that list. The following are some relevant estimates (USTR 2007 and 2008, OECD 2007, CMPI 2005, IACC 2005, Youill 2007a and b) on IP theft:

- international global counterfeit trade is over US$400 billion annually;
- approximately 5–7 per cent of the world trade is in counterfeit goods;
- global counterfeit drugs market estimated at US$32 billion in 2003 and US$40 billion in 2005;
- the entertainment industry loses over US$20 billion annually to piracy;
- in the US alone, over 750,000 jobs had been lost (time period unspecified) as a result of counterfeit merchandise (IACC 2005);
- some companies are losing 40 per cent of revenue to such theft;
- for the Asia Pacific Region alone, for the two years 2005 and 2006 the total estimated trade losses to copyright theft were just over US$6 billion in each year.

According to Interpol (www.interpol.int):

*Trademark counterfeiting and copyright piracy are serious IP crimes that defraud consumers, threaten the health of patients, cost society billions of dollars in lost government revenues, foreign investments or business profits and violate the rights of trademark, patent, and copyright owners. Fake products pose a significant safety threat to consumers worldwide. Unsuspecting customers and patients put their health, and even lives, in jeopardy each time they use fake medicines, alcoholic beverages, food products and travel in automobiles or aircraft maintained with substandard counterfeit parts.*

According to Smith (2007), 'The cost of piracy to the US economy, from a recently-released study, amounted to at least $58 billion in 2006, cost 373,375 jobs and $16.3 billion in earnings, and resulted in lost government tax revenue of $2.6 billion. Reducing piracy globally is an economic and policy necessity.'

The European Commission's report on counterfeiting and piracy for 2007 (EC 2008) shows that counterfeiting and piracy cases and actions within the EU had increased ten-fold since 1999. The costs to EU member states and companies have been estimated (IACC 2005) at £250 billion (€400 billion in 2005 terms). Tax revenue and excise losses were estimated then to be £30 billion (approx €50 billion). The OECD report (2007) on the Economic Impact of Counterfeiting and Piracy put the annual international trade in pirated goods as high as US$500 billion, which (if accurate) was larger than the individual GDPs of over 150 countries, including 21 of the EU member states. EUROPA (2008) cites similar data.

The accuracy of all the estimates quoted thus far in this chapter is open to challenge and the uncertainty is, perhaps, a reflection of the difficulty in obtaining comprehensive hard data. However, despite the uncertain data, the unanimous agreement of the various reports is that the negative impact of counterfeiting and piracy is huge and growing.

The counterfeiting industry has become a very lucrative business for organized criminal gangs, supported by a myriad of small-time distributors and outlets. The organized criminals often work in syndicates from region-to-region and country-to-country. For example, typically capital financing will be arranged in one country, production in another, supply chain and trans-shipment through various other countries, distribution and sales within target countries and banking of revenues somewhere else. Money laundering is usually an integral part of the process (OECD 2007, UFAB 2004, IACC 2005).

### Case 12.1   Operation Blackout, Asia-Pacific (Waring and Youill 2008)

The Motion Picture Association (MPA) announced in early February 2008 that Operation Blackout, an Asia-Pacific wide anti-piracy enforcement operation initiated by the MPA that ran from November 2007 to January 2008, resulted in the arrest of 675 suspected counterfeiters, seizures of more than 2.6 million pirated optical discs and 1,200 optical disc burners. The burners were capable of producing thousands of pirated movies a year and potentially millions in illicit revenue. Operation Blackout included 894 raids undertaken by enforcement authorities in 12 countries across Asia-Pacific. As with previous similar operations, the raids were aimed at targeting the producers, distributors and sellers of pirated movies.

### Case 12.2   Chinese Counterfeit Retail Goods (Waring and Youill 2008)

On 5 December 2007, US Government federal law enforcement officials announced the arrests of ten individuals on criminal charges related to the smuggling of an estimated $200 million worth of counterfeit goods. The arrests were the result of an undercover operation by Immigration and Customs Enforcement that began in June 2006.

Posing as a corrupt union official at the Port of Newark, a law enforcement agent reportedly received nearly half a million dollars in bribes from the arrested persons and co-conspirators. The money allegedly was paid to clear the illicit cargo – including counterfeit Nike, Burberry, Chanel, and Baby Phat footwear, apparel, and accessories – through customs undetected. According to the authorities, the Chinese-made counterfeits were shipped with falsified bills of lading through Port Newark to a number of warehouses throughout New York City, and the surrounding metropolitan area, where they were subsequently distributed to retail-level vendors.

## Case 12.3  Optical Disc Counterfeiting in Malaysia (Waring and Youill 2008)

In November 2007, Malaysian authorities raided three illegal optical disc manufacturing plants. They recovered $6 multi-million replication lines, several hundred infringing master copies and thousands of infringing optical discs containing both popular music and Hollywood movies. The Royal Malaysian Police, working with music industry anti-piracy operatives, acting on information received moved against the first illegal facility on 20 November. The raid netted three optical disc production lines and more than 6,000 infringing optical discs. A review of evidence recovered from the first facility led to the location of a second illegal optical disc factory in the same town. The police subsequently raided this facility and located a further two illegal production lines together with several hundred infringing optical discs.

The Royal Malaysian Police then passed the investigation and exhibits to the Ministry of Domestic Trade and Consumer Affairs who, together with music industry investigators, identified a third related illegal replication facility. When the authorities approached this optical disc plant they discovered the owners attempting to remove a sixth replication line in a heavy goods vehicle. This replication machinery was also seized during the course of the operation. Subsequent investigation revealed that the illegal factories were part of the same organized crime syndicate and the illegal compact discs that were being manufactured were destined for both local Malaysian and overseas markets.

Although an undoubted success as an anti-piracy operation, the Malaysian raids only removed a tiny portion of the overall DVD and CD counterfeiting activities in the region. This disparity highlights both the scale of anti-piracy and intelligence resources required, even to mount a very modest action, and the need for anti-piracy programmes to attack a wider range of targets than simply production facilities, as discussed later in Chapter 12.

There is also growing concern about fake pharmaceuticals in particular as these often have either attenuated or no pharmacological effect or else toxic side-effects. Cases of fake medications reportedly made in China or Hong Kong include anti-cancer drugs, anti-malaria pills and other medicines. Patients have died or been seriously harmed.

### Case 12.4   Fake Anti-Malarial Drugs (Newton et al. 2008)

Since 1998, the serious public health problem in South East Asia of counterfeit artesunate, containing either no or sub-therapeutic amounts of the active anti-malarial ingredient, has led to deaths from untreated malaria, reduced confidence in this vital drug, large economic losses for the legitimate manufacturers, and concerns that artemisinin resistance might be engendered as a result of patients receiving attenuated doses of the active ingredient.

With evidence of a deteriorating situation, a group of police, criminal analysts, chemists, palynologists, and health workers collaborated to determine the source of these counterfeits under the auspices of the International Criminal Police Organization (Interpol) and the WHO's Western Pacific Regional Office. A total of 391 samples of genuine and counterfeit artesunate collected in Vietnam (75), Cambodia (48), Lao PDR (115), Myanmar (Burma) (137) and the Thai/Myanmar border (16), were available for analysis. Sixteen different fake hologram types were identified. Tests confirmed that of specimens thought to be counterfeit (195/391, 49.9 per cent) on the basis of packaging contained either no or small quantities of artesunate. Chemical analysis demonstrated a wide diversity of wrong active ingredients, including banned pharmaceuticals, such as metamizole, and safrole, a carcinogen, and raw material for manufacture of MDMA ('ecstasy'). Evidence suggested that at least some of the counterfeits were manufactured in southeast PRC. This evidence prompted the Chinese Government to act quickly against the criminal traders with arrests and seizures.

## Links to Terrorism

In addition to the economic damage to countries and defrauded companies and the threat to people's health and safety, the most ominous development in the past decade has been the 'Al Qaeda connection' (Waring and Sayell 2009). Just as organized criminals are attracted to product counterfeiting, so too are international terrorists now also making and/or distributing such fakes as an easy, low-cost, inconspicuous and low-risk way to raise funds. The phenomenon of terrorist involvement in the counterfeit trade is not new but the Al Qaeda dimension is. There is some hard evidence and much circumstantial evidence to indicate that terrorists and criminal syndicates are now collaborating in this activity (OECD 2007, UFAB 2004, IACC 2005, Mukasey 2008, Youill 2008, Waring and Youill 2008, Waring and Sayell 2009). Examples include:

- terrorist bombing of HSBC Bank, Istanbul, November 2003. Arrested suspects had prior arrests for selling counterfeit goods in Istanbul;
- suspects arrested in Paris, October 2002, for goods counterfeiting had previous convictions for terrorist offences and belonged to the Salafist terrorist group;
- informed sources report that an identified terrorist in the Middle East who engages in counterfeit distribution has held meetings in the region with counterfeit syndicate members from several countries.

In summary, the nature of the problem in the European context (Waring and Sayell 2009) is:

- production and distribution of counterfeit goods undermines legitimate trade and markets and damages national economies as well as companies and people;
- in Europe, counterfeit goods are usually made outside EU and trans-shipped/sold into EU;
- multi-national separation of capital, production, supply chain and distribution (typically, manufacture in Asia, trans-shipment through Middle East/Mediterranean, sales into mainland EU);
- low risks and high returns are attractive to both organized criminals and terrorists;
- terrorists in particular require funding for their major logistics;
- countries with lax law enforcement, obscure legislation, weak judicial penalties, relaxed financial systems, weak trans-shipment controls, corrupt societies and porous borders are most attractive to both organized criminals and terrorists;
- for Western companies buying or sourcing in Asia, the risks to their corporate reputation and brand should not be under-estimated. Equally, Western luxury brands now want to sell into China and Asia generally to tap the new consumer wave there. Global brands and their reputations are at high risk from unscrupulous criminal gangs and lax regulatory enforcement in Asia (Youill 2006, 2007a).

## The Traditional Approach to Intellectual Property Risks

Most companies continue to seek solutions to their IP requirements either by contracting-out to service providers or by creating an in-house 'security' capability. However, in doing so they rarely take into account the political, economic, legal, social and global contexts in which the business operates and seeks to grow. Research and experience (Waring and Youill 2008, Youill 2005a and b, 2007b) reveal that such solutions are invariably:

- reactive;
- focussed on monitoring and on treating symptoms;
- short term in nature;
- narrow in scope;
- fragmented;
- not integrated with overall ERM;
- lacking in long-term cost-effectiveness.

Companies with IP to protect, as well as their service providers, often assume that low-level general security and litigation responses offer sufficient protection and that top-down corporate IP and brand protection is somehow unnecessary. Many service providers offering IP protection services describe what they do as 'enforcement', 'litigation support', 'investigations' and 'intelligence gathering', all of which are necessary but insufficient and indicate reactive piece-meal solutions to the problem.

Traditional in-house security solutions are often as ineffective as contracted-out services. Managements often have a poor understanding of the actual role and expertise of their security personnel, to whom they may have unwittingly entrusted IP and brand protection along with numerous other security responsibilities. Effective IP and brand protection are usually beyond the skills, experience and time resources of general security staff faced with many other legitimate demands. Highly trained and well-funded specialist

IP security strategists, operatives and investigators are required and few companies are willing to budget for this. Moreover, in times of increasing demands to show value for money and justification for one's existence in the firm, a number of different parties (senior executives, legal departments, security staff and external services) may share a common interest in 'looking good' in the eyes of the board, or put another way, image over substance. A predominant focus on investigations and raids fits in nicely with that culture, with its penchant for melodramatic events involving police raids, court cases and good media exposure. Everyone can, metaphorically speaking, 'slap each other on the back' and declare that a jolly good job has been done. However, in reality although investigations, raids and enforcement are indeed necessary, on their own they are extremely unlikely to stop or even deter the welter of IP threats against the company.

The nature of the problem may be seen by reference to Figure 12.1, which shows the main elements in the life-cycle of a product. Investigations, raids and enforcement focus predominantly on Distribution and Sales, primarily because that is where the existence of counterfeit products may be readily encountered and becomes visible. For example, evidence may emerge of counterfeit CDs and DVDs being sold in a number of shops and kiosks in a city neighbourhood. Often, a tip off will be received from someone among a network of paid informants, possibly someone even close to or sometimes working with the counterfeiters or their distributors. Truly, there is no honour among thieves! The aggrieved principal then carries out an undercover investigation to gather evidence of the times, dates and locations of specific transactions involving specific counterfeit products. A police raid is organized, illicit goods and records are seized and arrests are made. Court action for enforcement ensues and with luck some of the culprits will be fined. However, necessary as it is, such action will have virtually no effect on the overall manufacture, supply, distribution and sale of the offending products. There is no shortage of new counterfeiters or outlets willing to sell such goods.

Even when principals do venture back up the supply chain to try to root out the counterfeit mass production units (such as in cases 12.1 to 12.3), the effort, patience and coordination required are not for the faint hearted. Only a relatively small number of companies have injected the dogged determination, specialist human resources and funding to pursue counterfeit mass production units around the world. Few companies also seem to consider how it is possible for counterfeiters to be able to produce counterfeits that are so convincing in every detail. It is certainly not through acquiring a genuine article and then seeking to mimic it, although some poor quality counterfeits are done that way. Precision copies can only be produced from original genuine design drawings and specifications; so, where are the counterfeiters acquiring these? How is it possible for the latest Hollywood movie to be available unedited in pirated form on the Internet even before the final edited version has been released for public viewing, as has happened on numerous occasions? The original design theft and the pre-release movie theft are most likely occurring through industrial espionage during the Design, Prototyping and Piloting stage. This could involve, for example, an unscrupulous employee (whether opportunist or a deliberate plant), contractor or service provider, any one of whom could gain access to the necessary documents or computer files to copy. Thus, once again, we return to the absolute necessity of a robust system of due diligence background checks on all such persons (see Chapters 7 and 8) as well as robust access control and supporting IT, physical security and monitoring systems on site. However, as the following paragraph shows, IT security now also has to protect against remote computer hackers not only attacking the

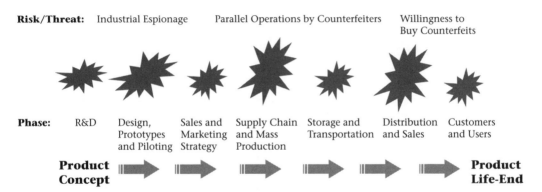

**Figure 12.1 IPR vulnerabilities in the product life-cycle**

*Source:* Waring (2009).

company's systems on its own sites directly but also attacking the laptops of travelling executives while off-site, via compromised Internet connections in hotels.

In some sectors, the R&D stage can also be vulnerable to industrial espionage. This is particularly so in the pharmaceutical and high tech industries. In pharmaceuticals, for example, pioneering research and R&D on new drugs usually take years and a huge amount of investment before finally a product gets to market and the company can recoup the investment many fold. The potential loss to the originator and the economy and the potential gain to the thieves and their country's economy is staggering. Riley and Walcott (2011) report that the total loss to the US economy from cyber theft of blueprints, chemical formulae and other IP from US corporate computers in 2010 was estimated by government officials to have reached US$500 billion. They refer in particular to an organized system of computer hacker units in China who are the biggest single threat of this kind to the US and the West. They cite the example of how such hackers had been remotely copying e-mails and data from executives of Western companies while they are away from the company's offices. They had done this by compromising the iBahn networks used to provide Internet services to hotels. In the pharmaceutical and biotechnology sector, companies targeted by the hackers included Abbott Laboratories, Boston Scientific and Wyeth (now part of Pfizer Inc).

However, in contrast to the pharmaceutical and high tech industries, the luxury personal goods sector has a rather blasé attitude towards the copying of its products and principals rarely pursue counterfeiters even when they openly advertise their products. One suggestion for this apparently surprising attitude is that in cost terms the genuine product's price mark-up is so high as to compensate for counterfeit losses, coupled with a 'symbiotic relationship' in which the counterfeiters (wittingly or not) are boosting the genuine brand and validating the genuine product's desirability. The genuine brand may therefore decide to tolerate the counterfeiters selling at much lower prices, especially as those buyers might never have been able to afford a genuine article.

# Key Principles for Improved Deterrence and Control for IPR

There are some guiding principles for intellectual property rights (IPR) action that apply anywhere in the world (Waring and Youill 2008). These are:

- pro-active, integrated and strategic approach required from government, law enforcement and businesses not just low level, reactive and piecemeal tactics; there must be a political will to succeed;
- relentless detection, identification and pursuit of IP criminals throughout the product's life-cycle;
- cut off snake's head not just the tail – seriously disrupt the counterfeiters' financing, production, supply chain, distribution and sales – no good just arresting local counterfeit goods sellers;
- cooperation and collaboration between government, law enforcement, business community and the public, for example zero tolerance campaign, public education, robust law enforcement;
- joined-up thinking required to tackle jointly: (a) organized crime (including counterfeiting; trafficking of goods, drugs, people, currency and arms; money laundering; Internet crime), (b) corruption and (c) terrorism;
- cross-border and multi-national cooperation and collaboration by law enforcement and counter-terrorist agencies essential;
- high integrity police, law enforcement and judiciary required;
- extremely tough penalties for convictions.

# New Approach to Intellectual Property Rights and Brand Protection

A credible strategy and strategic framework are required for long-term effective IP and brand protection and these rarely feature in either traditional in-house approaches or those from service providers. This new approach to IP and brand protection is first to examine all the factors, both internal and external, now and in the future that may impact upon the particular company and its IP and brands. This approach has the following features:

- proactive;
- focussed on tackling causes not symptoms;
- long term in nature;
- broad and comprehensive in scope;
- life-cycle approach and joined-up systemic thinking;
- integrated with overall ERM;
- long-term cost-effectiveness.

With a clear understanding of the company's risk exposures and contexts, a tailored IP protection 'blueprint' is then developed that establishes a coherent policy and strategy and a framework of best-practice standards and procedures at all levels of the company.

This approach allows the enterprise to prevent IP protection problems before they have the ability to significantly impact the company's brands and reputation.

The protection of a company's IP therefore requires a product life-cycle approach as depicted in Figure 12.1, which is holistic, strategic and takes account of multiple contexts and risk interactions. This life-cycle approach takes in the entire life of a product, starting from the earliest kernel of an idea for a product through R&D, design stages, piloting, component sourcing, production, marketing, sales, advertising, distribution and so on into the future.

# **13** *Ensuring Product Safety*

The previous chapter outlined the nature and scale of the threats to a company's IP and brands, through all forms of IP theft, particularly but not exclusively product counterfeiting. For example, patent infringement remains a huge area of IP threat but one that is beyond the scope of this book. The previous chapter also referred to the growing problem of product safety and the damage that dangerous counterfeit products can do to the principal's corporate reputation and brand name, but of course product safety issues may also arise from legitimate sources of production.

IP risks and product safety are traditionally dealt with as separate issues by manufacturers of legitimate goods. However, this is a somewhat artificial separation since there are many commonalities and crossovers between the risk management requirements of the two. For example, products, whether genuine or counterfeit, may exhibit defects or hazards. Design, materials and construction are directly germane both to IP risks and to product safety as well as to brand protection.

This chapter evaluates current approaches to product safety and highlights the need for a life-cycle approach akin to that required for IP risk management.

## Product Safety and Dangerous Goods

On average some two-thirds of all US product recalls are of imported goods and, of these, the majority are made in China (CPSC 2007). Since the beginning of 2007, there has been widespread media attention to a number of cases of alleged unsafe Chinese products exported to the West. These cases include: 20 million toys recalled by Mattel, 100,000 drink bottles recalled by Asda, pet food recall by Walmart in 2007, contaminated toothpaste and Bindeez/Aqua Dots toys recalled in US and Australia, and children's jewellery contaminated with cadmium withdrawn by Walmart in 2010. So far as is known, most of these are from legitimate producers. Counterfeit producers, however, are likely to show few qualms about the safety of what they produce. Dangerous fakes are known to include spare parts for cars and aircraft, as well as cosmetics, shampoos and pharmaceuticals.

The following two cases 13.1 and 13.2, so far as is known, relate to legitimate rather than counterfeit production.

### Case 13.1   Toys from China

In 2007, it was widely reported that Mattel made recalls of several different toys made in China, the most prominent recall being a large range of magnetic toys, especially the Polly Pocket range for young girls but also a smaller number of Barbie and Batman products. The magnetic toys had a design fault whereby the small magnets within the toy could readily break off and be swallowed by children, for example if they put the toy in their mouth. Several cases in the US were reported where surgery was required to remove the magnets. In 2006, the toy company Mega Brands Inc recalled 3.8 million Magnetix magnetic building sets following the death of one child and serious injuries to four others after swallowing magnets from these toys.

### Case 13.2  Toxic Jewellery

In 2010, it was widely reported that Walmart had withdrawn items of children's jewellery from its stores following an investigative report by the Associated Press (AP) into the amount of cadmium in these items produced in China. Most of the items independently tested for AP had very high levels of cadmium, a heavy metal with toxic and carcinogenic properties, which can leach out if children bite or suck the jewellery containing it. It was reported that the practice of using cadmium in such jewellery was commonplace among Chinese manufacturers. The metal also has been identified increasingly as an additive in toys made overseas which contain PVC plastics.

The US Consumer Product Safety Commission's (CPSC) Chairman Inez Tenenbaum issued a stern warning to Chinese manufacturers not to make the mistake of simply replacing toxic lead by other toxic metals such as cadmium, antimony and barium.

## Good Practice in Ensuring Product Safety

Ensuring product safety focuses on rigorous application of safety standards and assurance methods throughout the product life-cycle from concept, design, materials selection, fabrication, construction, prototype testing, production, marketing, sales, distribution, service life, maintenance, repair, disuse and ultimate disposal. Product recall policy must be both clear and appropriate. The overall life-cycle approach that is required to ensure product safety (Waring and Tyler 1997, Waring and Glendon 1998) is summarized in Table 13.1.

Although the life-cycle approach to product safety is now mature and widely used in the West and in developed countries, in the new industrial nations there may be a tendency to cut corners and turn blind eyes. Cheap labour and a contract-out culture may encourage false assumptions by principals that all necessary monitoring, tests and risk controls have been carried out by sub-contractors. As the cases cited below show, this may be illusory. In societies with lax regulatory enforcement and widespread corruption, many small production units remain unregulated and, for those that are regulated, false test certificates and safety documentation may be obtained easily.

**Table 13.1  Life-cycle approach to product risk management**

| Life-cycle Phase | Key Activities | Key Risk Management Requirements for Phase |
|---|---|---|
| Research | Basic research; R&D | Hazards data collection; identifying applicable product regulations |
| Design | Conceptual design; detailed design | Product risk profiling including misuse, application contexts and environments; hazards data analysis; design risk assessments, modifications and re-assessments; feedforward of data to manufacturing |
| Testing and Approvals | Laboratory tests e.g. NDT, flammability, toxicity; pilot scale trials; field trials | Hazards data analysis, Availability, Reliability & Maintainability (AR&M); design feedback; compliance with standards; feedforward of data to manufacturing; independent certifications |
| Manufacture | Raw materials to formulation; processing; finishing; packaging; batch marking | Quality assurance throughout manufacturing; compliance with standards; conformity assessments; technical data files |
| Product Launch | Labelling and manuals; advertising, marketing; contract terms; insurance | Appropriate instructions, warnings and safety data; ensuring accuracy of claims for product; contractual risk allocation to parties (for example, manufacturer, distributor, retailer, customer) and limited acceptance by manufacturer/principal |
| Service Life | Monitoring, reviewing; responding to customer complaints; keeping distributors informed | Policy and procedures for maintenance, design modifications, recalls, replacements, withdrawals; feedback of data to design |
| Decommission | Surveys; dismantling, demolition, scrapping; safe disposal | Policy and procedures for decommission; risk assessments including environmental effects; ensuring adequacy of risk control measures |

*Source:* Adapted from Waring and Glendon (1998), page 421.

## Case 13.3  Baxter and Contaminated Heparin

Heparin is a substance used widely as an anti-coagulant in medicine. It is derived typically from intestines and other offal from pigs. When the extraction process is done under properly managed factory conditions and product safety procedures, there should be little cause for concern about contamination. However, in parts of China, some larger suppliers to principals contract out their heparin production to middlemen 'consolidators' who in turn sub-contract to groups of smaller suppliers, many of whom are unregulated and lack the necessary knowledge, training, equipment or scruples required to avoid contamination. In many instances, the offal is simply boiled up in the back yards of villagers using *ad hoc* equipment and dubious chemicals to assist the process.

In late 2007 and early 2008, an escalating number of reports in the US began to emerge of patients experiencing serious allergic reactions and deaths following the use of heparin supplied by Baxter Healthcare Corporation, part of the global drug company Baxter International Inc. In March 2008, the US Food and Drug Administration (FDA) stepped in and ordered a major recall of the product. At least 81 patients died, although the final figure may have been as high as 140; at least 785 suffered serious injury.

A major official investigation by the FDA revealed that Baxter had contracted the US firm Scientific Protein Laboratories (SPL) to supply it with heparin sourced through its Chinese JV partner Changzhou SPL. During subsequent litigation by injured patients or the relatives of patients who had died, evidence emerged that the batches of heparin responsible had been adulterated with a substitute called over-sulphated chondroitin sulphate, which medical researchers had linked to the adverse reactions in patients.

On 9 June 2011, in the first of hundreds of civil actions against Baxter and SPL, the widow of a man (Steven Johansen) who had died following administration of the Baxter heparin product during kidney dialysis, was awarded US$625,000 in damages. The court heard that Baxter and SPL had failed to establish and apply quality and purity specifications and failed to trace and control their supply chain. The catalogue of failures by SPL was particularly damning, including as it did its failure to investigate heparin contamination cases involving a range of US pharmaceutical companies it had supplied. Some five weeks later, the same judge determined that although Baxter had been guilty of negligence it was not to the same degree as that of SPL which had acted with 'such gross negligence as to indicate a wanton disregard of the rights of others'. Accordingly, the judge held that plaintiffs could now lodge additional claims for punitive damages against SPL but not Baxter.

## Case 13.4   Sanlu, Fonterra and Contaminated Milk Products

The 'melamine in milk' scandal in 2008 and 2009, which involved the Chinese dairy products company Sanlu Group and its New Zealand co-owner Fonterra, had a primarily internal impact in China. Victims were consumers in China whereas in the Baxter heparin case the victims were patients overseas.

Some dairies in China apparently would dilute milk with water so as to increase the total volume and boost profits. However, the effect of dilution is to reduce the protein concentration of the milk and this is detectable by routine quality assurance and regulatory testing. To avoid detection, the companies started to add to the diluted milk a nitrogen-bearing organic substance (melamine) which would trick a routine Kjeldahl assay for total nitrogen (the proxy measure of protein content) and make the milk protein concentration appear normal, a problem acknowledged by WHO (2008).

Melamine is not a traditional, or recognized or indeed WHO/FAO approved food additive for human consumption and its use had previously been confined to plastics formulations and other industrial applications. Melamine in raw ingredients from China for use in the manufacture of pet food in the US had been blamed in 2007 for a large number of deaths of dogs and cats owing to kidney failure (WHO). Unfortunately, it appears that babies and infants are also particularly susceptible to melamine toxicity. In September 2008, large numbers of infants across China became seriously ill with kidney stones and renal damage after consuming milk made from melamine-contaminated powdered infant milk formula sold under different brand names. By the end of November 2008, some 294,000 infants had been made ill, over 50,000 had been hospitalized and six deaths had been confirmed (WHO 2008, USFDA 2008).

Although a number of dairy companies were implicated in the scandal, the main source of the contaminated milk products was confirmed by the Chinese authorities as the Sanlu Group Company. The latter was part-owned (43 per cent) by the New Zealand company Fonterra who had invested US$139 million in the company. Ironically, it was Fonterra that first alerted the Chinese Government to a potential health crisis on 2 August 2008, having noted a growing number of kidney stone cases reported during July. Fonterra pushed Sanlu for a product recall but none occurred so on 5 September Fonterra asked the Chinese Government to take action. Four days later, Chinese officials issued a warning about the melamine contamination and on 11 September Sanlu recalled 700 tons of its infant milk formula. Unfortunately, by this time the epidemic of cases had already taken hold.

Over the coming weeks, more than 60 arrests were made among Sanlu executives, distributors and others and many were charged with a variety of criminal offences relating to the contamination scandal. In January 2009, a total of 21 individuals were tried and convicted. The Intermediate People's Court in Shijiazhuang announced death sentences on Zhang Yujun and Geng Jinping and a suspended death sentence on Gao Junjie. Zhang had been the prime supplier of melamine formulations to the farming and dairy industry. The former chairwoman of the Sanlu Group, Tian Wenhua, received a life prison sentence. Two former deputy general managers of Sanlu, Hang Zhiqi and Wang Yuliang, received eight years and 15 years imprisonment respectively.

The Sanlu Group was declared bankrupt and liquidated in February 2009. Fonterra lost its investment. It is not known to what extent Fonterra undertook a due diligence examination of Sanlu before making that investment.

In summary of Part 4, the product life-cycle is the common vehicle for strengthening corporate approaches to IPR threats and to product safety. For IP risks, investigations and raids in the distribution and sales phase need to be supplemented by rigorous due diligence checks of personnel and contractors much earlier in the life-cycle, and especially R&D, design, prototyping and piloting. For product safety, rigorous due diligence checks and production audits of the full supply chain by the client principal may be all that stands between the latter and disaster, as many cases have shown.

# PART 5

# *Man-Made Disasters*

# **14** *Policy and Practice in Major Hazards Risk Management*

Disasters which, in a single incident, result in huge loss of life and/or major damage to property and/or the environment are either natural in origin (for example, typhoons, tsunamis, earthquakes) or man-made (for example, the Piper Alpha disaster, BP's Deepwater Horizon, the Chernobyl nuclear reactor meltdown and the PetroChina Jilin disaster). Occasionally but rarely, a natural disaster may trigger an additional man-made disaster. For example, the Richter scale 9.0 earthquake (the Great East Japan Earthquake) and subsequent tsunami which struck Japan on 11 March 2011 not only caused catastrophic loss of life and destruction but also damaged Tokyo Electric's Fukishima Daiichi nuclear power plant so badly that whatever structural and engineering protection had been built into the nuclear reactors was compromised, reactor core meltdown occurred, containment was lost and radioactive contamination spread over a wide area. Subsequent investigations have determined that safety features designed into the Fukushima plant were inadequate to protect against a combined earthquake and tsunami of this magnitude.

Man-made disasters emanate from inadequately controlled man-made major hazards which are characterized by (Waring and Glendon 1998):

- large-scale technology or technical activities;
- large-scale storage or use of high-energy sources and/or toxic and/or biohazard and/or radioactive materials;
- potentially large numbers of people at risk of being injured or killed in a single incident;
- potential widespread environmental and/or property damage resulting from a single incident;
- special implications for major hazard management, risk assessment and risk control concerning normal, abnormal and emergency conditions.

Typically, when a man-made disaster strikes, high-energy transfer occurs in a relatively defined area in a short space of time, for example major fire, explosion, structural collapse, transportation crash. Sometimes, however, a disaster can be 'slow motion' and possibly unannounced, for example the release of toxic substances from a factory into the local environment over a long period which results in irreversible health damage to the local population. A number of alleged incidents of this type have occurred in China.

The main kinds of site, installation or activity where man-made major hazards are likely to arise are:

- nuclear installations;
- chemical process factories handling large quantities of flammable, highly flammable and/or toxic materials;
- offshore oil and gas installations;
- onshore oil and gas installations, oil refineries and petrochemical plants;
- water treatment plants using bulk chlorine as a sterilizing agent;
- bulk storage of explosive, flammable or highly flammable materials;
- civil transportation (railways, urban rapid transit railways, passenger ferries, ocean-going liners, airliners).

## The Development of Major Hazards Policy

Disasters involving man-made major hazards have reflected industrial growth and the vast increase in scale of high-energy industrial processes and high-energy inventories on a single site, particularly since the Second World War. This much was acknowledged explicitly in paragraphs 296 and 297 of the Robens Report (Robens 1972), which paved the way for the wholesale modernization of health and safety legislation in the UK via the Health and Safety at Work etc Act 1974. The latter Act, which came into effect on 31 July 1974, introduced general duties for ensuring health and safety imposed on employers, directors and other senior persons and on persons in control of premises, as well as making available a range of enforcement instruments and much tougher penalties than hitherto had been the case. It is perhaps a bitter irony that on 1 June 1974, barely two months before the Act came into force, the Nypro caprolactam plant at Flixborough in the UK blew up. As Professor Bryan Harvey CBE, the Deputy Director-General of the new enforcement body the Health and Safety Executive (HSE), commented some time later in the presence of the author, if the Flixborough Disaster had occurred on the 1 August 1974 and not the 1 June, the owners and operators Nypro would almost certainly have faced prosecution on indictment under the new duties and penalties of the Health and Safety at Work Act.

### Case 14.1  The Flixborough Disaster 1974 (Parker 1975)

The Court of Inquiry report into the Flixborough disaster (Parker 1975) states in its introduction that on 1 June 1974, the Flixborough plant of Nypro (UK) Ltd was 'virtually demolished by an explosion of warlike dimensions'. Of people working on the site at that time, 28 were killed and a further 36 were injured. The blast resulted in another 53 people recorded over a wide area suffering moderate injuries, plus hundreds more with minor injuries that were not recorded. In addition to personal injuries, property damage was extensive and a preliminary survey identified 1,821 homes and 167 shops and factories as having suffered damage.

The Court of Inquiry noted that whatever happened during the final shift prior to the explosion can never be known for certain, as the explosion not only killed everyone in the control room but also destroyed all relevant instrumentation and records. The work of the Court and its appointed technical experts was therefore daunting, as they tried to piece together as robust an explanation of the disaster as possible with limited hard data. As a record of a forensic inquiry involving complex technical and scientific issues and several competing hypotheses, the report was masterful and set a standard for subsequent major accident inquiries.

The Nypro operation fitted quite well the warning in the Robens Report about the vast increase in scale of high-energy industrial processes and high-energy inventories on a single site. Between 1967 and 1972, the plant had been expanded and developed so that annual output capacity increased from 20,000 tons of caprolactam to 70,000 tons. Caprolactam, a compound used in the manufacture of polyamides or 'nylon', was produced at the expanded plant by first oxidizing the hydrocarbon cyclohexane to produce the ketone cyclohexanone and converting it to caprolactam. This chemical process required very large inventories of cyclohexane to be stored on site and, further, very large quantities had to be circulated through the reactors under raised pressure and temperature. Any leakage would be highly dangerous, since if the highly flammable cyclohexane vapour met a source of ignition an explosion would be inevitable.

The report concluded that a temporary by-pass pipe intended to isolate one troublesome reactor (Number 5) in the reactor train had failed and, as a result, a large volume of cyclohexane had been released as a vapour cloud which eventually met a source of ignition. Expert witnesses estimated that the force of the explosion was equivalent to between 15 and 45 tons of TNT. The by-pass had failed because it was a modification which had not been designed, constructed and tested to take account of the requirements for pressure systems containing such hazardous materials. The individuals carrying out the modification work had not been trained generally in the hazards of uncontrolled modifications or advised or supervised specifically regarding the safety requirements relating to the Reactor Number 5 by-pass. The report noted that at the time of the explosion the key post of Works Engineer, which carried the responsibility for such critical safety work, had been vacant for some months. A management reorganization was underway but 'there was no mechanical engineer on site of sufficient qualification, status or authority to deal with complex or novel engineering problems and insist on necessary measures being taken'. Referring to the rigging up of the by-pass, the report also notes that none of the senior personnel, who were chemical and not mechanical engineers, 'were capable of recognizing what was in essence a relatively simple mechanical engineering problem, let alone solve it'.

The Flixborough disaster was a wake-up call for the process industries and the engineering professions and provided a focus for re-evaluating the technical, managerial and training requirements for major hazard sites. Nevertheless, following Flixborough, it was to take another ten years before the first specific UK regulations on major hazards arrived (Control of Industrial Major Accident Hazards Regulations 1984), prompted also by the first EU Major Hazards Directive 82/501 ('Seveso I') in 1982 and another 15 years beyond that before new regulations (Control of Major Accident Hazards Regulations 1999) taking into account the EU Major Hazards Directive 96/82 ('Seveso II') of 1996. The Seveso Disaster refers to the chemical plant accident and release of dioxin into the environment at the Hoffmann-La Roche site at Seveso in Italy in 1976.

During his career, the author has contributed either directly or indirectly to a number of official public inquiries in the UK into man-made major hazards or disasters involving them and to the subsequent preventive activities. These contributions include:

- Research from 1969–1970 at the Gas Council into combustion of North Sea gas and development of safer burners for domestic appliances, as directed by the Morton Report (Morton 1970) into the safety of natural gas following a number of fatal domestic explosions.

- Following the fire at King's Cross London Underground Station in 1988, led a consultant team examining fire safety preparedness of operational staff at stations, whose report was submitted in evidence to the Fennel Inquiry into the disaster (Fennell 1988). Subsequently, from 1989–1995, acted as a consultant to London Underground Ltd on improving its SMS and safety culture and developing its first Safety Cases presaging the Railways (Safety Case) Regulations 1994.

- Following the Piper Alpha disaster in 1988 (see Cullen 1990), assisted from 1990–1994 a number of offshore oil and gas operators and drilling contractors with installations in the North Sea, Irish Sea and further afield in improving their offshore SMS and developing their first Safety Cases under the Offshore Installations (Safety Case) Regulations 1992.

- Following two fatal explosions at different sites of a leading manufacturer and global supplier of industrial explosives, carried out a company-wide review of safety systems.

- Submitted a review report to the Sea Empress Environmental Inquiry Committee on consultants' submission on the effectiveness of national and local contingency plans, including the Joint Response Centre, following the grounding of the Sea Empress oil tanker in Milford Haven harbour in February 1996 (see Edwards 1998).

- Headed a consultant team from 1998–2003 advising a petrochemical company in improving its safety and environmental management systems and developing its Tier 2 compliance with the Control of Major Accident Hazards Regulations 1999.

- Member of a consultant team from 1999–2003 advising various MoD establishments on risk management with respect to the Specific, Measured, Appropriate, Realistic and Timed (SMART) Procurement initiative and Integrated Project Teams for the development of military platforms for air systems and sea systems, including for one agency the integration of management systems for major hazards, fire safety, general health and safety and environmental protection.

The examples selected by the author in this chapter, as well as the comments and opinions expressed, reflect that personal experience and his conviction that the unforgiving nature of man-made major hazards make it imperative that they require always to be under highly disciplined and competent management.

## Major Hazards Control in Practice

In view of the explicit and unambiguous major hazards legislation imposed on site operators in most countries, one might imagine that the level of implementation would be consistently high. However, in the author's experience in a variety of regions and countries in evaluating and advising on major hazards safety management, compliance is patchy (Waring 2005). In most cases it is generally adequate but with room for improvement but in some cases it is dangerously inadequate. The apparent dilemma for developing countries is self-evident: in the race for industrial and economic growth, should they turn a blind eye to the delays and extra costs that first-world major hazards risk control entails and run the risk of major disasters, or should they follow the first-world approach and potentially have slower industrial and economic growth? In the author's opinion, the dichotomy is false and little more than an excuse to disguise ignorance and laziness as economic necessity.

In addition to the Flixborough Disaster, examples of man-made major accidents have already been cited in earlier chapters (Table 1.1, cases 3.2, 4.5, 6.1, 6.2 and 8.3) and the whole of Chapter 15 is dedicated to the Mari-Vassilikos Disaster of 11 July 2011. Further examples are:

## Case 14.2   BP Grangemouth Fires and Explosion 1987 (HSE 1989)

On the 13 March, 22 March and 11 June 1987, a series of fires and an explosion occurred at two sites in Scotland operated by BP Oil (Grangemouth) Refinery Ltd killing a total of four men, injuring others and causing extensive damage to plant as well as off-site damage.

In the first incident at Grangemouth, refinery staff and maintenance contractors from outside had been working for several days to isolate a flare line and then dismantle it. Confirmatory checks on the plant that the line was isolated and not under pressure were inadequate and the necessary Permit-To-Work (PTW) system, while functioning, was not based on sufficient knowledge of the actual hazards. As a result, although the fitters reported suspicious drips of liquid from the pipe flange they were working on, the PTW authorized person concluded that it was just minimal residual liquid and that the line was not under pressure. The fitters carried on their work after receiving his assurances but the flange suddenly released and a large volume of flammable liquid poured out under pressure onto the working platform and the ground below. The spreading pool of liquid created a cloud of flammable vapour above it. The official inquiry report (HSE 1989) concluded that when the vapour cloud met a source of ignition, it was almost certainly a mobile diesel-engine air-compressor used to supply air to the fitters' breathing apparatus. Forensic examination showed that the generator's spark arrestor had been missing. The conflagration killed two workers and injured two more.

The second incident, again at the Grangemouth site, also involved essential repairs but this time to a hydrocracker unit. After the repairs, the unit was re-commissioned at 22.00 hours on Saturday 21 March and production was steady. At about 01.30 hours the next morning, automatic alarms sounded, the plant tripped out automatically and the system started to depressurize. A temperature cut-out (TCO) was noted as having caused the shut-down but the operators thought this was a spurious event as they could find no evidence of excess temperature that could have triggered it. The TCO was manually over-ridden to enable hydrogen circulation to recommence and at about 02.00 hours the plant was brought back up to operating pressure ready to restart the reactor. Following procedure, the operators waited for the hydrocracker supervisor to arrive before introducing feedstock. The incoming day shift at 06.00 hours were told by the outgoing night shift that the plant was still on standby and that there was nothing to report other than a slightly higher vibration than normal on one compressor.

At 07.00 hours, there was a violent explosion followed by an intense fire. The explosion was heard and felt some 30km away. A high-pressure separator which was at the centre of the explosion had disintegrated and such was the force of the explosion that one fragment weighing nearly 3 tonnes was found 1km away. Other large fragments rained down on neighbouring premises. Although the nine operators working at the hydrocracker unit at the time escaped with no or minor injuries, a contractor was killed.

According to the official investigation (HSE 1989), the proximate cause of the explosion was over-pressurization of one of the high-pressure separators following gas breakthrough from an associated separator. In addition, there was a number of design and functional failures of various safety devices (such as pressure-operated relief valves), fault detection systems and alarms. A variety of human factors and safety management issues was also cited, including:

• inadequate training;
• false beliefs and assumptions about the need for routine monitoring of interlocks, alarms and trips on hydrocracker units;
• failure to reassess periodically relevant human factors, especially regarding control rooms;
• failure to act on potential gas breakthrough warnings raised in safety audits in 1975 and 1980;
• inadequate safety reviews prior to plant modifications;
• absence of a full safety analysis of the inherent hazards, consequences and safeguards required in the operation of hydrocracker units.

The third incident involved a fire at a crude oil storage tank at BP's Dalmeny terminal on 11 June 1987. One of seven floating roof tanks, each with a capacity of 70,000 tonnes, was scheduled for a clean out of the sludge that typically accumulates at the bottom of such tanks. In the particular tank, an estimated 1,000 tonnes of sludge was present. Work began on 2 June with a team of eight operatives from the appointed contractor, who had significant experience in the industry and at this site. The tank was not totally free of all flammable or other vapours, that is, not gas-free but the risk of a flammable atmosphere forming was not considered sufficient to warrant either mechanical ventilation or rigorous gas monitoring. The sludge clearance routine was to use two teams of four operatives who alternated every four hours. Three men in the team worked inside the tank while the fourth stayed outside to monitor progress and safety and liaise with the BP safety services operative.

On 11 June, a team changeover had occurred at 12.30 hours. At 13.20 hours, the outside man looked in and shouted an alarm, having spotted a ring of fire surrounding the three men inside. Two ran in one direction and escaped but the third went in the opposite direction and died from asphyxiation and burns. After an extensive investigation, it was concluded that the proximate cause of the fire was a lighted cigarette being smoked by one of the contractor's team inside the tank (HSE 1989). It was established that at various times three of the contractor's employees had smoked cigarettes inside the particular tank and smoking had also been commonplace among contractor employees at the Dalmeny site. Although the workmen had a personal duty to rigorously follow safety procedures and 'no smoking' rules, it was also a duty of their employer (the contractor) to have a robust SMS including tough selection, disciplinary and dismissal procedures, safe systems of work, competent supervision and close monitoring of operatives in hazardous settings. Further, the site operator (BP) had a duty to be rigorous in the selection and appointment of contractors, including requiring them as a condition of contract to demonstrate that they would apply a robust SMS in all respects, and monitoring and control of contractors while they are on site.

Commenting on the common factors of all three incidents, the official investigation report (HSE 1989) noted that formal safety reports required from site operators must be reviewed periodically and revised so as to identify and eliminate defects and deficiencies in plant and SMS. Paragraph 5 of the report states: 'HSE emphasize that safety reports for existing plant must reflect actual conditions and be based on appraisal of the plant as it is functioning at the time. A management view of how it should ideally be will not suffice.' BP were subsequently fined £750,000. The damage to their prestige and reputation was incalculable.

Three further major hazard incidents occurred at BP Grangemouth during May and June of 2000. Although there were no serious injuries, the incidents prompted a major investigation, the report on which (HSE 2003) cited weaknesses in the SMSs, failure to learn from previous incidents and safety culture weaknesses. BP was fined a total of £1 million.

With all of the above in mind, it is perhaps somewhat incredible that BP should then in 2005 experience a broadly similar disaster with 15 deaths, 180 injuries and plant damage at its Texas City refinery (USCSHIB 2007). For a major oil and gas company with global safety standards proclaimed on its website to have such a 'failure of hindsight' (see Chapter 3 and Fischhoff 1975, Toft 1990, Toft and Reynolds 1997) is truly remarkable. Even more astonishing was BP's Deepwater Horizon disaster in 2010 in the Gulf of Mexico, which involved 11 deaths, 17 injured and an environmental catastrophe, the total financial cost of which to BP stands at the time of writing at in excess of US$41 billion, including US$30 billion in civil claims and US$4.5 billion in criminal penalties. BP has arguably the world's longest corporate experience in offshore oil and gas (exploration and production) E&P, including safety requirements, and of all companies it should have been able to ensure that all the post-Piper Alpha safety discipline (see also case 6.1) had been fully implemented. Also, as a major partner in the original Five Star Safety Audit System, still widely used by many large organizations around the world, it is some irony that BP itself had been unable to translate excellence in safety auditing into excellence in actual safety. Moreover, the US official inquiry into the Deepwater Horizon disaster found widespread safety management failures had led to the failure of the well blow-out preventer and to how its immediate impact was dealt with. In both the Texas City and Deepwater Horizon cases, the words from the Grangemouth inquiry report (HSE 1989) resonate: 'A management view of how it should ideally be will not suffice.'

## Case 14.3   The Buncefield Explosion and Fire of 2005 (Newton 2008, HSE et al. 2011)

The Buncefield oil storage depot is a large fuel oil storage and transfer 'tank farm' situated approximately 5km east of the town of Hemel Hempstead in Hertfordshire, UK, approximately 1km west of the major M1 motorway and about 4km north of the main outer orbital motorway of Greater London, the M25. Near to the complex are a number of hamlets, residences, businesses, farms and public highways and immediately to the west of the complex lies the Maylands Industrial Estate which was home to 630 businesses and some 16,500 employees. In December 2005, there were three operating sites within the Buncefield tank farm complex:

- Hertfordshire Oil Storage Ltd (HOSL), a JV between Total UK Ltd and Chevron Ltd and run day-to-day by Total.

- British Pipeline Agency Ltd (BPAL), a JV between BP Oil and Shell Oil UK.
- BP Oil UK Ltd.

The complex overall had hazardous planning consent to store up to 194,000 tonnes of hydrocarbon fuels and all three sites were designated 'top tier' in terms of required compliance with the Control of Major Accident Hazards Regulations 1999 (COMAH). Fuel came into the three sites via three pipelines linked back to various oil refineries across the UK. Although the majority of fuel left the complex in road tankers, jet aviation fuel went via two pipelines into the West London (Walton) Gatwick pipeline system and then to London Heathrow and Gatwick airports.

At 06.01 hours on Sunday 11 December 2005 the first of a series of explosions occurred, the main one centred on the Maylands Industrial Estate car parks. The explosions measured 2.4 on the Richter scale and were heard 200km away in the UK, there also being reports from Holland. A huge fire engulfed more than 20 large fuel storage tanks across a large part of the complex. Despite the efforts of some 180 fire-fighters from the Hertfordshire fire brigade, supported by involvement of nearly 1,000 more fire-fighters as well as police forces from across the UK, it took them 32 hours to extinguish the main blaze while the overall fire burned for five days and destroyed most of the complex. The huge smoke plume was large enough to be seen across most of South East England.

It was fortunate that the incident occurred on a Sunday morning when few people were in the vicinity and when most of the businesses on the Maylands Industrial Estate were closed for the weekend. While no one was killed in the incident, 43 people suffered minor injuries and many others reported longer-term stress or psychological disorders. Some 2,000 local inhabitants had to be evacuated from their homes and the M1 and other roads were closed. There was widespread damage to surrounding property and homes close to the complex were either destroyed or severely damaged. The lives and amenity of local residents whose homes were damaged were severely disrupted for a long time after the incident. Further afield, lesser damage to property was reported from up to 8km away. Official estimates put the cost to local businesses alone at £70 million, while large compensation claims (4,140 in total) against the site operators amounted to £625 million. The total estimated cost, excluding rebuild costs of the complex, was estimated at £894 million (Newton 2008).

To investigate the disaster, the Government immediately set up the Buncefield Major Incident Investigation Board (BMIIB) under the chairmanship of Lord Newton and aided by the HSE and the Environment Agency as the joint Competent Authority under the COMAH Regulations. The BMIIB issued a series of reports (Newton 2008). In essence, the triggering event of the disaster was the overflow of one fuel tank which went on undetected for some considerable time (about three hours) because a number of automatic fuel level detection systems and associated alarms and cut-outs did not work. Some 250,000 litres of petrol are estimated to have overflowed. The overflowing fuel released a white flammable vapour cloud that spread out over a 360 mile radius, and was visible as evidenced by CCTV footage. Members of the public off-site and tanker drivers on-site reported the vapour cloud to site employees and the fire alarm button was pressed at 06.01 hours. The vapour cloud was most probably ignited by a spark from the start-up of the firewater pump linked to the fire alarm.

In addition to numerous technical defects identified as root causes by the Competent Authority in its investigation report (HSE et al. 2011), SMS at the HOSL site were also defective. In particular, the company's own statutory COMAH safety report that it was required to prepare and follow in managing major hazards was largely aspirational and 'did not reflect what actually went on at the site', a criticism remarkably similar to that made by the official inquiry into BP Grangemouth in case 14.2 (HSE 1989). Total, through Total employees, had the over-riding responsibility for safety management on the HOSL site but did very little, with the SMS lacking any real depth about the control of major hazards. HOSL had a board of directors but no employees yet it had the legal responsibility for the control of a major hazards site, including the preparation and submission of the COMAH safety report. In fact, the safety report was prepared by a contractor and was never scrutinized by the HOSL board. The board only met twice a year and its hands-off approach was 'clearly insufficient oversight to achieve the stringent managerial framework required for the control of a major hazards site'. There was 'an unjustified confidence' within Total and HOSL in the safety and environmental performance at the site. As paragraph 88 in HSE et al. (2011) notes regarding Buncefield, 'Good process safety management does not happen by chance and requires constant active engagement.' This entrains all levels of personnel including clear and positive safety leadership from the board.

Five companies were prosecuted for their part in creating the disaster and in February 2011 were fined a total of £5.35 million plus £4.08 million costs. The main penalties were: Total (£3.6 million fine plus £2.6 million costs), HSOL (£1.45 million fine plus £1 million costs) and BPA (£300,000 fine plus £480,000 costs).

## Case 14.4   Middle East Oil Refineries

In the late 1990s, the author acted as a consultant on major hazards management to the Oil Refineries and Distribution Company (NIORDC), then part of the National Iranian Oil Company. This was at a time of significant change in Iran: recovery from the devastation of the Iran–Iraq War, a rising population, the second Five Year Plan was underway with a specific aim of reducing Iran's dependence on oil exports and, for the first time post-1979 revolution, a more open-door policy and willingness to establish links with Western expertise and investors. Certainly, NIORDC senior personnel were aware that in the 15 or so years that the country had been in virtual lockdown (revolution, Iran–Iraq War, five year post-war period), there had been not only considerable changes in approaches to major hazards risk control generally in the world but also Iranian refineries themselves were now racing to expand output using increased processing temperatures and pressures but with growing concern about possibly inadequate risk controls in some instances. Peyvandi (1996) and others at an NIORDC safety conference in Tehran in 1996 (see Waring 1996b) provided some revealing data on the issue of rapid expansion and processing variables, as discussed on pages 315 and 316 of Waring and Glendon (1998). The potential problems were similar to those that had arisen in the West by the 1970s and noted in the Robens Report (see earlier in this chapter).

As part of the NIORDC safety development programme, the author ran a five-day course on major hazards risk management for some 20 senior managers from all eight refineries, who came together for this at the most geographically central refinery at Shazand Arak. The participants were all very experienced in the industry and at least half had studied and/or worked in the West. There was a genuine desire to apply the most up-to-date safety methods and techniques and the tutorial and syndicate work went well. As a former BP enterprise before the 1979 revolution, NIORDC personnel were still imbued with a certain admiration and respect for the technology and systems that BP had left behind, as several participants made clear to the author. They expressed some astonishment that the BP Grangemouth accidents (case 14.2) could possibly have occurred and, in a curious way, this realization seemed to spur them on to taking the course very seriously. After all, if an industry leader such as BP could experience serious problems regarding major hazards in refineries then any refinery company was surely vulnerable.

The course addressed a fairly classical post-Flixborough UK approach to major hazards, with an emphasis on a life-cycle 'cradle-to-grave' approach as described in HSE (1995), the ALARP Principle, major hazard analysis techniques, refinery processes and procedures most at risk and risk reduction and control methods. The participants were asked to identify what they considered the most hazardous part of their typical refineries and then, as a syndicate exercise, to carry out a preliminary hazard analysis that could be developed later into a more formal HAZOPS. They selected the hydrocracking reactors.

The discussions on emergency procedures and emergency planning were illuminating. It transpired that on-site emergency arrangements were fairly limited in scope and amounted to little more than an *ad hoc* fire brigade. There was no off-site emergency plan for summoning and coordinating emergency services or keeping the highways clear of traffic, concerned relatives and morbid sightseers. All decision-making of significance had to be referred all the way to Tehran several hundred kilometres away. Furthermore, immediately adjacent to a number of refineries were petrochemical plants that took some of their feedstock from the refinery next door but there were no formal safety communication channels between the two let alone a joint emergency plan. The concept of a major incident occurring in one plant then enveloping the plant next door to create a double disaster had not been considered.

A lively debate ensued between two factions among the participants about how much, if at all, additional major hazards measures were really needed. One faction, referring back to the Iran–Iraq War and the fact that almost every morning the refineries in the west of the country would be raided by Iraqi jets, noted that within two hours of being bombed and strafed the redoubtable staff would have plugged all the shrapnel and other holes in the fuel oil tanks with wooden bungs they had ready while the engineers would patch up the processing plant as best they could, just so long as production could continue. Their argument was, in essence, one of: 'With that experience, we know all about hazards and risks. We can face any disaster and win.' The other faction countered with, 'Yes, but that was wartime and who wants to live on a knife edge like that now in peacetime when we can do so much to control major hazards and prevent disasters?'

At the end of the course, there was general consensus that it had been a success and that the participants now had a good grounding in major hazards risk management which they could develop onwards themselves. Having returned to the UK, the author was disconcerted to learn that a few months after the course a fire and explosion had occurred in a cracker unit on the very refinery where the course took place, regrettably with several people killed or injured. Those Iranians of a cynical or superstitious nature (see case 6.6) might well have thought at the time, 'Aha, it's the British again. If that consultant had not come here telling us about major hazards, this incident would never have happened. Kar-e inglis hast!' To the author, however, the incident merely points up the unforgiving nature of major hazards if they remain inadequately controlled. Time and major hazards wait for no man, in the sense that since a major hazard incident may occur at any moment this requires the most robust precautions to always be in place and not neglected, or left to a later and possibly more convenient time, or ignored on the grounds of an incident being only a remote possibility.

In summary, the underlying generic causes of man-made disasters encompass some, if not most, of the following:

- failures of hindsight and organizational learning failures – see Chapter 3;
- bounded rationality and too many false assumptions about hazards, risks, consequences and cause-and-effect relationships – see Chapter 3;
- weak safety culture, especially with a production emphasis justifying safety lip-service, complacency and a failure to recognize and address human factors – see Chapter 4;
- fatalism in those cultures subscribing to the belief that events are not ordained or controlled by humans but by fate or a supra-human god and therefore human controls are superfluous – see Chapter 4;
- weak SMS including inadequate training, inadequate skilled resources, defective safety procedures, defective risk assessment and risk control methodologies, defective routine safety monitoring;
- over-reliance on periodic external certification of plant at the expense of permanent internal review and revision of the SMS and formal assessments of safety and risks that reflect the actual conditions on site rather than an idealized expectation (see Piper Alpha, for example).

## The European Union and United Kingdom Approaches to Major Hazards

The thrust of the EU Major Hazards Directive 82/96 EC of 1996 (the so-called Seveso II Directive) is, firstly, to prevent major accidents occurring and, secondly, limit their impact. The Directive applies to specified dangerous substances listed in Annex 1 of the Directive that are present in quantities that equal or exceed specified threshold amounts. Presence includes processing, creation, use, handling and storage. The scope excludes military establishments, their installations or their storage facilities among others but it is common practice for military sites, facilities and platforms to adopt the principles voluntarily.

For sites where the Directive applies, the member state government 'shall ensure that the operator is obliged to take all measures necessary to prevent major accidents and to limit their consequences for man and the environment'. Among obligations of operators is the requirement (Article 7) to draw up, maintain and revise as necessary a MAPP 'designed to guarantee a high level of protection for man and the environment by appropriate means, structures and management systems'. Note the word 'guarantee'. Proximity of other sites, especially if they also have major hazards, must be addressed in order to prevent a domino effect (Article 8) and the public must be suitably informed. Operators must prepare, review and revise as necessary a detailed safety report (Article 9) demonstrating: the effectiveness of the MAPP and its associated SMS, as detailed in Annex III; systematic identification and assessment of major hazards and the corresponding safety measures; adequate safety and reliability in the design, construction, operation and maintenance of any installation, storage facility, equipment infrastructure relevant to major hazards; and adequate internal and external emergency plans.

The UK has one of the longest histories of major hazards management and was a major contributor to the framing of the Directive. The UK's developed approach to major hazards, which meets the Directive, is enshrined in COMAH 1999. The 1999 Regulations were amended in 2005 to broaden their scope and reflect lessons learned from major accidents in Europe since COMAH was introduced. As cases 14.2 and 14.3 show, the UK authorities have long demanded that operators and duty holders must avoid treating compliance with major hazards safety requirements as merely an administrative exercise in which they can prepare safety reports that reflect idealized aspirations rather than on-the-ground reality. It is usually insufficient, for example, to make risk assessments and risk decisions based on a limited HAZOPS on some of the plant, draw up a motherhood-and-apple-pie SMS manual, put all these documents in the filing cabinet and largely ignore them for year after year. To be of any value and to fully comply with regulatory requirements, formal safety reports must be substantial, meaningful and realistic and need to reflect current expert thinking and advances in safety knowledge and technology. The life-cycle approach as set out, for example, in the HSE Guide 'Out of Control' (HSE 1995) plus an array of complementary hazard identification and risk assessment techniques need to be applied.

In addition to COMAH, since the early 1990s the UK has also adopted a more rigorous 'safety case' approach to major hazard exposures in particular industries, notably offshore oil and gas and railways. The 'safety case' approach originated in the UK's civil nuclear industry and remains the safety 'backbone' for all nuclear installations. In simple terms, a 'safety case' is a documented statement which seeks to demonstrate on safety grounds (both to the operator and to the regulatory authority) why a particular installation should be allowed to operate or continue to operate. It is normal routine to have a set of interlinked safety cases which relate to different phases of the installation life-cycle (for example, design, projects, operations) as well as safety cases for special operations. As a safety risk justification document (usually a substantial and interlinked set of documents), the statements in a safety case must be both lucid and defensible and therefore be based on evidence such as formal risk assessments using the ALARP principle. The statements on the SMS must represent reality and not idealized aspirations.

Further detailed discussion of safety cases is beyond the scope of this book and readers are referred specifically to Chapter 12 Safety Cases and Safety Reports in Waring (1996a), as well as Chapters 10 and 12 of Waring and Glendon (1998).

In terms of knowledge about causes of man-made disasters, the control of major hazard risks and the required preventative methodologies, techniques and technology, these are amply available to the relevant industries and have been well tried and tested over many years. The findings of official inquiries into man-made disasters have become quite repetitive in that respect. With such a mature state of development in the requirements for effective safety management and technology for major hazards, coupled with an equally mature understanding of why such controls continue not to be implemented in many cases (as evidenced by disaster inquiry reports), the scope for new insights has lessened. Whereas invaluable incremental improvements continue in the area of safety technology, perhaps more knowledge is still needed on what will motivate major hazard site operators to behave more responsibly and address the risks seriously (Waring 2013). This aspect is part of the wider problem of organizations failing to take risk management seriously, as discussed in earlier chapters.

# **15** *The Mari-Vassilikos Disaster, 11 July 2011*

On the 11 July 2011, a quantity of mixed munitions and explosives stored unsafely at the Mari Naval Base in Cyprus exploded. A total of 13 people (seven naval personnel and six civilian fire-fighters) were killed. The Vassilikos power station, operated as the island's main power station by the Electricity Authority of Cyprus (EAC) and which is adjacent to the Mari site, was virtually destroyed thereby knocking out 60 per cent of the country's electricity supply. Fortunately, the heavy fuel oil tanks on the EAC site did not ignite or explode as, by luck, they were shielded by the power station building which took the brunt of the blast from Mari. Sixty-eight people were recorded as receiving injuries and there was significant property damage to homes and businesses over a radius of several kilometres. The loss of such a large proportion of the islands' electricity supply, followed by many months of intermittent supply from other power stations, had a dramatic impact on business activity, employment and the functioning of the public sector, to the extent that it accelerated the economy's fall into recession. The disaster presents a sobering case of the mismanagement of man-made major hazards which was accentuated by incompetence, political intrigue, evasion of responsibility and a culture of perceived self-interest taking precedence over the objective requirements of public protection when it came to decision-making and action prior to the explosion.

## Background to the Explosion

On 20 January 2009, the Monchegorsk, a Russian-owned, Cypriot-flagged cargo vessel on its way from Iran to Syria was intercepted by the US Navy in the Red Sea on suspicion of being in violation of UN Security Council Resolution 1747 which places arms exports from Iran under sanction. The ship's captain was ordered to change direction once in the Mediterranean and to proceed to the port of Limassol in the Republic of Cyprus. Once the ship had docked in late January, Cypriot officials inspected the cargo of 98 containers on 29 January and 2 February and requested an assessment of the inspection reports from the UN Sanctions Committee as to whether Resolution 1747 provisions had been breached and what should be done next. The Sanctions Committee confirmed the breach and on 13 February 2009 the 98 containers were confiscated by the Cyprus Government and unloaded. It later emerged that the total consignment amounted to some 2,000 tonnes of various explosives, including 65 containers of gunpowder. It was decided as a temporary measure to transfer the containers to the Evangelos Florakis Naval Base at Mari, along the coast east of Limassol. Here, the containers were stacked in the open while the Government decided what action to take.

A number of friendly countries offered Cyprus immediate technical expertise and assistance to dispose of the dangerous cargo safely. For example, a US diplomatic cable on 29 January 2009 disclosed by Wikileaks referred to a US offer of technical assistance and other cables also referred to Cyprus's rejection of help from the US and from Germany. The UN headquarters in New York even suggested that a prompt by the UN Sanctions Committee might inspire Cyprus to accept one of the many offers of third-party assistance to dispose of the cargo. A subsequent request by the Sanctions Committee early in 2011 to visit and inspect the containers was also turned down by Cyprus (Hazou 2011b). However, on 13 February the then Defence Minister Costas Papacostas stated publicly and rather boldly, 'the material is completely safe, there is no risk' and 'it could even be placed in residential areas without any risk'. Thus, despite the international clamour to assist, there was no apparent recognition at ministerial level that the cargo was a major hazard or that any further safety measures were needed and therefore there was no rush to remove or neutralize the hazard. Much speculation in the media, based on Wikileaks's disclosures of US diplomatic cables, was raised at the time (and subsequently) that the deeper reason behind the blasé attitude of government ministers was the over-riding concern of President Dimitris Christofias, a career communist and well-known supporter of Russia and anti-Western regimes such as Syria, Iran, Cuba and Venezuela, not to upset President Assad of Syria or the Iranians by destroying the cargo. It was one thing to have to accept the Monchegorsk into port and offload the cargo; it was quite another to destroy it or allow others to destroy it.

It was widely reported that the Cyprus National Guard felt that it had neither the facilities nor the technical resources to be responsible for the cargo and its storage. A lengthy article in the *Cyprus Sunday Mail* of 17 July 2011 by Elias Hazou (Hazou 2011a), which quoted leaked minutes of Government inter-ministerial meetings on the subject, elaborated that on 28 May 2009, army commander Petros Tsalikidis warned of the specific danger of continuing to leave the containers exposed to the elements, including high temperatures in summertime. Nevertheless, a joint ministerial meeting on 6 August 2009 ordered that the cargo remain at Mari until the President had completed his official visit to Syria and the UN General Assembly in October 2009. However, a decision was not immediately forthcoming after the President's return. When the defence ministry wrote to the foreign ministry in November 2009 to express concern over the continuing delay about the unsatisfactory storage of the cargo, it received a reply to the effect that the political reasons for storing the cargo at Mari had not changed. A further request from the defence ministry in June 2010 received the same answer from the foreign ministry in July 2010.

The matter was not examined again until February 2011 at a meeting of the Defence Minister, Foreign Minister and the President's diplomatic office but again a decision was deferred. As the year progressed into summertime, with temperatures typically reaching 40 degrees C or more in early July, it is alleged that senior officers at the naval base sent repeated written expressions of concern to defence headquarters including a request to construct proper sheltering for the containers but to no avail. The base was advised instead to spray cold water on the containers. On 3 July, naval personnel noticed that two of the containers had buckled, indicating that some sort of exothermic chemical reaction was occurring inside, and on 4 July there was a small explosion in one of these containers which breached the container wall. On 5 July, the defence ministry instructed the National Guard to submit a written report on these incidents but this was not delivered before the major disaster on 11 July. The author's observation in Chapter 14 that 'time and major hazards wait for no man' is particularly poignant (that is, that man-made major hazards may erupt at any moment, thus scotching any assumption or expectation that deferring decisions on control measures will be of no consequence).

The principles for the safe storage of explosives are well known and the rules and procedures followed by military establishments in most countries are highly disciplined. Some years ago, one of the world's leading explosives manufacturers suffered two fatal explosions at different sites within a few months of each other. The company operated a number of sites in the UK, including toluene nitration plants as well as mixing and filling stations. The company was prosecuted and the author was commissioned to carry out a company-wide review of its safety systems, in part so that the company could produce a defence report to the court showing that it had already learned lessons and was active in trying to improve its systems. The following are the well-known principles which the author advocated (Waring 2011b):

- Explosives facilities, whether manufacturing and/or storage, should be sited remotely from dwellings and other sites, especially those with major hazards of their own or which are critical to the country's infrastructure.
- Sites should be selected that have as many natural or man-made blast barriers as possible, so as to deflect blast upwards.
- Distance and separation of inventories should be accompanied by storage units and cover that together avoid explosives 'sweating' or other adverse temperature/humidity effects.
- Inventories should be kept to a minimum.
- Modern technology should be used to monitor stability of explosive materials.
- SMS, safety procedures and safety culture at the site need to reflect the actual risks to life and limb on the ground and not be idealized aspirations or be diluted or ignored to suit commercial, political or other considerations.

The last bullet point, in respect of political considerations, was especially relevant to the Mari explosion. Also, as demonstrated by the cases in Chapter 14, so often even when competent personnel do exist at site level they are not always matched by equally competent or well-motivated superiors at headquarters somewhere else. See, for example, case 14.3 (Buncefield) where the board of HOSL was disengaged from its major hazard responsibilities for the site. Safety risk assessments and decisions based on them should be undertaken by competent persons at site level, with external assistance if necessary. SMS and protocols at site level should take precedence over 'political' or other questionable considerations higher up the tree. Civil servants and politicians clearly are unlikely to possess the technical knowledge and competence to know whether explosives are safe or not. They are prone to make naïve, and possibly fatal, assumptions.

## The Fire and Explosion on 11 July 2011

At 04.00am of 11 July 2011, a fire started at the Mari naval base. National Guard soldiers present tried to put the fire out but were unsuccessful and at 04.27am the local Fire

Department received a call about the fire. Senior defence officers arrived at the site at about the same time. By 05.00am, the fire was out of control.

At 05.53am, there was a massive explosion involving the munitions containers. Fires continued until finally brought under control at between 12.00 and 12.30pm. Twelve persons were already dead and a further 15 had been injured at the site, one of whom subsequently died. Both the Mari installation and the adjacent Vassilikos power station were devastated. Many homes in the nearby village of Mari were wrecked and property was damaged over a radius of several kilometres with dozens of people injured to varying degrees. An early official estimate of the cost of local property damage was put at about €2 million. Some 150 Mari residents had to be evacuated as their homes had been destroyed or badly damaged.

## The Government's Immediate Response

At 10.30am on the morning of the explosion, President Christofias visited the scene. He commented to TV and newspaper reporters present that the disaster was 'of biblical proportions' and was a black day for Cyprus. Cynics noted that by invoking the bible perhaps he was trying to suggest at the earliest opportunity that it was an act of God and therefore not attributable to any human involvement and especially governmental decisions or indecision.

Within days, the Government had established two parallel official inquiries into the disaster. The first was to be a criminal investigation by the police to determine whether criminal offences had been committed and who was accountable for them. Any legal proceedings arising would take some time beyond the criminal investigation itself. Meanwhile, in parallel with the criminal investigation, there would be a general investigation. The Attorney General stated that 'the investigative committee will examine this catastrophe in its entirety from when these containers arrived until after the explosion'. He added that no person or office no matter how high would be excluded from the investigation and the Chairman of the investigative committee and the criminal investigators would jointly determine the extent and type of individual responsibility for the disaster.

The person appointed by the cabinet was Mr Polis Polyviou, a respected lawyer with extensive experience in banking and finance issues. At the time, many (including the author) expressed concern about whether Mr Polyviou had the right credentials for heading an inquiry that would probably have to grapple with complex scientific and technical matters. Concern was also expressed at the small size of the investigating team, which appeared to be primarily Mr Polyviou himself, and the extremely short deadline he had been given or had set himself (three months) compared to other disaster inquiries in other countries. In the final analysis, however, such concerns proved to be unfounded as evidenced by his official report (Polyviou 2011) discussed below.

In addition to the two inquiries appointed by the cabinet, the parliamentary House Defence Committee decided to conduct its own investigation and submit a report in evidence to the Polyviou Inquiry. The joint Health and Environment Committee also examined aspects of the disaster, particularly the decisions and actions of the Fire Service.

## Public Outrage

Public protests arose very quickly after the disaster. Anger was directed at the Government and in particular the President personally, whom protesters accused of causing the disaster through incompetence, bad motives and years of indecision. A large crowd of protesters gathered outside the Presidential Palace in Nicosia on the evening of 12 July. By the evening of 15 July, the nightly numbers outside the Presidential Palace had grown to well in excess of 10,000 protesters from all walks of life and political persuasions hurling highly critical and inflammatory insults at the President and demanding that he resign. By 18 July, the number of protesters had risen to 12,000. It should be remembered that Cypriots tend to be conservative and are not noted for staging large-scale protests of this kind. By all accounts, this was the largest public protest of any kind in the history of the Republic. With a total population of barely 840,000, for thousands to gather in this way was quite extraordinary.

Public anger against the President had been fuelled by his address to the nation on 14 July, which was widely condemned as being evasive and making clichéd platitudes about finding those responsible. His address contained no form of an apology. The nightly protests outside the Palace continued for several weeks with protester numbers varying between 1,000 and 12,000.

Meanwhile, as the Polyviou Inquiry prepared to start, two cabinet ministers resigned (apparently forced or 'encouraged') and a public drama of denials, mutual accusations and recriminations among ministers, former ministers, politicians, defence officials, military officers and fire service heads then ensued. In the developing game of 'pass the blame parcel', no one wanted to be left holding the parcel.

## The Polyviou Inquiry and Report

The Inquiry amassed and examined a vast number of documents and also interviewed a large number of witnesses from across the spectrum of government ministries, public services, National Guard and the EAC. Witnesses included President Christofias as well as present and former ministers who had been party to the deliberations over two-and-a-half years about what to do about the munitions consignment.

Both in his testimony to the Inquiry and in public statements (which he either made himself or through his spokesman Stefanos Stefanou), the President sought to deny that he ever personally knew that the containers were likely to blow up unless removed or destroyed. The line was that the President was cut off from such matters which correctly were technical matters for the defence ministry and also that whatever decisions or actions he took were in the national interest. However, Polyviou's 600-page report was clear and damning in attributing to the President directly a 'serious personal responsibility for the tragic event and its consequences'. He noted that although military officers had evaluated a number of potential sites to keep the containers and had advised that the Mari base was the most suitable, the Minister of Defence had agreed with this advice and the decision to go ahead was at least approved or endorsed by the President who held the ultimate authority for the decision. A plea of ignorance was no defence for the President, especially in the light of evidence that the National Guard commander Tsalikidis had given specific warning of the dangers. A combination of laxity, negligence and inaction then ensured that the containers remained in limbo at Mari for some two-and-a-half years in unsafe conditions. In one especially damning passage, Polyviou stated:

> My conclusion is that the main responsibility for the tragedy and its aftermath burdens the President of the Republic ... I deem that the actions, acts and decisions of the President do not correspond to the minimum diligence expected of him, whether it be with regard to the public interest, the economy of the country, but above all the safety of the citizens of the Republic ... The bottom line is that the President of the Republic ... failed to see to it, or even take the most basic of steps, to ensure the safety of citizens, and in particular the safety of servicemen and fire-fighters.

Polyviou also found that the acts and omissions of the former Defence Minister Costas Papacostas, the former Foreign Minister Markos Kyprianou and the head of the President's diplomatic office Leonidas Pantelides all contributed to this 'accident waiting to happen'. For the President's part, he refused point-blank to accept any personal blame or responsibility and accused Mr Polyviou of exceeding his brief, despite the fact that he had been given a virtual *carte blanche* to investigate and comment without restriction.

In addition to examining the causes leading up to the explosion, the Polyviou Report examined at length what the EAC did in relation to compliance with the EU Major Hazards Directive (EU 1996) at the Vassilikos power plant next door to the Mari naval base. Chapter 7 and pages 540–583 in chapter 9 of the Report deal with this aspect in detail. The Report is especially scathing about the EAC's claim not to know anything about the location of the explosives containers at Mari and their proximity to the Vassilikos site:

> Chapter 7, page 486: I cannot accept the ... assertions. We are talking about a huge volume of containers, placed one above the other. Not only was the cargo within view of the power station but any reasonable person could note the distance between the nearest container and the EAC power station. Did the responsible officers of EAC know nothing? Could they not have raised questions about the containers' contents? ... I can only express my amazement and wonder ... there was gross negligence.

> Chapter 9, page 579: I know that the Director General of EAC before me did not accept the position that the EAC knew or should have been aware of the danger. I do not agree, because senior officers of EAC from 13 February 2009 had enough information and evidence of the risk. Quite simply, the real danger was not further investigated or evaluated correctly.

The Report found that the EAC site was subject to the EU Major Hazards Directive and that it was incumbent on EAC to comply, especially Article 8 (preventing 'domino' effects from any nearby major hazards). The risks of an individual major hazard site are greatly affected by other major hazard sites nearby. Not only can an incident at one site trigger an incident at the next one but also, and more importantly, the scale of a domino disaster is likely to be much larger than simply the sum of the two. Thankfully, this did not happen in the Mari-Vassilikos case (just a matter of luck) but the whole thrust of disaster prevention by the two sites, individually and jointly, should have been based on the potential geometric risk.

The EAC's 'Safety Report' in 2007 for the Vassilikos site as required under Article 9 did indeed identify the Mari naval base as a potential source of domino effect hazards, including projectiles 'and other exogenous factors'. However, this was not amplified or developed and the arrival in 2009 of the explosives containers at Mari did not provoke (as it should have done) a formal review and revision of the Vassilikos site Safety Report, including risk re-assessment and new control measures (Waring 2011c). The Polyviou Report found that the Labour Inspection Department (one of the two joint regulators) compounded the problem by wrongly telling EAC in February 2010 that the pre-2009 Safety Report still stood.

The Polyviou Report noted that there was confusion and a blinkered approach by various parties regarding the bi-directionality of domino effects. Mari was seen as being potentially vulnerable to major hazard threats from Vassilikos but not vice-versa. Further, the Vassilikos external emergency plan was only to be triggered in the event of an actual major accident and not if precursor factors were identified, for example the buckling of the explosives containers in Mari in the days prior to the explosion. In Mr Polyviou's words, the explosion and the domino effects were an 'accident waiting to happen'.

Mr Polyviou spotted some glaring holes in the testimony of senior EAC officials. For example, he noted that it was undisputed that the EAC Plant Director sent a report to his HQ in February 2009 that showed his awareness of the arrival and location of the munitions at Mari next door. Yet the current EAC Director told the Inquiry that no documents on this were traceable. When Mr Polyviou asked at the hearing why there was no record of the Plant Director's report, the EAC Director gave a truly astonishing answer (Psyllides 2011):

*What we heard came from statements to the media, which in fact said that the material was inert and could even be stored in the city centre. There was no reason to investigate any further. We were reassured by the statements.*

Although the EAC had no responsibility for the explosion at the Mari Naval Base, it definitely did have its own major hazard responsibilities for its own site. It was sheer luck that its fuel tanks did not go up when the blast from Mari struck Vassilikos. The EAC Director's reported statement taken at face value is terrifying in its demonstration not only of serious management failures with documentation control on high-risk issues but also of a woeful ignorance of the major hazard risk exposures and control requirements. Worse, it revealed a very casual attitude and a willingness to accept hearsay statements of reassurance on such critical matters from media reports instead of the EAC making its own due diligence enquiries and protective arrangements as required by the EU Directive (EU 1996). That Directive demands that operators, including EAC, 'guarantee a high level of protection for man and the environment'.

## Wider Criticisms by the Polyviou Report

Chapter 11 of the Report addressed what Mr Polyviou saw as the root cause of why the explosives were left so long in the open at Mari, and why the underlying principles of the EU Seveso Directive (that is, (a) prevention, (b) limit effects), were misunderstood and ignored by EAC. His analysis and comments on what he regarded as a deep malaise within Cypriot society verge on a polemic. In paraphrase, he alleged that a relentless pursuit of vested self-interests by politicians and officials coupled with their incompetence, empty rhetoric and a 'reduced perception of duty and selective observance of morality and legality' had resulted in a deeply cynical and mistrustful populace. As Polyviou noted and Professor Phedon Nicolaides (2011) reiterated, the problem in a system based on favouritism and cronyism is that no one has any incentive to speak out and point up obvious wrongdoing, mistakes or risks. No one wants to take personal responsibility so decision avoidance, *laissez-faire* and buck passing become the norm along with lack of transparency and a generalized corruption of the spirit:

> *Page 593–594: The responsibility for the disappointing state of affairs ... is now understood by all as timeless and accumulated. The tragedy at the Mari naval base reflects not only a colossal failure in this case but the failure of the political system in general. In this case, nothing worked ... Many public servants and the military showed sloppiness, avoiding responsibility and demonstrating self-evident cowardice against political leaders. There was complete collapse of the system (which of course is staffed and led by people, political officials and civil servants). It was very naïve to believe that the recent tragedy is a single or an unexpected event.*

To all intents and purposes, in Chapter 11 of the Report Mr Polyviou could have been describing the problems of sovereign corruption as defined in Chapter 9 of this book and further exemplified in relation to the Cyprus Property Scandal in Chapter 11 of this book. The abject failure and unwillingness of successive governments and their relevant ministries and departments to solve the title deeds and property fraud scandal is symptomatic of the same malaise identified by Polyviou as underlying the Mari disaster.

The Report demands serious reforms and not 'wishful thinking and empty findings'. Cronyism and clientism must go and be replaced by a fully transparent and merit-based system. Among the 13 recommendations in Chapter 10 of the Report is one for the establishment of an Independent Commission Against Corruption (see reference to the ICAC concept in Chapter 9 of this book), among other functions, to encourage public spirited 'whistle blowers' to report wrongdoing. However, the Polyviou Report is not binding and as the President had dismissed Chapter 11 of the Report and rejected the finding that he is primarily to blame for the disaster, it may be some time if ever before the Report's recommendations are accepted much less implemented. Ironically, in Cyprus the Report is likely to become a victim of the very malaise that its own Chapter 11 condemns. Nevertheless, in world terms, the Report is an important text in the library of man-made disaster reports.

Unfortunately, the Polyviou Report is available only in Greek. In the developed world, it is normal practice for major disaster reports commissioned by a government to be made public at least in English so that, hopefully, the whole world can avoid similar disasters. The author therefore had to obtain his own unofficial translation from which extracts above have been drawn.

## The Criminal Investigation

The criminal investigation recommended that criminal charges should be brought against 12 individuals but proceedings against four of them were not started. On 24 January 2012, eight officials were formally charged with manslaughter and causing death through a negligent act in relation to the Mari disaster. They were:

- The former Minister of Defence, Costas Papacostas, and the former Foreign Minister, Markos Kyprianou.
- Three senior National Guard officers in post at the time of the disaster: former National Guard Commander Petros Tsalikidis, former Deputy Chief Commander Savvas Argyrou and Colonel Georgios Georgiades, Deputy Commander of the third support brigade and former Commander of the ordnance corps.
- Three senior Fire Service officers, Chief Andreas Nicolaou, Deputy Chief Charalambos Charalambous and Commander of the disaster response unit Andreas Loizides.

In June 2012, the charges against Colonel Georgios Georgiades were dropped on instruction from the Attorney General. Former National Guard commander Petros Tsalikidis (a Greek national) was to be tried not in Cyprus but in Greece for the same offences. Despite the damning conclusion of the Polyviou Inquiry that the President was primarily responsible for causing the disaster, he was not among those recommended for prosecution and was not charged. A huge public debate ensued about whether constitutionally he enjoys immunity from prosecution. The consensus of legal opinion reported thus far is that he does enjoy such immunity in relation to his carrying out his presidential work and duties. At the time of writing, the court cases were still proceeding.

## The Costs of the Disaster

Cyprus is one of the smallest member states in the EU with a population of about 840,000 (the size of a medium city in most EU countries) and a GDP of only some €18 billion. By way of comparison, the Athens Larger Urban Zone has a population of 4.1 million. The Cyprus population and economy rely heavily on a narrow range of sectors, primarily tourism, property and offshore financial services. Whereas larger, diverse economies may be able to absorb fairly rapidly the impact of a disaster such as Mari-Vassilikos, Cyprus simply does not have the economic capacity and the adverse impact continues to affect every citizen and resident, whether directly or indirectly.

Apart from the deaths and injuries, and the damage to local properties, homes and businesses within the blast radius, the population as a whole suffered electrical power cuts for several months after the explosion while EAC did its best to plug the capacity gap. Large industrial generators were imported to form part of the response. However, while the power crisis remained throughout the hottest summer months, many businesses and government offices were working short time so as to reduce power demand. There was an inevitable downturn in the economy which tipped the country further into recession and rising unemployment. Up until February 2013, every electricity consumer was paying higher EAC charges as contribution towards the higher generating costs resulting from the Vassilikos damage and disruption.

The damage to the Vassilikos power station was estimated at €700 million soon after the disaster. Subsequent estimates put the rebuild cost at €300–€400 million. In December 2012, it was reported that as far as insurable costs are concerned (excluding uninsured and uninsurable losses), an out-of-court settlement between the EAC, its insurers and the Government had been reached whereby the insurers would pay a total of €132.5 million and the Government would pay the insurers €99 million as compensation in recognition for its contributory responsibility for the explosion. The state also faced a compensation claim of some €200 million from EAC to cover its uninsured losses. Cyprus's application to the EU Solidarity Fund for financial aid linked to the Mari disaster was rejected on the grounds that the disaster was man-made and not a disaster of nature for which the Fund was intended.

A study by the University of Cyprus in August 2011 estimated that the energy crisis resulting from the damage to Vassilikos would lead to a 2.4 per cent drop in the country's annual GDP and a 1 per cent point rise in unemployment. By the end of the last quarter of 2012, the unemployment rate had risen to 14.7 per cent from all causes. As early as the end of July 2011, the Mari disaster was cited by the international credit ratings agency Moody's as a factor in it downgrading Cyprus's Government bonds from A2 to Baa1. Over the nine months following Mari, for other reasons including financial imprudence and mismanagement, Cyprus Government bonds and the country's three main banks were relegated to 'junk status,' the lowest level possible, a downward trend that continued into 2013.

The emotional and health costs to those injured and the families of those killed or injured have also been incalculable. Victims continue to express anger and outrage at the Government and establishment. Many have also reported financial hardship as a result of the disaster. On 30 March 2012, the parliamentary House Defence Committee was informed by its Chairman of a number of cases of injured victims or their relatives who could no longer work as a result of the disaster. Some had been made redundant because of health problems reportedly linked to the disaster and in one case a woman had to give up her own job to look after her injured husband. Apparently, all had been abandoned by the state in terms of financial support.

The political costs at various levels were significant. Among the population, there was a sea change in support for the President and his AKEL (communist) Party as evidenced in opinion polls and in municipal elections across the country, when AKEL administrations which had been incumbent for years and sometimes decades were voted out. His public statements on, and attitude towards, the disaster, his failure to deliver an unequivocal apology and his avowed insistence that he was entirely innocent contrary to the evidence, undoubtedly added to a widespread unpopularity and rejection of AKEL by voters. In May 2012, the President announced that he would not stand for re-election as President in 2013.

Internationally, the President and the Government have also been damaged politically. The revelations about the political motivations for keeping the explosives at Mari for so long (that is, not wanting to upset Syria, Russia and Iran), and the US diplomatic cables disclosed by Wikileaks which painted President Christofias in very unflattering terms, made him appear parochial, evasive, stubborn, dogma-driven and untrustworthy. Such an image was unhelpful while the Government continued to evade repeated demands from the EU for Cyprus to curb its massive public debt. The predicted application for an EU bailout was formally made on 26 June 2012. Thus, on this and other major issues, Cyprus needed as many EU friends as it could muster and not to alienate them.

# Present and Future Risk Exposures

In addition to Vassilikos, EAC operates a number of other power stations and the stored fuel inventories at each are likely to bring them within the scope of the Seveso Directive. If any of the EAC sites holds inventories of designated dangerous substances, such as fuel oil, that exceed the EU Directive's threshold quantities then each site has a present and ongoing obligation to comply with the Directive. The public need to be assured that EAC has fully complied with the EU Major Hazards Directive at each of these sites.

Moreover, on top of human and environmental safety as demanded by the EU Seveso Directive, as a strategic utility provider EAC has a further (governance) obligation to protect its operations, its shareholders, its customers and the economy from unnecessary loss and damage. Therefore, it was expected that EAC would create a comprehensive and robust risk management system for all its sites, addressing prevention as well as emergencies and crises and covering all manner of threats and major accident scenarios.

What of the future? The pre-existing plan to add a Liquefied Natural Gas (LNG) terminal to Vassilikos for receipt of bulk gas by ship and/or from offshore gas production installations is apparently still on track. The advent of offshore gas extraction south and south east of Cyprus will also almost certainly result in onshore gas reception and processing terminals in Cyprus, including gas liquefaction plant. Thus far, these new plants are being concentrated at and around Mari. All such developments will have a huge impact on the major hazard profile of the overall site or complex of sites and the 'safe operating envelope'. The threshold quantities of LNG specified in Annex 1 of the Directive are 50 tonnes (Article 6 Notification and Article 7 MAPP compliance) and 200 tonnes (Article 9 Safety Report compliance).

LNG presents awesome explosion risks. As a gas liquefied under pressure, any rupture of a tank, pipe or seal can lead initially to Boiling Liquid Expanding Vapour Explosion (BLEVE) followed by a much more serious Unconfined Vapour Cloud Explosion (UVCE) or air-fuel explosion. The high-pressure shock wave can be devastating. Remote locations and strict safety controls for such facilities are therefore *de rigueur*.

Cyprus is no stranger to disaster in modern times. Its people have acquired a certain toughness, some might say obstinate resilience, following the 1974 invasion and a *de facto* territorial partition in all but name. The Helios airliner crash of August 2005, in which many Cypriots lost their lives, is still a raw and controversial subject. The Mari-Vassilikos disaster too will linger on for a long time in the public psyche. At the time of writing, the criminal prosecutions are still proceeding but, even once concluded, it is doubtful that the accusations and controversy will subside rapidly. In line with Government policy of 'no transparency', there have been no public statements or reports (official or unofficial) providing any details of any remedial action by the Cyprus authorities to prevent a recurrence at Mari or a similar occurrence elsewhere. The case not only highlights the maxim that 'time and major hazards wait for no man' but also demonstrates that failure to follow with good discipline the well-known principles and practices of major hazards risk control is likely to end in disaster. Sovereign corruption mixed with ineptitude and political expediency is a toxic combination that cannot co-exist safely with the effective control of major hazards.

# *Conclusion*

The terms 'governance' and 'risk management' have become somewhat over-exercised clichés and platitudes. Most people, including corporate boards, say that they believe in the need for good governance and the effective management of risks. Their corporate brochures, mission statements, annual reports, websites and PR emissions are full of it. In reality, however, only a minority of organizations makes any serious and sustained attempt to put their fine words into practice. The evidence is all around. The high-profile cases of risk management failure and poor governance, as in the many examples described in this book, are but the tip of the iceberg. When even the gods of the corporate world are shown to have feet of clay (as in the mass of well-known and 'blue chip' organizations which continue to feature in corporate scandals and collapses), it does not inspire confidence that the myriad of other less well-endowed organizations can do any better at risk management and governance.

The seeds of risk mismanagement, tunnel vision and quackery, which lead to much damage to businesses, their corporate reputations, their revenues and share values and, in some cases, to corporate disasters, lie in the fertile mix of faulty risk cognition, human weakness and fallibility, dysfunctional organizational cultures and toxic power relations as identified in Waring and Glendon (1998) and in many of the chapters in this book. As summarized in Chapter 3, the poor quality of risk management in large organizations is associated with:

- bounded rationality, narrow risk-related experience, untutored view/ignorance, unchallenged dogma;
- failure to recognize risk interdependencies;
- arrogance among directors and senior executives and an often unwarranted belief in their own risk expertise;
- reaction rather than pre-emption: 'It can never happen to us', decision-avoidance, ignore risk issues and they will solve themselves;
- biases towards finance, insurance and risk transfer, risk quantification, single metrics and salvation models; ignoring people risks and HR risks;
- personal agendas and self-serving calculation: an apparatchik 'herd' culture; cynical, temporary 'presenteeism' encouraging lip service, soft-pedalling and decision-avoidance on risk issues;
- a chancer culture of 'What can we get away with?' and casino-style gambles on major issues with little or no cogent risk evaluation;
- inadequately qualified risk managers.

All of the above may lead to a lack of due diligence in a broad sense. For this situation to change fundamentally for the better, a radical revision of corporate and managerial thinking and attitude will be required. It is still commonplace in many countries for senior executives to regard risk management and governance as optional extras or as alien topics that do not form part of 'normal management' and which therefore they consider are not part of their job function. Despite the obvious limitations, many of them believe that their own prior knowledge and experience are sufficient. As noted in Chapter 2, they often put forward the self-deception that their many years' experience helping to run successful businesses is proof enough that they know all about risk management. For example, while drafting this concluding section, the author was invited to participate in a supposedly high-level conference within the EU on crisis management and corporate risk. The organizers confided that, from experience, they had grave doubts that board directors and other senior executives would be likely to attend unless it was held during the evening because otherwise it would interfere with their normal daily priorities. Unless and until directors and senior executives perceive and accept that risk management and governance are not an optional extra to be relegated to an out-of-hours activity but an essential, integral part of competent management and their responsibilities and duties towards shareholders and other stakeholders, the present malaise will continue indefinitely.

The question arises as to how it may be possible to make a step change in the right direction. In keeping with his view that salvation models and quick fixes rarely work, the author believes that all business, management and finance degree courses, whether undergraduate, post-graduate masters or MBA, should have a substantial compulsory element devoted to risk management. By making it compulsory rather than elective, the false impression that risk management is just another optional extra is avoided. In addition, membership criteria for relevant professional bodies in business, management and finance should specify clearly that only a qualifying degree which incorporates the compulsory risk management module is acceptable, unless the applicant is prepared first to obtain an additional qualification specifically in risk management. Further, for those professional bodies which operate a Continuing Professional Development requirement, members should be required to demonstrate completion of a minimum number/frequency of short or special courses on risk management topics in any one reporting period.

Moreover, organizations themselves should require all members of their board risk committees and board audit committees to undergo at least a basic course or courses in ERM, ISO 31000 principles, due diligence requirements and crisis management/business continuity planning. This would avoid such committees trying to 'wing it' on the basis of members' untutored knowledge and experience (however substantial), which is likely to be incomplete or faulty.

As in so many aspects of business life, either doing little or nothing on risk management or expecting to muddle through without proper understanding of the subject or of protective requirements are no longer options that companies can get away with readily. It is no more compulsory for an organization not to experience corporate damage and disaster than it is compulsory for an individual not to experience ill-health. Good governance and robust risk management do not just happen by chance. They require commitment, effort, knowledge and expertise. Owners, shareholders, employees and other stakeholders surely deserve no less.

# Glossary

**B**

**bounded rationality:** the inherent limitations on what an individual or group can know and understand about a particular topic. Decision-making is thus constrained by limited information (which also may be inaccurate or biased), limited capacity to process that information (which capacity may also be subject to biases) and limited time.

**business continuity:** ensuring that during and following a crisis an organization is able to continue functioning with minimal disruption to its business.

**business continuity plan:** a formal plan for business continuity ready to be activated by a designated authorized person at a time of crisis.

**C**

**caveat emptor:** let the buyer beware. A legal principle, especially in civil and common law, meaning that, before making a transaction, a buyer has a primary duty to protect his own interests by considering both the obvious and likely risks of buying a particular item.

**chancer:** an English colloquial term for someone who, by nature and habit, tends to gamble that they can do something daring (which is also possibly wrong, disreputable, illegal or just plain stupid) and avoid getting caught or harmed. A chancer is usually driven by the prospect of an attractive reward for such risky behaviour and the expectation that he will get away with it.

**control:** action taken by a system to maintain its activity or output at a pre-determined level, rate or quality.

**corporate fraud:** the abuse of position, or false representation, or prejudicing the rights of an organization's owners, shareholders, investors, customers or employees for personal gain. The essence of such fraud is a deliberate act of deception, within or by a corporate entity, intended to permanently deprive another party of a valued asset (for example, money, shares, property, pensions) which is rightly theirs.

**corporate governance:** the set of values, principles, systems and processes by which companies are directed and controlled in order to protect the interests of owners, shareholders and other stakeholders. Corporate governance is a primary responsibility of the board of directors.

**corruption:** (1) UNCAC definition: an abuse of (public) power for private gain that hampers the public interest. (2) EU definition: requesting, offering, giving or accepting, directly or indirectly, a bribe or any other undue advantage (to any public official), or prospect thereof, which distorts the proper performance of any duty or behaviour required of the recipient of the bribe. Some jurisdictions treat all forms of such behaviour as corruption, even involving companies or individuals and no public official.

**corruption of the spirit:** corruption exhibited by a culture in which officials lack the will or encouragement to act professionally, ethically and efficiently or to challenge manifest wrongdoing.

**crisis:** for an organization, a period of intense and often dramatic conflict and uncertainty about a topic which is central to the organization's current existence and involving loss of control and, if unresolved, possible collapse and chaos. Frequently, a crisis involves acutely unstable conditions and often leads to enforced major change in the organization.

**crisis management plan:** a formal plan for managing specifically identified crisis scenarios/contingencies and ready to be activated by a designated authorized person at a time of crisis.

**crisis management planning:** the process of formally planning the arrangements, procedures, resources, key responsibilities and specified authorities to be activated at a time of crisis.

**culture:** a set of unwritten and usually unobtrusive attitudes, beliefs, values, rules of behaviour, ideologies, habitual responses, language, rituals, 'quirks' and other features which characterize a particular group of people; cultures may be identified at different levels, for example nations, localities, societies, professions, organizations, departments, interest groups.

**D**

**double selling:** a type of fraud, especially relating to immovable property transactions, in which a vendor sells a property to Party A and then, unbeknown to the latter, sells the property again to Party B (often for a higher price) but fails to return Party A's money.

**due diligence:** the exercise by a party to an activity, relationship, contract, transaction or deal which seeks to demonstrate an appropriate and adequate degree of searching examination of an individual or entity to establish their probity, honesty and *bona fides*, and to uncover any hidden relevant facts, from which it may be reasonably deduced whether or not that party should proceed with the activity, relationship, contract, transaction or deal.

**E**

**Enterprise Risk Management (ERM):** a corporate approach to managing risk that recognizes the full range of significant risk exposures relevant to the particular organization, as well as their interactions and corporate implications.

**F**

**fraud:** the abuse of position, or false representation, or prejudicing the rights of someone for personal gain. The essence of such fraud is a deliberate act of deception intended to permanently deprive another party of a valued asset (for example, money, shares, property) which is rightly theirs. Most jurisdictions automatically treat all fraud as a criminal offence as well as a civil offence but a few jurisdictions are reluctant to treat fraud as warranting criminal investigation and proceedings.

**H**

**hazard:** a physical entity, substance, condition, activity or behaviour which is capable of causing harm.

**hazard identification:** the process of identifying a hazard and analyzing how it may cause harm, as a preliminary step in risk assessment.

**HAZOPS:** Hazard and Operability Studies designed to check systematically, and challenge assumptions about, the operational safety of process plant and equipment.

**heuristic:** assessment using experience or rules-of-thumb.

**I**

**intellectual property:** tangible and intangible assets which have been created by artistic or intellectual endeavour, for example books, writings, fine art, computer programs, inventions, chemical formulae, designs, formulations.

**Intellectual Property Rights (IPR):** the accumulated laws and precedents that seek to confer protection on the rights of owners of intellectual property.

**intellectual property risk:** the array of threats by which someone's or an organization's ownership or exploitation rights of intellectual property may be compromised.

**K**

**Key Risk Indicator (KRI):** an indicator or measure of risk judged by a particular organization's management to be of major importance to its overall context.

**L**

**letter rogatory:** a formal request sent by the authorities of one jurisdiction to their counterparts in another jurisdiction requesting assistance and provision of information about specified matters and questions relating to criminal investigations and legal proceedings in the first jurisdiction.

**M**

**major accident hazard:** a hazard which, in a single incident, could result in the death or injury of large numbers of people and/or major damage to property and/or environment. Such hazards may be either natural in origin or man-made. Typically, man-made major hazards are named and defined by legislation, for example EU Major Hazards Directive.

**Major Accident Prevention Policy (MAPP):** the specific and appropriate means, structures and management systems established by the operator of a major hazard installation, which are designed to guarantee a high level of protection for man and the environment.

**management system:** (1) A notional system relating to management of an organization or operation. (2) A structured systematic means for ensuring that an organization or a defined part of it is capable of achieving and maintaining high standards of specified performance.

**N**

**Non-Executive Director (NED):** a director appointed to the board of an organization but having no executive role, responsibilities or authority. A NED usually has lengthy experience elsewhere as an executive director and is appointed to offer independent advice to the board on matters of governance and risk, such as business strategy, remuneration policy, mergers and acquisitions.

**Non-Performing Loan (NPL):** a loan where the borrower has failed persistently to service the debt according to the agreed schedule of repayments.

**O**

**organizational culture:** a set of unwritten and usually unobtrusive attitudes, beliefs, values, rules of behaviour, ideologies, habitual responses, language, rituals, 'quirks' and other features which characterize a particular organization or a defined part of it.

Organizational culture both influences attitudes and behaviour of the organization's individual members as well as being reinforced by their collective attitudes and behaviour.

**organizational learning:** a cumulative, reflective, experiential process through which all members of an organization learn to understand and continuously interpret the organization, its strengths and weaknesses and its successes and failures, so as to modify systems and behaviour and improve outcomes.

# P

**pandemic:** an epidemic in which a potentially fatal disease spreads rapidly across multiple countries and infects large numbers of people.

**Permit-to-Work (PTW):** in operational safety management, a procedure which seeks to prevent accidents during highly hazardous activities by requiring a sequence of documented safety checks and formal authorizations before, during and on completion of a specified piece of work.

**Ponzi scheme:** a type of 'pyramid structure' corporate fraud in which investors' earnings and returns statements are falsely inflated while their investments are actually being used to pay the earnings of earlier investors. Usually necessarily involves illicit money movements, false accounting and false investment statements. Ultimately, all Ponzi schemes collapse. Classic Ponzi schemes were operated by Madoff and Stanford International.

**pure risk:** an absolute risk or one which relates only to harm. With a pure risk, the best that can happen is that nothing bad happens.

# Q

**quack:** a person who claims specialist knowledge or skills but who lacks requisite qualifications.

**quackery:** the application of unqualified beliefs and opinions to matters requiring specifically relevant professional qualifications, especially where people's health, safety and lives may be endangered by an unqualified opinion or action.

# R

**res ipsa loquitur:** the thing speaks for itself. A legal principle, particularly in common law, which suggests that the likely explanation for what someone said, or did, is self-evident.

**risk:** (1) The probability or likelihood that (for a pure risk) a specified hazard will result in a specified undesired event, or (for a speculative risk) a specified event or course of action will result in a specified gain or enhancement and/or specified loss or detriment. (2) For pure risks, the product of the potential severity of hazard consequences and the probability that the undesired event will occur.

**risk acceptability:** use of criteria, usually formally agreed criteria, to determine whether a particular level of risk is acceptable. Often assumes that acceptability determined by risk specialists broadly matches public acceptability but this assumption may not be born out.

**risk acceptance:** the fact of accepting a particular risk or level or risk. May not mean that all those accepting a risk actually regard the risk as acceptable if their options are constrained or compromised or they are under duress.

**risk appetite:** the propensity, usually of a corporate board, to take speculative risks. Risk appetite varies according to factors such as board composition, recent company history and events, tradition, state of external economy and markets.

**risk assessment:** the process of estimating and evaluating a risk in order to determine whether current risk strategies are appropriate and adequate.

**risk evaluation:** the process of interpreting risk estimates and the overall results of a risk assessment.

**risk financing:** a strategy seeking to deflect the financial impact of specified undesired events occurring by the application of financial instruments such as insurance policies, investment instruments and captive funds.

**risk management:** the overall process of ensuring that risk exposures are managed in the most cost-effective and cost-efficient way.

**risk reduction:** a strategy seeking to reduce risk levels by prevention and control techniques.

**risk retention:** a strategy seeking to accept specified risk exposures, possibly involving captive insurance.

**risk strategy:** an approach to risk seeking the best combination of avoidance, deferment, reduction, retention, transfer, sharing and limiting of risk exposures.

**risk tolerability:** acceptability of a given level of risk on the grounds that the probability of an undesired event is sufficiently low and (for speculative risks) significant benefits are also derived.

**risk transfer:** (1) Seeking to transfer by contract term the liability for a specified risk from one party to another. (2) Seeking through an insurance policy to deflect the financial impact of specified undesired events occurring; only applies to insurable risks.

**rogue trader:** an individual who, while employed to buy and sell stocks, shares and securities, engages in improper transactions over a period of time, which result in large financial losses for the employer and clients. The activities of Nick Leeson at Barings Securities are often taken as the quintessential example of rogue trading.

**S**

**safety case:** a documented statement seeking to demonstrate on safety grounds why a particular major hazard installation should be allowed to operate or continue to operate. The statement is usually accompanied by a large inter-linked compilation of documents including major hazard risk assessments.

**safety culture:** those aspects of an organization's culture which affect health and safety.

**Safety Management System (SMS):** a structured systematic means for ensuring that an organization or a defined part of it is capable of achieving and maintaining high standards of health and safety performance.

**salvation model:** a model which proponents imagine and expect will offer instant and long-term protection without too much effort.

**self-regulation:** the purposeful and active interpretation and practical implementation by an organization of goal-directed legislation which applies to it, as opposed to waiting for external compliance enforcement by regulatory authorities.

**share ramping:** a type of corporate fraud in which false share sales occur between related companies having the same controlling owner so as to inflate share values.

**sovereign corruption:** a situation in a country where the scale of state-inspired corruption of all kinds (petty, grand, corrupted spirit) and its tentacles is vast and all-pervasive throughout society.

**speculative risk:** a risk which may have both beneficial and/or detrimental outcomes, for example risks related to investment, human resources, product innovation, mergers and acquisitions.

**strategic risk:** a risk which may damage or disrupt significantly an organization's overall business/corporate strategy or the organization itself.

**sub-system:** an identifiable component of a system which itself has all the characteristics of a system.

**subjective risk:** a personal view of a risk. In a sense, all risk is subjective as risk is a perceptual and cognitive phenomenon, that is, it exists entirely in the minds of individuals.

**system:** a concept of a recognizable whole consisting of a number of parts which interact in an organized way; characterized by inputs, outputs, processes, a boundary, an environment, an owner, emergent properties, control and survival; addition or removal of a component affects both the component and the system.

**T**

**threat:** an alternative term for hazard used in some areas of risk such as security.

**V**

**Value At Risk (VAR):** a measure of the risk of loss on a specific portfolio of financial assets.

# References

Anderlini, J. 2009. A cautionary tale from China, *Financial Times*, 27 July 2009.

Anderson, R.C. and Reeb, D.M. 2003. Founding family ownership and firm performance: evidence from the S&P 500, *Journal of Finance*, 58, 1301–1328.

Ansari, A.M. 2006. *Confronting Iran*. Cambridge MA, USA: Basic Books, Perseus Books Group.

Arnold, S. 2007. Making sense of an organizational crisis: the experience of hospital employees working during the SARS outbreak. Pages 221–247. In Glendon, A.I. Thompson, B.M. and Myors, B. (eds). *Advances in Organizational Psychology*. Brisbane: Australian Academic Press.

ASNZ 4360 2004. *Risk Management*. Standards Australia.

Banbury, S. and Tremblay, S. 2004. *A Cognitive Approach to Situation Awareness: Theory and Application*. Farnham, UK: Ashgate Publishing.

Barton, D. Coombes, P. and Chiu-Yin Wong, S. 2004. Asia's governance challenge. *The McKinsey Quarterly*, 2, 55–61.

Basel II 2004. *Basel II Accord*. Basel Committee on Banking Supervision, Basel, Switzerland.

Beer, M. Eisenstat, R.A. and Spector, B. 1990. Why change programs don't produce change, *Harvard Business Review*, 68(6), 158–166.

Bignell, V. and Fortune, J. 1984. *Understanding System Failures*. Manchester, UK: Manchester University Press.

BoBS 1995. *Report of the Inquiry into the Circumstances of the Collapse of Barings*. Chairman E.H. George. 18 July 1995. Board of Banking Supervision. London: The Stationery Office.

Bohdjalian, S. 2012. Commentary: Cyprus banks should offload distressed property, page 26, *Financial Mirror*, 11–18 April 2012.

Bovard, J. 2008a. Your money, *South China Sunday Morning Post*, 5 October 2008.

Bovard, J. 2008b. The Lehman collapse – are human failings in risk decisions controllable? *Asia Risk Newsletter*, 4, 1–2.

Bovingdon, T. 2012. The wronged man, interview with Michael Woodford, *Risk Management Professional*, June, 12–13, London: Institute of Risk Management.

BS 25999-2 2007. *Specification for Business Continuity Management*. London: British Standards Institution.

Burke, R.J. Clarke, S. and Cooper, C.L. (eds). 2011. *Occupational Health and Safety: Psychological and Behavioural Aspects of Risk*. Farnham, UK: Gower Publishing.

Burke, R.J. and Cooper, C.L. 2010. *Risky Business*. Farnham, UK: Gower Publishing.

Burke, R.J. Martin, G. and Cooper, C.L. 2011. *Corporate Reputation – Managing Opportunities and Threats*. Farnham, UK: Gower Publishing.

Christou, J. 2009. Couple awarded house after long legal battle, *Cyprus Sunday Mail*, 4 January 2009.

Chrysafis, A.C. 2010. *Corruption, The Vanishing Cyprus series*, press article released June 2010 via info@evandia.com.

CIPD 2008. *The 2008 Retention and Recruitment Survey*. London: Chartered Institute of Personnel and Development.

COMAH 1999. *The Control of Major Accident Hazards Regulations 1999* (revised 2005). London: The Stationery Office.

Coombes, P. and Chiu-Wong, S. 2004. Chairman and CEO – one job or two? *The McKinsey Quarterly 2004*, 2, 43–47.

COSO 2004. *Enterprise Risk Management – Integrated Framework.* Committee of Sponsoring Organizations of the Treadway Commission (COSO), September 2004.

CPAG 2007. *Cyprus Property Pitfalls – A Time for Action,* Cyprus Property Action Group, Available at www.cyprus-property-action-group.net.

CPAG 2011. *Complaint about the Non-Compliance of Cyprus with EU Law.* Submission to the Commission of the European Communities on the EU Unfair Commercial Practices Directive 2005/29/EC. 3 November 2011. Cyprus Property Action Group, Available at www.cyprus-property-action-group.net.

CPI 2011. *Corruption Perceptions Index 2011.* Transparency International, International Secretariat, Alt-Moabit 96, 10559 Berlin, Germany.

CPSC 2007. *2007 China Program Plan.* International Consumer Product Safety Program, US Consumer Product Safety Commission, Bethesda, MD.

Cullen 1990. *Report of the Official Inquiry into the Piper Alpha Disaster,* chairman Lord Cullen. London: The Stationery Office.

CySTAT 2012. *Preliminary Results of the Census of Population 2011.* Cyprus Statistical Service, Ministry of Finance, 1444 Nicosia, Cyprus.

der Partogh, M. 2012. Cyprus Airways: shape up or shut down, editorial, page 6, *Financial Mirror,* 11–18 April 2012.

Dickerson, J. 2011. *Every Day's a Monday.* London: Olympia Publishers.

DoLS 2012. *Property Sales in Cyprus 2011.* Department of Land and Surveys, Ministry of Interior, Nicosia, Cyprus.

Douglas, M. 1992. *Risk and Blame: Essays in Cultural Theory.* London: Routledge.

EC 2008. *Report on Community Customs Activities on Counterfeit and Piracy, Results at the European Border 2007.* Brussels: European Commission.

Edwards, R. 1998. *The Environmental Impact of the Sea Empress Oil Spill,* Final Report of the Sea Empress Environmental Evaluation Committee, chairman Professor Ron Edwards CBE. London: The Stationery Office.

Elliott, D. Swartz, E. and Herbane, B. 2002. *Business Continuity Management – A Crisis Management Approach.* London: Routledge.

EU 1982. *EU Major Hazards Directive (the 'Seveso I' Directive) 82/501EC.* European Commission, Brussels.

EU 1996. *EU Major Hazards Directive (the 'Seveso II' Directive) 96/82EC.* European Commission, Brussels.

EU 2008. *Report on Community Customs Activities on Counterfeiting and Piracy, Results at the European Border 2007.* European Commission, Brussels.

EU 2011. *The EU Corporate Governance Framework.* Green Paper, COM(2011) 164 final, European Commission, Brussels, 5 April 2011.

EUROPA 2008. *Conference on Counterfeiting and Piracy, Frequently Asked Questions.* 13 May 2008, EUROPA, European Commission, Brussels.

Fennell, D. 1988. *Report of the Official Inquiry into the King's Cross Fire,* chairman Desmond Fennell QC. London: The Stationery Office.

Fischhoff, B. 1975. Hindsight does not equal foresight: the effect of outcome knowledge on judgement in uncertainty. *Journal of Experimental Psychology, Human Perception and Performance,* 1, 288–299.

FRC 2005. *Internal Control: Revised Guidance (Turnbull) for Directors on the Combined Code,* October 2005. London: Financial Reporting Council.

FRC 2010. *The UK Corporate Governance Code,* June 2010 (amended September 2012). London: Financial Reporting Council.

FSA 2011. *Report on the Failure of the Royal Bank of Scotland (RBS),* December 2011, FSA Board, chairman Adair Turner. London: Financial Services Authority.

FSA 2012. FSA bans and fines former Royal Liver Assurance finance director George McGregor £109,000, *FSA/PN/022/2012.* London: Financial Services Authority.

Georgiou, A.K. 2010. *Corporate Governance and its Effect on the Performance of Family and Non-Family Companies Listed on the Cyprus Stock Exchange,* doctoral thesis paper, Institute for Work-Based Learning, Middlesex University, England.

Gibson, K. 2002. A case for the family-owned conglomerate, *The McKinsey Quarterly 2002,* 4, 126–137.

Gilman, L.F. 2010. *Due Diligence – A Strategic and Financial Approach,* 2nd edition. Durban, South Africa: LexisNexis South Africa.

Glendon, A.I. 2004a. *Comparing Organizational Risk Perceptions in Hong Kong and Australia,* 28th International Congress of Psychology, Beijing.

Glendon, A.I. 2004b. *Understanding and Managing Risk Perceptions,* 36–43 in conference proceedings of Maximizing Trade – Minimizing Risk, Quarantine and Market Access Conference 2003, Canberra, Australia, 24–25 September 2003.

Glendon, A.I. 2008. Safety culture and safety climate: how far have we come and where could we be heading? *Journal of Occupational Health and Safety Australia and New Zealand,* 24(3), 249–271.

Glendon, A.I. Clarke, S. and McKenna, E. 2006. *Human Safety and Risk Management (2nd edition).* Boca Raton, FL: CRC Press/Taylor & Francis.

Glendon, A.I. and Waring, A.E. 1997. *Barings: A Case of HR Mismanagement?* 31–40 in conference proceedings of ANZAM 97 Conference, Management Theory and Practice – Moving into a New Era, Monash University and Macmillan Australia.

GRECO 2005. *Second Evaluation Round, Evaluation Report on Cyprus,* GRECO Eval II Rep (2005) 3E, 10 March 2006, Groupe d'Etats Contre la Corruption, DG 1 Legal Affairs, Department of Crime Problems, Council of Europe, Strasbourg.

GRECO 2010. *Third Evaluation Round, Evaluation Report on Cyprus and Incriminations* (ETS 173 and 191, GPC 2), (Theme 1), 1 April 2011, Groupe d'Etats Contre la Corruption, DG Human Rights and Legal Affairs, DG Monitoring, Council of Europe, Strasbourg.

Gwyther, M. and Anderson, E. 2012. The MT Interview; Michael Woodford, *Management Today,* 28–32, March 2012.

Harding, D. and Rouse, T. 2007. Human due diligence. *Harvard Business Review,* April, 85(4), 124–131.

Hazou, E. 2011a. State apathy of the criminal kind, page 4–5, *Cyprus Sunday Mail,* 17 July 2011.

Hazou, E. 2011b. Cyprus side-stepped law, UN over blast containers, page 6, *Cyprus Mail,* 27 July 2011.

HKCCG 2005. *Hong Kong Code of Corporate Governance,* Hong Kong Exchange and Clearance, January 2005.

Ho, S.S.S.M. 2007. Opinion: are split CEO/Chairman roles good for corporate governance? *Asia Risk Newsletter,* 3, 1–2.

HOCTC 2009. *Banking Crisis: Dealing with the Failure of UK Banks,* 7th report of session 2008-9, report HC416 1 May 2009, House of Commons Treasury Committee. London: The Stationery Office.

Howarth, N. 2011. *Buying Property in Cyprus: Golden Commandments*, Available at: www.cyprus-property-buyers.com.

Howarth, N. 2012. British pensioner hospitalized after brutal attack, 6 March 2012, Available at: www.news.cyprus-property-buyers.com.

HSE 1989. *The Fires and Explosion at BP Oil (Grangemouth) Refinery Ltd, Report of the Investigations*, Health and Safety Executive. Sudbury, UK: HSE Books.

HSE 2003. *Major Investigation Report: BP Grangemouth, Scotland, 29 May to 10 June 2000*, a public report prepared by the HSE on behalf of the Competent Authority 18 August 2003, Health and Safety Executive and Scottish Environmental Protection Agency. Sudbury, UK: HSE Books.

HSE et al. 2011. *Buncefield: Why Did it Happen? The underlying causes of the explosion and fire at the Buncefield oil storage depot, Hemel Hempstead, Hertfordshire, 11 December 2005*, the Competent COMAH Authority (Health and Safety Executive, Environment Agency and Scottish Environmental Protection Agency). Sudbury, UK: HSE Books.

IACC 2005. *The Negative Consequences of International Intellectual Property Theft: Economic Harm, Threats to Public Health & Safety and Links to Organized Crime and Terrorist Organizations*, White Paper, International Anti-Counterfeiting Coalition, Washington DC, January 2005.

IMF 2011. *Cyprus: Selected Issues Paper*, IMF Country Report No. 11/332, November 2011. Washington DC: International Monetary Fund.

Interpol 2007. *Intellectual Property Crime Conference June 2007*, Intellectual Property Crime Unit, Interpol General Secretariat, Lyon, France.

IRM 2010. *A Structured Approach to Enterprise Risk Management (ERM) and the Requirements of ISO 31000*. London: Institute of Risk Management.

IRM 2011. *Risk Appetite and Tolerance*, Guidance Paper. London: Institute of Risk Management.

IRM 2012. *Risk Culture – Resources for Practitioners*, Guidance Document. London: Institute of Risk Management.

ISO 2009. *ISO 31000 Risk Management – Principles and Guidelines*. Geneva, Switzerland: International Organization for Standardization.

ISO 2012. *ISO 22301 Business Continuity Management*. Geneva, Switzerland: International Organization for Standardization.

Khurana, R. 2007. *Searching for a Corporate Savior: The Irrational Quest for Charismatic CEOs*. Princeton NJ, USA: Princeton University Press.

Leeb, S. 2006. *The Coming Economic Collapse – How You Can Thrive when Oil Costs $200 a Barrel*. New York: Warner Business Books/Grand Central Publishing.

Leeson, N. 1996. *Rogue Trader*. London: Little Brown.

Leigh, D. and Evans, R. 2007. BAE accused of secretly paying £1 billion to Saudi Prince, *The Guardian*, London, 7 June.

London Stock Exchange 1998. *The Combined Code, Report of the Committee on Corporate Governance*. London: Gee Publishing.

Maclean, B. and Elkind, P. 2004. *The Smartest Guys in the Room: The Amazing Rise and Scandalous Fall of Enron*. New York: Portfolio Trade, Penguin Group (USA) Inc.

Menon, A. 2004. Gamble that went wrong, *The Straits Times*, Singapore, 3 April.

Mintzberg, H. 1994. Rethinking strategic planning, part 1: pitfalls and fallacies, *Long Range Planning*, 27(3), 12–21.

Morton, F. 1970. *Report of Inquiry into the Safety of Natural Gas as a Fuel*, chairman Frank Morton, Ministry of Technology. London: The Stationery Office.

Mukasey, M. 2008. *Speech by US Attorney General Michael B. Mukasey*, US Department of Justice, Tech Museum of Innovation, San Jose, CA, 28 March.

Neocleous, A. 2000. *Introduction to Cyprus Law*, (ed.) D. Campbell. New York: Yorkhill Law Publishing.

Newton 2008. *The Buncefield Incident 11 December 2005, Final Report of the Buncefield Major Incident Investigation Board*, chairman Lord Newton, Health and Safety Executive, Rose Court, 2 Southwark Bridge, London SE1 9HS.

Newton, P.N. Fernandez, F.M. Plancon, A. Mildenhall, D.C. Green, M.D. et al. 2008. A collaborative epidemiological investigation into the criminal fake artesunate trade in S E Asia, *PLoS Medicine*, 5(2), e32.doc101371/journal.pmed.0050032.

Nicolaides, P. 2011. Comment: indecisive, woolly system made tragedy inevitable, page 15, *Cyprus Sunday Mail*, 9 October.

OECD 2007. *The Economic Impact of Counterfeiting and Piracy, Part 1 Overall Assessment*. Paris: OECD.

O'Hare, S. 2011. Former expat prisoner writes book, Personal Finance section,*The Daily Telegraph*, London, 1 December.

Olympios, M. 2007. Old habits, new hypocrisy from FBI, Corporate Governance, page 4, *Financial Mirror*, 6-12 June.

Parker, R.J. 1975. *The Flixborough Disaster*, Report of the Court of Inquiry, chairman R.J. Parker QC, Department of Employment. London: The Stationery Office.

PAS 200. 2011. *Crisis Management: Guidance and Good Practice*. London: British Standards Institution.

Pearce, J.L. 2000. Employability as trustworthiness. Pages 79–90. In Carrie R. Leana and Denise M. Rousseau (eds). *Relational Wealth: The Advantages of Stability in a Changing Economy*. New York: Oxford University Press.

Pettigrew, A. McKee, L. and Ferlie, E. 1992. *Shaping Strategic Change*. London: Sage.

Peyvandi, M.H. 1996. *Management Views on Operational Units*, Safety and the Petroleum Industry Seminar, NIORDC, Tehran, 8–10 January 1996.

Polyviou, P. 2011. *Report of the Inquiry into the Disaster on 11 July 2011 at the Naval Base 'Evangelos Florakis' at Mari*, chairman Polis Polyviou, Government of the Republic of Cyprus, Nicosia, 30 September 2011 (in Greek).

PRCCCG 2002. *PRC Code of Corporate Governance for Listed Companies in China*, China Securities Regulatory Commission, State Economic and Trade Commission, January 2002.

Psyllides, G. 2010a. Developer under police scrutiny, *Cyprus Mail*, pages 1 and 3, 6 August.

Psyllides, G. 2010b. Developer put on the stop list, *Cyprus Mail*, page 5, 7 August.

Psyllides, G. 2010c. €100,000 award in property case, *Cyprus Mail*, pages 1 and 5, 22 September.

Psyllides, G. 2011. EAC was 'reassured' by army statements on safety of the cargo, *Cyprus Mail*, page 4, 17 September.

Riley, M. and Walcott, J. 2011. China-based hacking of 760 companies shows cyber Cold War, *Bloomberg News*, Available at: www.bloomberg.com/news/.

Robens 1972. *Safety and Health at Work*, Report of the Committee 1970-72, chairman Lord Robens, Cmnd 5034. London: The Stationery Office.

Romano, R. 2004. *The Sarbanes-Oxley Act and the Making of Quack Corporate Governance*, Finance Working Paper 052/2004, European Corporate Governance Institute, September 2004, Social Science Research Network, Available at: http://papers.ssrn.com.

SCCG 2005. *Singapore Code of Corporate Governance*, Council for Disclosure and Corporate Governance, Accounting and Corporate Regulatory Authority of Singapore, September 2005.

Shea, H. 2006. *Corporate Governance and Social Responsibility of Family Firms in Hong Kong: A Case Study of Hutchison Whampoa Limited (HWL)*, October 2006, Social Science Research Network, Available at: http://papers.ssrn.com.

Simon, H.A. 1972. Theories of bounded rationality. Pages 161–176. In MaGuire, C.B. and Radner, R. (eds). *Decisions and Organization*. Amsterdam: North Holland Publishing Co.

Smith, E.H. 2007. *International Piracy: The Challenges of Protecting Intellectual Property in the 21st Century,* submission by the International Intellectual Property Alliance to the Sub-Committee on the Courts, the Internet and Intellectual Property, US House of Representatives, Washington DC, 18 October 2007.

SOASAC 2006. *Guidelines to the Integrated Risk Management of the Central Enterprises,* State-Owned Assets Reform Document No. (2006) 108, 6 June 2006, State-Owned Assets Supervision and Administration Commission of the State Council, People's Republic of China.

SOX 2002. *Sarbanes-Oxley Act 2002.*

Stavrakis, C. 2012. *Economy in Politics and Politics in the Economy.* Nicosia: Laser Graphics Ltd. Cited in press report 'Corruption in Cyprus at all levels says former Minister', *Cyprus Mail,* 20 February 2012.

Stockwatch 2009. *Property Market at Risk from Unsold Houses.* 22 July 2009. Larnaca, Cyprus: Stockwatch Ltd, Available at: www.stockwatch.com.cy.

Toft, B. 1990. *The Failure of Hindsight,* PhD Thesis, Department of Sociology, University of Exeter, UK.

Toft, B. 1996. Limits to the mathematical modelling of disasters. Page 99–110. In C. Hood and D. Jones (eds). *Accident and Design: Contemporary Debates in Risk Management.* London: UCL Press.

Toft, B. and Reynolds, S. 1997. *Learning from Disasters: A Management Approach,* 2nd edition. Leicester, UK: Perpetuity Press.

Turnbull, N. 1999. *Internal Control: Guidance for Directors on the Combined Code, Report of the Working Party on Internal Control,* chairman Nigel Turnbull. London: Institute of Chartered Accountants in England and Wales.

Turner, B.A. 1988. Connoisseurship in the study of organizational cultures. Pages 108–122. In A. Bryman (ed.) *Doing Research in Organizations.* London: Routledge.

Turner, B.A. 1992. *Organizational Learning and the Management of Risk,* proceedings of British Academy of Management 6th Annual Conference, Bradford University, 14–16 September 1992.

Turner, B.A. 1994. Causes of disaster: sloppy management. *British Journal of Management,* 5, 215–219.

UFAB 2004. *Counterfeiting and Organized Crime,* Union des Fabricants, Paris.

UNCAC 2004. *UN Convention Against Corruption,* resolution 58/4 of 31 October 2003, UN Office on Drugs and Crime (Vienna), United Nations, New York.

UNCAC 2008. *UN Convention Against Corruption, Implementing Procurement-Related Aspects,* UN Commission on International Trade Law, Conference, second session, Nusa Dua, Indonesia, 28 January–1 February 2008.

US Department of Justice 2012. *Allen Stanford Sentenced to 110 years in Prison for Orchestrating $7 billion Investment Fraud Scheme.* Justice News 12-756. 14 June 2012. Office of Public Affairs. Washington DC: Department of Justice.

USCSHIB 2007. *Refinery Explosion and Fire, BP Texas City 23 March 2005.* Investigation Report No. 2005-04-I-TX. March 2007. US Chemical Safety and Hazard Investigation Board. Washington DC.

USFDA 2008. *Interim Safety and Risk Assessment of Melamine and its Analogues in Food for Humans,* 31 October 2008, US Food and Drug Administration, US Department of Health and Human Services, Washington DC.

USTR 2007. *Special 301 Decisions, IIPA 2005-2006 Estimated Trade Losses Due to Copyright Piracy and Estimated Levels of Copyright Piracy,* Office of the US Trade Representative, Washington DC.

USTR 2008. *Special 301 Report for 2008,* Office of the US Trade Representative, Washington DC.

Vassiliades, A. 2009. Title deeds saga: at risk of creating a legal and social minefield, *Financial Mirror,* 2–8 December.

Wallis, D. and Allason, S. 2011. *European Property Rights and Wrongs* (eds) D. Wallis and S. Allanson. Helsinki: D.Wallis and Conexio Public Relations.

Walton, M. 2007a. Leadership toxicity – an inevitable affliction of organizations? *Organizations and People*, 14(1), 19–27.

Walton, M. 2007b. Toxic leadership. In Gosling, J. and Marturano, A. (eds) *Leadership: The Key Concepts*. Oxford: Routledge.

Walton, M. 2010. Senior executives: behavioural dynamics. *HRM Review*, August, 10–18.

Wang, I. 2005. High accident rate takes its toll on growth, *South China Morning Post*, 16 June.

Waring, A.E. 1996a. *Practical Systems Thinking*. London: Thomson/Cengage.

Waring, A.E. 1996b. *Safety Management Systems in the Oil, Gas and Related Industries*, Safety and the Petroleum Industry Seminar, National Iranian Oil Refineries and Distribution Company, Tehran, 8–10 January 1996.

Waring, A.E. 2001a. Critical issues for effective risk management. *Corporate Governance*, 13(April) 1–3.

Waring, A.E. 2001b. *Forging a Culture of Responsible Risk-Taking*, IIR Enterprise-Wide Risk Management Conference, 10–11 December 2001, London (reprinted in *Foresight, the Journal of Risk Management*, Part 1, pp. 11-14, Feb 2002 and Part 2, pp. 11–13, March 2002).

Waring, A.E. 2005. *Public Policy and Management of Disaster Reduction*, paper presented at the Asian Conference on Disaster Reduction, organised by PRC and UN, 27–29 September 2005, Beijing, abridged as Managing Disaster Reduction, *Catastrophe Risk Management*, March 2006.

Waring, A.E. 2006a. Demonizing Iran: a comforting illusion, The Risk Watch Column, *Financial Mirror*, 7–13.

Waring, A.E. 2006b. *Enterprise Risk Management and the Business Risk Management Framework*, Enterprise Risk Management Forum 2006, AARCM and the PRC State Owned Assets Supervisory Committee of the State Commission, Beijing, 15–16 September 2006.

Waring, A.E. 2006c. *Paper 1 Risk Management Issues Facing Chinese Enterprises, Paper 2 Risk Management in Practice*, Dialogue on Risk Management with Chinese Corporate Leaders, China Institute of Directors, Stock Exchange, Shanghai, 13 October 2006.

Waring, A.E. 2007a. *Family Businesses, Governance and Risk Management: European Experience*, 2nd Asia-Pacific Corporate Governance Conference, Hong Kong Baptist University, 23–24 August 2007.

Waring, A.E. 2007b. SOX and quack governance, The Risk Watch Column, *Financial Mirror*, 7–13 November.

Waring, A.E. 2007c. *Enterprise Risk Management: Countering Tunnel Vision and Quack Governance*, paper presented at CFO Southeast Asia Summit, Singapore, 19 November 2007.

Waring, A.E. 2009. Closed presentation on IPR risks to corporate audiences, Far East.

Waring, A.E. 2010. Risk myths and delusions, The Risk Watch Column, *Financial Mirror*, 21–27 April.

Waring, A.E. 2011a. Fighting the 'chancer' culture, The Risk Watch Column, *Financial Mirror*, 18–24 May.

Waring, A.E. 2011b. The gamble that cost lives, The Risk Watch Column, *Financial Mirror*, 13–19 July.

Waring, A.E. 2011c. Reflections on the Polyviou Report, The Risk Watch Column, *Financial Mirror*, 2–8 November.

Waring, A.E. 2013. *Man-Made Disasters: Lessons for Governance, Safety Culture and Risk Management*, paper presented at 2nd Cyprus Safety Platform Symposium on Man-Made Disasters, European University Cyprus, Nicosia, 30 January 2013.

Waring, A.E. and Glendon, A.I. 1998. *Managing Risk – Critical Issues for Survival and Success into the 21st Century.* London: Thomson Learning/Cengage.

Waring, A.E. and Sayell, S. 2009. *Fakes and Cyprus: Their Role in Organized Crime and Terrorism*, paper presented at IPR Seminar, sponsored by US Embassy and Turkish Cypriot Chamber of Commerce, Nicosia, Cyprus, 10 April 2009.

Waring, A.E. and Tunstall, S. 2005. *Operational Risk – Implications for You and Your Customers*, paper presented at GARP Asia–Pacific Convention, 26–27 October 2005, Hong Kong (abridged as The Implications of Operational Risk, *Strategic Risk*, 36–37, April 2006).

Waring, A.E. and Tyler, M. 1997. Managing product risks. *Risk Management Bulletin*, 2(5), 4–8.

Waring, A.E. and Youill, R. 2008. *Intellectual Property, Reputation and Brand Issues Affecting Trade with Asia,* paper presented at CIRCLE Conference on International Consumer Behaviour and Retailing Research, University of Nicosia, Republic of Cyprus, 26–29 March 2008.

WEF 2008. *Global Risks Report 3rd Edition 2008*, World Economic Forum, Cologny, Geneva, Switzerland.

WEF 2011. *Global Risks Report 6th Edition 2011*, K. van der Elst and N. Davis (eds), World Economic Forum, Cologny, Geneva, Switzerland.

WEF 2012. *Global Risks Report 7th Edition 2012*, World Economic Forum, Cologny, Geneva, Switzerland.

Westley, F.R. 1990. The eye of the needle: cultural and personal transformation in a traditional organization. *Human Relations*, 43(3), 273–293.

WHO 2008. *Expert Meeting to Review Toxicological Aspects of Melamine and Cyanuric Acid*, World Health Organization in collaboration with FAO, Ottawa, Canada, 1–4 December.

Youill, R. 2005a. *Money Laundering and Counterfeiting*, Forfeiting the Proceeds of Counterfeiting Crimes conference, Sponsored by the US Department of Justice, Hong Kong.

Youill, R. 2005b. *Effective Tactics to Combat Product Counterfeiting*, US Ambassador to the Philippines Round Table Seminar on Counterfeiting Issues in the Philippines, Manila, Philippines, November 2005.

Youill, R. 2006. *Music Piracy in SE Asia – A Situational Overview*, Briefing for the US Trade Representative's Office, Issues relating to the Counterfeiting of US Manufactured Goods in South East Asia, Singapore, May 2006.

Youill, R. 2007a. *Counterfeiting and Organised Crime in Asia*, speaker and moderator, ASEAN-US Department of Justice sponsored anti-counterfeiting conference for Asia–Pacific law enforcement agencies, Bangkok, Thailand, October 2007.

Youill, R. 2007b. *Fighting Music Piracy – An Industry Perspective*, Anti-piracy and Anti-counterfeiting training seminar for Indonesian National Police, Jakarta, Indonesia, April 2007.

Youill, R. 2008. pers comm, June 2008.

Yuanyuan, H. 2004. Tighter control on SOEs to control risk, page 2, *China Daily*, 14 December.

# Index

**A Short Guide to Facilitating Risk Management**
**Engaging People to Identify, Own and Manage Risk**
Penny Pullan and Ruth Murray-Webster
Paperback: 978-1-4094-0730-0
Ebook: 978-1-4094-0731-7


**A Short Guide to Operational Risk**
David Tattam
Paperback: 978-0-566-09183-4
Ebook: 978-1-4094-2891-6


**A Short Guide to Reputation Risk**
Garry Honey
Paperback: 978-0-566-08995-4
Ebook: 978-0-566-08996-1


**A Short Guide to Risk Appetite**
David Hillson and Ruth Murray-Webster
Paperback: 978-1-4094-4094-9
Ebook: 978-1-4094-4095-6


Visit **www.gowerpublishing.com** and

- search the entire catalogue of Gower books in print
- order titles online at 10% discount
- take advantage of special offers
- sign up for our monthly e-mail update service
- download free sample chapters from all recent titles
- download or order our catalogue